D0918449

Studies in Eighteenth-Century

British Art and Aesthetics

PUBLISHED UNDER THE AUSPICES OF THE

WILLIAM ANDREWS CLARK MEMORIAL LIBRARY

UNIVERSITY OF CALIFORNIA, LOS ANGELES

Studies in Eighteenth-Century British Art and Aesthetics

Edited by
RALPH COHEN

Clark Library Professor, 1980-1981

UNIVERSITY OF CALIFORNIA PRESS
BERKELEY • LOS ANGELES • LONDON

University of California Press
Berkeley and Los Angeles, California

University of California Press, Ltd.
London, England

Copyright © 1985 by The Regents of the University of California

Library of Congress Cataloging in Publication Data
Main entry under title:

Studies in eighteenth-century British art aesthetics.

(Publications from the Clark Library professorship,
UCLA; 9)
 1. Arts, British—Addresses, essays, lectures.
2. Arts, Modern—18th century—Great Britain—Addresses,
essays, lectures.   3. Aesthetics, British—Addresses,
essays, lectures.   I. Cohen, Ralph, 1917-   . II. Title.
III. Series.
NX543.S78   1985   700'.1   84-2693
ISBN 0-520-05258-7

Printed in the United States of America

1 2 3 4 5 6 7 8 9

CONTENTS

ACKNOWLEDGMENTS

I am indebted to the Chancellor of the University of California, Los Angeles, and the Clark Library Committee for their invitation to serve as Clark Library Professor during 1980-81. The hospitality shown me by the director, Robert Vosper, the librarian, Thomas Wright, and the staff made my stay a memorable one, and I am grateful to them for their help, generosity, and graciousness.

My tenure as Clark Professor marked my return to a university with which I was associated for many years, and I appreciated the opportunity to renew the association with it and to deepen my attachments to many friends who remain part of it. Although such attachments may thrive on physical proximity, there is an interior closeness that no physical distance can obscure.

I thank the scholars who consented to participate in the year's seminar and I regret that some of the performance aspects of the lectures are lost in book presentation. This was especially the case with Selma J. Cohen's program because she arranged with the Dance Department at UCLA to offer a number of eighteenth-century dances to illustrate her talk. Such activities enhanced the spoken word and were enthusiastically received by the audience.

I wish it was possible to include some of the exchanges between audience and speakers to show the interest and excitement the lectures produced. But, if that sense of immediacy is lost, perhaps another will be found in a reading of the essays.

CONTRIBUTORS

M. H. Abrams, Class of 1916 Professor of English, Cornell University, is the author of *The Mirror and the Lamp* and *Natural Supernaturalism,* among others.

Harold Bloom is University Professor of Humanities at Yale University. His most recent works are *Agon: Towards a Theory of Revisionism* and *Breaking of the Vessels.*

Ralph Cohen, Kenan Professor of English, University of Virginia, is the author of *The Art of Discrimination* and *The Unfolding of the Seasons.*

Selma Jeanne Cohen, Dance Perspectives Foundation, New York, is the editor of *International Encyclopedia of Dance* and the author of *Next Week, Swan Lake: Reflections on Dance and Dances.*

Carole Fabricant, Professor of English, University of California, Riverside, is the author of *Swift's Landscapes.*

Frances Ferguson is Professor of English, University of California, Berkeley. She is the author of *Wordsworth: The Language as Counter-Spirit.*

Joseph Kerman, Professor of Music, University of California, Berkeley, is the author of *The Beethoven Quartets* and *Opera as Drama.*

Ronald Paulson is Thomas E. Donnelley Professor of English at Yale University and is the author, most recently, of *Literary Landscape: Turner and Constable* and *Representations of Revolution (1789-1820)*.

Dora Wiebenson is Professor of Architectural History, University of Virginia, and recently edited *Architectural Theory and Practice from Alberti to Ledoux*.

I
INTRODUCTION

Ralph Cohen

Seven of the eight essays published in this volume were originally delivered as lectures at the William Andrews Clark Memorial Library during the academic year 1980-81 (the exception is Carole Fabricant's contribution). The subject set by the Library was "English [British] Art and Aesthetics in the Eighteenth Century," and it sought to provide a series that would appeal not only to scholars but to interested nonscholars as well. The lectures, therefore, were to deal with specific arts and to call attention to aesthetic issues pertinent to them. Eighteenth-century writers often wrote of the "sister arts" poetry and painting, and modern scholars have produced a number of studies of those arts and of aesthetic subjects such as the sublime and the beautiful. As this would have meant confining the series to analyses of what critics wrote about these arts rather than analyzing the arts from a modern viewpoint, I thought it more appropriate to my aim to present examples of eighteenth-century arts—the dance, poetry, architecture, music, landscape—and to have scholars inquire into some of their governing principles.

One of the surprises of such a series is to observe the interweaving of themes and arguments as experts in quite different fields develop aesthetic issues. Each of the contributors saw—but did not hear—the original essays, and they refer to one another's

1

papers. It seems desirable, therefore, in this Introduction to explore the themes, the agreements, and the disagreements they reach.

It should be noted that although the set subject was "English" art and aesthetics many of the contributors found it necessary to discuss the interaction, the interrelation, between British and German or British and French artists and philosophers. The reasons for this are self-evident: there was an intellectual commerce between English and Continental thinkers and artists. Sometimes the movement was, as in philosophy, from Shaftesbury to Baumgarten, from England to Germany; at other times, for example, in architecture, it was from France to England. Meyer Abrams traces the development from Baumgarten to Kant of two innovative aesthetic models and notes their relevance for English aesthetics of the nineteenth and twentieth centuries. Dora Wiebenson points to the construction material — pisé — popularized in France at the end of the eighteenth century by François Cointeraux who came to England in the 1790s "to demonstrate his product" in the building of cottages. So, too, eighteenth-century English ballet, although it had a promising beginning with the Englishman John Weaver, came under the French influence of Jean Georges Noverre. And Joseph Kerman, in his discussion of late eighteenth-century music, is concerned with the "modern view of classical music." His inquiry goes into the nature of musical analyses and interpretation and, although he does not concentrate on English music, his study does have applicability to the hermeneutics of interpretation to which any inquiry into the eighteenth century is committed.

The other essays, however, do confine themselves to aspects of British aesthetics, even though Carole Fabricant and Frances Ferguson find that such aesthetics inevitably lead to Kant. But if these critics find Kant the chief figure in aesthetic theory at the end of the eighteenth century, they arrive at their conclusions independently. Abrams had traced in *The Mirror and the Lamp* the mimetic and pragmatic orientation of critical theory in the eighteenth century, showing how, in the latter part of the century, such orientation changed into one that was "Romantic, or expressive." In his present paper, he supplements his earlier argument by pointing to two innovative procedures that developed primarily in German philosophy which he identifies as the contemplation model and the heterocosmic model. Both are perceptual paradigms, but the first refers to perceivers who identify the work by an act of contemplation that is disinterested, "focused exclusively on the isolated object as its own end, or for its own sake." The second, the heterocosmic model, claims that each poem is its own world, analogous to the ordinary world, but complete in itself, "that is, subject only to laws specific to its individual cosmos."

For Abrams, Kant is the philosopher who became "the main conduit" of the contemplation model: "for Kant the pure judgment of taste 'combines delight or aversion immediately with the mere *contemplation* [*blossen Betrachtung*] of the object irrespective of its use or any end.' This judgment 'is the one and only disinterested [*uninteressiertes*] and *free* delight,' in that it is 'purely contemplative [*bloss kontemplativ*],' hence without desire, indifferent 'to the real existence of the object,' and totally independent of reference to the 'external' ends of utility, pleasingness, or moral good." Kant also supported the heterocosmic model. But what is important is the fact that "both models originate in views about God," and that both models have features that have long histories, the contemplation model in pagan metaphysics, the heterocosmic model in the God of Genesis.

Abrams traces the continuity of features of these two models to show their history and their specific application to the arts in the eighteenth century. He is not interested, in this paper, in explaining why the models became aesthetic but, rather, what the consequences of this situation were. He is, in other words, desirous of expanding our knowledge of aesthetics by explaining certain continuities and innovations that have been overlooked in studies of eighteenth-century aesthetics. But, even more, he wishes to argue that the contemplation and heterocosmic models have become important in the twentieth century. For us, these models possess "profound metaphysical and theological pathos." "It is," he declares, "the same pathos that empowers the concept, which has endured from Plato through the Christian centuries, that perfection and ultimate value inhere solely in a metaphysical absolute or deity who is purely otherworldly, serenely integral, self-sufficient and self-bounded, and for those reasons, to be contemplated and revered above everything in the fragmented, incoherent, and conflict-ridden world in which we find ourselves."

It is one of the advantages of the Clark series that these essays move from generalizations about all the arts to studies of aesthetic issues in particular arts. Thus Fabricant finds an English tradition for the contemplation model; she finds a pattern in statements about landscape that resemble those outlined by Abrams. In the course of the eighteenth century religious moralizing is gradually supplanted by the "aesthetic and sensuous properties of the landscape." Moralizing does not completely disappear, but it loses its dominance. She points out that the meditation upon landscape became associated, as the eighteenth century wore on, with the *appearance* of meditation, with "the aesthetic effect it had on the (properly stationed) spectator." The procedures governing this change involved not only deceptive landscape but verbal allusions to past concepts "without, however, necessarily bringing to bear the network of assumptions and values that originally informed the passages." It is appropriate to note here that this point addresses the functions that quotations from past works possess. It is obvious that any quotation is divested of its original context, but does it divest itself of its own temporality, of introducing into a contemporary text certain elements of the past that are inherent in the implications and references of the quoted material?

Fabricant is interested in explaining the reasons for the new emphasis on the aesthetic values of landscape. She suggests that the references to the eye's freedom to roam at large can be understood as a political maneuver.

Addison, the well-to-do exponent of middle-class culture, combines the grandeur and majesty normally linked to a traditional aristocracy with the liberty and mobility more congenial to the nouveaux riches — to an expanding, prosperous capitalist class in the process of moving up into the world of (partly by appropriating portions of the landscape once exclusively owned by) the aesthetically cultivated, landed gentleman.

So, too, the spectator of prospects functioned like a lord overseeing his creation; he "was able to 'command' a view of the country stretching out beneath him and thereby exert control over it in much the same way that the aristocratic class (at least through the seventeenth century) ruled over those on the lower rungs of the social hierarchy." She indicates the paradox involved in the spectator losing himself in the act of aesthetic surrender and at the same time asserting control over the landscape. She is here noting an exception to the two models developed by Abrams, for in those the spectator is disinterested, detached, not involved in an act of "aesthetic surrender" that asserts control.

Fabricant shrewdly notes that for Addison, symbolic features of the landscape, such as mountains, "became one object among many in the natural world which were vulnerable to the spectator's restless eye and to the estate owner's desire for visual and territorial expansion. They became objects that could be moved about — and *re*moved — at will, given sufficient amounts of money and proper instruments of demolition." Moreover, the emphases on motion and change lent support to the "middle-class denigration of idleness and unprofitableness, and to its exaltation of industry, enterprise, and thrift."

The exaltation of novelty, variety, and movement in the early part of the eighteenth century led to a devaluation of certain aspects of the "natural and the human landscape" by the eighteenth-century spectator. The "obvious and telling examples were the habitats and the environs of the poor," and Fabricant quotes Mrs. Piozzi's travel through Lyons in 1784. But Dora Wiebenson offers some counterexamples in discussing the architecture of the small house. She declares that the 1780s in England marked a new period in the publications dealing with cottages and small houses. She writes:

The major social changes that had been developing earlier, such as the divisions of agrarian society into landowners, tenant farmers, and laborers, and into poor parish gentry and wealthy "county families," both occurring in the 1770s, may have begun to be reflected by the 1780s in a change in aesthetic values toward the more personal and less intellectual concept of the picturesque as well as toward a desire for social reform.

Mrs. Piozzi's statements, therefore, may represent a view that was developed much earlier and that shows little knowledge of the alterations in building plans and in aesthetic values that were beginning to take place as a result of changing social conditions.

Fabricant points to the perceptual procedure of the typical eighteenth-century spectator in "scene-hopping," "usually placing himself in a situation where he could view many different angles and features of the landscape while neither his mind nor his eye would have to 'waste it self on any particular Object.'" This "visual restless" cannot be related to paradigms of contemplation; it needs to be compared with contemporary procedures of constructing poetry that are additive rather than organic, as exemplified, for instance, in Pope's "Essay on Criticism."

She draws attention to certain landscape and architectural features that led to a sense of restriction, of the ejection of the servants from the main hall, of the failure of poets "to see" the actual lives of rural workers. But here, again, we seem to need more information about the houses of the rural poor. According to Dora Wiebenson publications that describe farm houses and cottages seem to be directed to members of the middle class or of the poor gentry who could afford them, but it seems not unlikely that rural workers did live in some of these cottages. John Wood, for example, in *A Series of Plans for Cottages or Habitations of the Labourer* published in 1781, offered plans for "dwellings intended to be built by landowners and occupied by their tenants." These dwellings, remarks Wiebenson, "represent the extreme extension of Palladianism"; "the point of view is far from that of the original promoters of Palladianism, who were concerned only with the style of significant public and private monuments. Wood's book implied a new recognition of social groups and of social reform in this type of publication."

Rural laborers had indeed been overlooked in the earlier part of the century, as Fabricant indicates. But, as Wiebenson points out, by the 1780s a change had begun to take place, and John Wood was a leader in planning cottages for laborers:

"the LABOURERS, [whose cottages] were become for the most part offensive both to decency and humanity; . . . the state of them and how far they might be rendered more comfortable to the poor inhabitants, was a matter worthy the attention of every man of property not only in the country, but in large villages, in towns, and in cities." These were the same structures [writes Wiebenson] that had been hidden from sight in the vast estates designed from 1720 to 1780, and concern for them indicates an entirely new attitude on the part of the architect — a concern with public welfare and with housing not only on country estates but also in urban centers, where the great estate developments had just begun.

In this architectural concern for the rural laborers we can see an instance of the humanitarian impulse for a class overlooked and disregarded earlier in the century. Perhaps the enclosure laws and the consequent movement from rural to urban areas led to a new view of those involved in such transitions. But it is also possible that until the principles supporting the great chain of being were undermined, the lower orders lacked an awareness of self necessary to encourage their prospect of improvement.

The acceptance of the domiciles as well as the behavior of the lower classes as appropriate subject matter for aesthetics in architecture and painting was achieved at the end of the century. But such concern was at odds with the view that aesthetic observation involved not an interested but a disinterested spectator. The contributors to this volume describe the political and aesthetic reasons for such conflicting views which are to be found in works from the various arts. Edmund Burke's *Enquiry into the Origin of our Ideas of the Sublime and Beautiful* (1757) reveals just this dilemma. On the one hand, Burke sought to reinforce the aesthetic objectivity and political implications of Addison's views of perception; on the other, he sought to show the social utility of the sublime. Ferguson finds in the *Enquiry* a revision of the explanations of perception offered by Addison. He had insisted on perception as an individual's act even though he described sight metaphorically "as a more delicate and diffusive kind of Touch, that spreads its self over an infinite Multitude of Bodies, comprehends the largest Figures and brings into our reach some of the most remote Parts of the Universe" (411 *Spectator*). Although Addison is interested in exploring the pleasures of the imagination, he is thoroughly aware that such pleasures arise from "the actual View and Survey of outward Objects: and these, I think, proceed from the Sight of what is Great, Uncommon or Beautiful" (412 *Spectator*). Objects are large—huge heaps of mountains, prospects of an open "Champain Country," a wide expanse of water—or objects are uncommon—monsters or the imperfections of nature—or objects are beautiful and, although any object may at some time appear beautiful, "we find by Experience, that there are several Modifications of Matter which the Mind, without any previous Consideration, pronounces at first sight Beautiful or Deformed" (412 *Spectator*).

Ferguson finds Burke converting Addison's position into a much more mechanistically directed empiricism. Burke uses a vocabulary that locates the basis for reactions only in objects: "Burke's practice is always to derive the mental reaction from the physical rather than the reverse." For her, Burke uses his mechanist, empirical approach to achieve objectivity; he, like Addison and Hume, posits uniformity among responders. In her discussion of Burke's view of the sublime she declares that "one rather peculiar aspect of Burke's account is that the effects of the sublime are seen as of particular social utility." Fear creates the first gods, but Providence "ensures the preservation of the social network." This seems at odds with Fabricant's view that insofar as the Burkean sublime refers to the humanly ungovernable, it begins a counterempirical tendency. But, as explanations of the development of British aesthetics, such antithetical positions can both be defended since there was no single development but rather several directions proceeding simultaneously. Ferguson points out that Kant, in the *Critique of Judgment,* praised Burke's empiricism but resisted and undermined it by arguing that individual responses did not show the uniformity claimed for them. Moreover, the disinterestedness that Kant wishes to impose on aesthetic judgments remains problematical. According to Ferguson, "the question that haunts the *Critique of Judgment* is whether or not social existence renders such disinterestedness an empty and purely theoretical notion."

Neither disinterestedness nor imitation are notions that Ronald Paulson finds especially pertinent to an analysis of the paintings of Joseph Wright and William Hogarth, contemporaries of Burke. Although the "visual arts, and painting above all, had been the exemplary form" for the contemplation model, according to Abrams, Paulson does not consider this model as dominant in the paintings he discusses. His procedure is to examine a number of Wright's paintings in order to arrive at some conclusions about the nature of his compositions. He notes that usually "included in Wright's subject pictures is a contrast between the human and the natural, the man-made and the unchanging, as in the ingot, the lamp, the illuminated air pump and the real sun or moon. . . . In fact, Wright's concern for the subjectivity of perception, his recognition of the inadequacy of reason to define experience, is frequently as observable as his intense interest in clarity of expression, in the technique of craft, and in the application of reason to the exploration of nature."

Paulson's point is that the great paintings do not embody principles expressed in treatises like those of the Richardsons or Burke: the "great paintings tend to be the ones that question principles." He points out that writers on aesthetics in the first half of the eighteenth century—Shaftesbury, Hutcheson, and Richardson—"all argue that the harmony perceived as beauty of form is also perceived as virtue of the person." Hogarth, whose *The Analysis of Beauty* (1753) seems to accept the equation of virtue and beauty, undermines "such ontological security" in his paintings and engravings. Indeed, the plates in this volume call into question the words of the text; the plates reveal that under a paradigm of beauty is a living, sensuous reality:

In Hogarth's own terms . . . the revelation is the living, breathing, sensuous reality that is beneath — and preferable to — even the greatest but dead art object.

Paulson believes that Hogarth is disagreeing here with the inherited equation of formal and moral beauty and is ridiculing the disinterestedness that separates aesthetics from moral considerations or "that includes this detachment in the aesthetic experience, which is distinct from either the moral or the purely existential experience." He finds Hogarth at one stage of aesthetic theory, Burke at another: "what Burke regards as sublimity Hogarth clearly regards chaos, or (as he put it in *The Analysis*) 'variety uncomposed, and without design, [which] is confusion and deformity.'" Between Hogarth's *The Analysis* and Burke's *Enquiry* only three years intervene, so that we can see the contrary aesthetic currents that are flowing between a discussion of painting and more general principles of art and nature.

What Hogarth depicts as the end of all coherent values [see his *Tail Piece, or The Bathos* (1764), fig. 6], Burke obviously sees (at the moment at least — perhaps less so later when the French Revolution emerged to test his theory) as the highest sort of aesthetic object. He would like to maintain the relationship between aesthetics and morality, as he wishes to retain the reality of the beauty or sublimity he envisions in the object itself. To do this he has to postulate a uniformity of response to it and a continuum of the object and the responding subject. Although, as Frances Ferguson has said in her paper in this volume, Burke "stipulates that a human observer be the passive instrument of the external object," he leaves it not very clear how any but the most overwhelming "object" can fulfill the requirement. His argument requires that "the *mind* is so entirely *filled* with its object, that it cannot entertain any other nor by consequence reason on that object which employs it."

Paulson argues that Wright's paintings embody as well as comment on aesthetic experience in the second half of the eighteenth century. Wright emphasizes "contingency and differences." Wright paints "from different assumptions than those enunciated by Reynolds." Paulson makes particular reference to Wright's portrait of Brooke Boothby (1780-81, fig. 2). He remarks that "while Reynolds ostensibly paints the living image, Wright finds a model in the tradition of funerary sculpture."

Paulson traces this funerary sculpture in eighteenth-century England, and remarks that the form adopted and explored for beauty in the 1760s and 1770s has as a model—or at least an analogue—tomb sculpture, "which was per se a filling of absence, a surrounding of emptiness, a representation of transition." Paulson extends his study beyond this one art. He wishes to move beyond portraiture to the verbal arts of the novel and biography: "it is interesting to note that the most distinguished practitioners of these forms questioned their efficacy in precisely the way we have seen Wright and other painters of history question the central mystery of their representations. It is the same sense of frustration at being unable to capture the past fully and permanently, whether in writing or images, that gives the elegiac tone to Sterne's *Tristram Shandy* and Wright's *Blacksmith's Forge.*"

The questioning of forms that Paulson finds in the paintings of Joseph Wright, the antiempirical emphasis, Harold Bloom finds in William Collins's "Ode to Fear." Bloom finds that this poem is governed neither by the concept of imitation nor by a contemplative or heterocosmic paradigm. Rather, he reads "Ode to Fear" "rhetorically and psychologically, so as to contrast within it the representations of two related but distinct poetic modes, Sensibility (as Northrop Frye suggested we call it) and Romanticism." Bloom argues that the experimental writings of the poets of the Age of Sensibility and of Romanticism were considerably in advance of the criticism and psychology of the same time. He finds this criticism marked by conservatism (Hazlitt being a "formidable exception"), and he, like Paulson, suggests that experimental works of art such as this poem imply relations unconsidered by the critics of poetry or painting. In this sense a study of eighteenth-century writings on aesthetics cannot be adequate without a study of the aesthetic implications of actual works of art.

Bloom grants that there exists an affinity between Collins and Burke in terms of "the effect of things on the mind over a clear idea of things themselves," though it would appear that Collins's antiempiricism is at considerable odds with Burke's mechanism. Bloom finds in "Ode to Fear" a division, what he calls "a making by breaking, or catastrophic creation." This division is identifiable in Collins's personification of fear: sublime personification is "an uneasy transitional phase or crossing between Associationist topos and Romantic trope."

Although Bloom gives a Freudian rather than an Associationist reading of the poem, he feels this historical procedure is justified because

Associationist categories and the Freudian mechanisms or fantasies of defense rely implicitly on rhetorical models, these being the topoi or commonplaces for Associationism and the prime tropes or figures for Freud. Romanticism is of course the connecting link here between topos and trope, association and defense, or to phrase this more saliently, Collins's "Ode to Fear," though a monument of and to Sensibility, is itself a version of that connecting link, a poem verging on High Romanticism and kept back from it mostly by two barriers. Call one of these decorum or diction, and the other Collins's own anxieties, human and creative, and you may be calling a single entity by two misleadingly different names.

Bloom's essay may appear only incidentally pertinent to the subject of aesthetics, but it is indeed relevant to the powers of an aesthetic. Bloom is primarily concerned with the power of the strong poet to achieve his own poetic voice through and against the voices of his poetic model—in Collins's case, Milton. "What Collins could not learn," he writes, "was what Wordsworth had to invent, a transumptive or time-reversing kind of troping as original as Milton's own, yet plainly *not* Miltonic." Bloom accepts the traditional distinction between Sensibility and Romanticism and his study seeks to explain why a subtle poet was unable to make the break that later poets did. Collins, Bloom argues, sought to reassert the will to take up "the transcendental possibility of poetry" as he knew it in Spenser, Shakespeare, and Milton. But his "will" was troubled; it lacked the wholeness necessary for visionary poetry: "Collins's synecdoches are wounded aggressivities, turned in against themselves, sadomasochistic vicissitudes of the thwarted poetic drive against time's 'It was.'"

This explanation of the poet divided against himself draws attention to an important problem in aesthetic analysis: the relation of the modern critic to an eighteenth-century work. Bloom proceeds from premises—Freudian premises—that the earlier time did not possess. While the critic situates the poem in the middle of the eighteenth century, he illustrates from his modern assumptions his view of the constituent features of the poem and the intentions of the poet. These, in the case of Bloom, are so clearly applicable only to verbal and rhetorical arts that it makes generalizations about all the arts unfeasible.

Joseph Kerman's essay, however, is an attempt to argue that modern theories of late eighteenth-century music tend to be governed by twentieth-century premises and that we need some sort of compromise between present views and past behavior. His aim is to have "a developing modern view of classical music"; he notes that we call late eighteenth-century music "classical" "not because of what it looked back to, but because of the way we look back to it." The way we look back to the "classical" music of Haydn and Mozart is through the contemplative and heterocosmic models described by Abrams: the "pithy characterization by Professor Abrams" [writes Kerman] "applies just as well to the vision of the musical analysts, the problem of artistic form and content is solved (when it is posed at all) by equation, by decreeing that expression, meaning, beauty, and so forth, must reside in the music's internal relations and nowhere else."

. . . analysis as a critical theory can absorb organicist theories of art much more easily than other theories we have learned to identify through Abrams' work—more easily than expressive theories, for example, or than the mimetic, imitative, didactic theories that still dominated the thought of the late eighteenth century. Music-analytic writings say nothing about the work of art as an expression of the composer's imaginative vision, his ideology, or indeed any other such personal category. They say nothing about how music might uplift, educate, or please the nonprofessional listener.

Are the "mimetic, imitative, didactic theories" that dominated late eighteenth-century music the only alternatives to modern organic theories offered as explanation? Kerman has reservations about this; in his analysis of the books by Charles Rosen and Leonard Ratner he makes clear that a commitment to organicism involves some reference to eighteenth-century assumptions just as scholarship based on collecting eighteenth-century statements about music must, to be viable for modern readers and listeners, include modern assumptions about how to interpret compositional organization.

How can the hermeneutic dilemma be resolved with regard to musical explanation? The dilemma arises from the circularity of offering explanations of late eighteenth-century music in terms of modern hypotheses or in terms of selected eighteenth-century explanations that have little persuasive power for modern scholars and readers. The solution that Kerman recommends is a kind of practical compromise. The analysis of particular compositions — his example is *Eine kleine Nachtmusik* — ought to be made in terms of a reception that would include the experience of the less learned as well as the learned listener of the period. Mozart's "less learned" listener probably appreciated an agreeably varied series of topics as well as symmetry, especially in recapitulations: "That he [the less learned eighteenth-century listener] cared about the recapitulation resolving or interpreting anything is vastly to be doubted. He would have appreciated the raucous passage at the end of the first movement, and also the parallel place at the end of the last movement; at any rate, these we can at least feel fairly sure he would have apprehended."

As for the features of this music for the connoisseur, I suppose I am making two contrary points about them. They can be missed by the connoisseur, the specialist, or the musicologist who concentrates on Kurth's "outer form," or formula and pattern, at the expense of "inner form." However, in a classical work of this kind they amount to no more than occasional touches. They can hardly be said to permeate the entire fabric of the music.

This approach to music analysis involves assumptions about the reception given it by different audiences at the time of its early performances as well as those of our own time. The speculations involved are buttressed by assumptions that a classical composition is a mixture of conventional topics and formulas and certain unifying procedures that were accessible to a nonlearned audience: "Whatever late eighteenth-century art was, it was not (and is not) esoteric."

What inferences can we draw from these essays about art and aesthetics in eighteenth-century Britain? The first is that scholars are not yet ready to make aesthetic generalizations that include all the arts in eighteenth-century England. Moreover, different works in the same art—for example, the dance—were governed by different aesthetic hypotheses. It is apparent, too, from these essays, that aesthetic hypotheses that were consciously developed do not suffice to characterize the processes of composition and the interrelations among the arts. Much was written about poetry and painting, but relatively little about the relation of poetry to the architecture of the cottage. The dance is clearly related to the drama, the opera, and music, but the nature of these interactions needs further study.

The essays, especially those of Fabricant and Ferguson, make clear that aesthetic premises are tied to political assumptions, and it may very well be that the prevalence of the contemplation and heterocosmic models at the beginning of the nineteenth century involves as well a change in political assumptions. But the critics do not always agree on what political assumptions are connected with aesthetic premises. Here a greater knowledge of historical relations seems pertinent for the making of such inferences. Many of the essayists assume that Kant's *Critique of Judgment* superseded earlier aesthetic assumptions, though Wiebenson finds that the aesthetics of the cottage at the beginning of the nineteenth century merges two contradictory styles developed during the preceding century, so that in architecture, at least, we have a new aesthetics based on new functions of the old, rather than a supplanting of the old. And this does seem to be the way in which the contemplation and heterocosmic models proceed. They are subordinate in the eighteenth century and become dominant in the nineteenth.

Indeed, the problems involved in aesthetic change, in the development, continuity, and discontinuity of aesthetic premises, are sufficiently adumbrated so that the reader is made aware of the puzzling nature of aesthetic history. John Weaver's possibilities as an innovative choreographer were aborted when he abandoned the theater. *The Analyses of Beauty* (1753), Hume's "Of Tragedy" and "On the Standard of Taste" in his *Four Dissertations* (1757), Burke's *Enquiry* (1757; 1759 2d ed.) all appeared in the same decade. The kinds of conversation that took place within these works are not discussed in the essays, but the sense of multiple aesthetic possibilities, of agreements and disagreements among eighteenth-century writers is ever-present.

The usefulness of general aesthetic principles can only be tested in the practice of artists. In the essays by Paulson, Bloom, and Kerman particular works are analyzed, calling into question the usefulness of general principles. But perhaps it is more appropriate to say that they raise questions not about the usefulness of general principles but about the appropriate formulation and application of such principles. They recognize the difficulty of making generalizations even about particular arts in the eighteenth century; nevertheless, they demonstrate again and again that generalizations about landscape gardening, architecture, dance, literature, painting, or music are not purely artistic. They possess social and political implications as well. These essays convey a sense of the variety of aesthetic possibilities and limitations that confronted writers and artists during the eighteenth century. They describe some of the shifts that took place as the century wore on. But if they demonstrate such changes, they also demonstrate the diverse explanations of change offered by modern critics. Such differences, however, are not merely posited. I have tried to show that throughout the essays included here there is a conversation, sometimes implicit and occasionally explicit, carried on by the participants. I invite the reader to share in this conversation.

II

FROM ADDISON TO KANT: MODERN AESTHETICS AND THE EXEMPLARY ART

M. H. Abrams

The era from Addison to Kant was one of unprecedented interest in the fine arts, and of unexampled expansion and innovation in the philosophical and critical theory of the arts. Eighteenth-century theorists had inherited from the Renaissance treatments of a single art, above all of poetry, in which the writers for the most part had explicated and played changes upon the vantage points and analytic terms they had found in their Greek and Roman progenitors. From the time of the Greeks, what we call "the arts" had been classified with crafts such as carpentry and cookery, and had only occasionally and in limited aspects been linked one to another. In the course of the eighteenth century, however, the various arts (especially poetry, painting, sculpture, music, and architecture), so patently diverse in their media and modes, in the skills they require, and in the occasion and social function of individual works, came to be systematized as "the fine arts," or simply as "art."[1] They were treated for the first time, that is, as a single class of products, sharing an essential feature that made them sui generis. By the middle of the century, Baumgarten had provided the new science of the arts-in-general with the coined name "aesthetics," and had made it, enduringly, a part of any philosophical system that undertook to account for our major modes of experiencing and dealing with the world. By the end of the century, Friedrich Schelling, in his *Transcendental Idealism* (1800), made the dialectical process of imagination in producing a work of art into the central and controlling concept of his entire metaphysics—in his words, "the general organon of philosophy and the keystone of its arch."[2]

Despite these drastic changes in the professional philosophy of art, the working premises of practicing critics, through much of the century, continued to be primarily pragmatic, based on Horace's *Art of Poetry* and classical theories of rhetoric, but incorporating concepts derived from Aristotle and Longinus. In general terms: a work of literature or of art was conceived to be, as Aristotle had said, an imitation, but with its materials selected, altered, and ordered in order to achieve predetermined ends, or effects. These ends were to move and give pleasure to the audience; variable stress was also given to the Horatian *utile*, that is, the moral and intellectual improvement of the audience. The excellence of a work, in its specific genre, was theoretically to be measured by the kind and degree of its emotional and pleasurable effectiveness. A primary criterion was that of "truth" to the nature that art imitates; this truth, however, was not verity, but "verisimilitude" or "probability," which is truth adapted to the responsiveness of the audience. That is, the people, objects, and events imitated in a work, though they deviate from history and may violate the known constitution and course of nature, must be so rendered that the audience will accept them as credibly like the world if the work is to achieve its justifying end of effecting pleasurable emotions.

Almost three decades ago, in *The Mirror and the Lamp*, I undertook to chronicle the shift in critical theory, beginning in the latter eighteenth century, from the mimetic and pragmatic orientation to the Romantic, or expressive orientation. According to this view, a work of poetry or art is not primarily an imitation, but the expression of the emotions or of the feelingful imaginative process of the artist. Its cardinal criterion, consonantly, is no longer its truth, in the sense of a credible correspondence to reality, but its sincerity, or the genuineness of its correspondence to the feelingful state of mind of the artist; often, the work is regarded also as a revelation of the unique personality of the artist.

It needs to be stressed, however, that this shift took place by an expansion and change in function of concepts and terms which were already present in the inherited vocabulary of eighteenth-century criticism. The notion, for example, that the language of poetry, in addition to its representational function, can express emotions and manifest the *ethos,* or character of the speaker, was entirely traditional, though it had earlier been used not to define poetry but to discuss style, or else to specify the matching of an utterance to the state of mind of a character within a poem. And in stressing the requirement that the poet evoke emotions in his audience, pragmatic theorists often added Horace's corollary, *si vis me flere,* that is, "if you wish to move me, you must first yourself be moved." In short, the change from a mimetic and pragmatic to an expressive theory was an evolutionary process, in which, in response to altering social circumstances, sensibility, and artistic practices, certain terms that had hitherto been marginal and subordinate became central and controlling, and so effected an internal revolution in critical theory.

The case, however, is quite different for two other eighteenth-century innovations that are my particular concern here. Both of these introduced new sets of terms, without precedent in the traditional critical vocabulary, for specifying the nature and criteria of a work of art. Both innovations are the achievement mainly of philosophers rather than practicing critics; they did not emerge fully as the express and inclusive premises of critics, and also of artists, until after the Romantic period, in the mid-nineteenth century; and their full effect was delayed until they reemerged to constitute, in diverse developments, the dominant modes of critical theory and discussion of the arts after the third decade of the present century. If these innovations are taken into account, it can be claimed that eighteenth-century theorists supplemented the traditional repertory of critical discourse with the major alternative concepts that have been exploited by critics and aestheticians up to the very recent past.

PARADIGMS OF CRITICISM AND MODELS OF ART

For easy reference, let us call these innovative elements "the contemplation model" and "the heterocosmic model" for a work of art. I cite two twentieth-century examples of each model.

In his influential *Speculations* (1924), T. E. Hulme, after defining "contemplation" as "a detached interest," wrote:

The object of aesthetic contemplation is something framed apart by itself and regarded without memory or expectation, simply as being itself, as end not means, as individual not universal.[3]

And in 1960 Jerome Stolnitz began his *Aesthetics and Philosophy of Art Criticism* by defining "the aesthetic attitude" as "disinterested and sympathetic attention to and contemplation of any object of awareness whatever, for its own sake alone." To apprehend a work of art with the attitude appropriate to it, consequently, is to see "the work as a self-contained object which is of interest in its own right." And to talk "about works of art as aesthetic objects" is to talk "about what is within the work itself. . . . [The work] has a significance and value which is inherent in itself alone."[4]

In both these passages the terms are the common currency of modern critical discourse, and the predications are often taken to be timeless truths about the nature and perception of works of art. They are, however, recent and radical novelties in the two-thousand-year history of art criticism. Prior to the eighteenth century, it had occurred to no philosopher or critic to assert that a work of human art is to be attended to with a "contemplation" that is "disinterested," and "for its own sake alone"; or to identify the work as an object "framed apart by itself" and regarded "as being itself, as end not means"; or to distinguish sharply between what is inside and outside a work, and to claim that, since the work is "self-contained," properly aesthetic criticism must confine itself solely to its "inherent," or internal, "significance and value."

The key term in these commentaries is "contemplation," and the shift in theory that the word signals is not a reorganization within the inherited critical system but the introduction of a new paradigm for dealing with a work of art. Traditional critical theory, from Aristotle on, had assumed a construction paradigm. The Greek and Latin terms for "poem" (*poiema, poema*) signified a "made thing"—made, that is, by the poet ("maker") in accordance with an "art" (a craft, or skill) for selecting materials to imitate, and for rendering and ordering these materials toward the end of achieving appropriate effects on the audience. And

traditional treatises did not distinguish between their function as
a guide to the poet in making a good, or successful, poem and as
a guide to the reader in judging whether the made poem is good.
This paradigm, which is assumed throughout Aristotle's *Poetics,*
becomes blatantly explicit in Horace's *Ars Poetica,* which later
critics applied to painting and the other arts as well as poetry. For
the *Ars Poetica* is a how-to letter addressed to a poetic novice,
advising him how to construct a poem that will achieve maximal
and enduring effects on the widest possible audience. In sharp
contrast, Hulme and Stolnitz take for granted a perceptual paradigm for art, and within this paradigm they formulate the mode
of perception by reference to a contemplation model. That is,
they assume that the representative situation, in establishing
what constitutes a work of art, is one in which a perceiver confronts a completed work, however it got constructed; and they
define the way he perceives that work as a "contemplation" that is
"disinterested," or "detached," and is focused exclusively on the
isolated object as its own end, or for its own sake.

To introduce the second eighteenth-century innovation by a
twentieth-century instance, here is what A. C. Bradley said about
the distinctive nature of a poem in an essay written in 1901:

Its nature is to be not a part, nor yet a copy, of the real world (as we
commonly understand that phrase) but to be a world by itself, independent, complete, autonomous; and to possess it fully you must enter that
world, conform to its laws, and ignore for the time the beliefs, aims, and
particular conditions which belong to you in the other world of reality....

[Poetry and reality] are parallel developments which nowhere meet
...they are analogues.... They differ... because they have different
kinds of existence.[5]

The paradigm is a perceptual one, as in the preceding examples,
but Bradley formulates the nature of the perceived poem on a
heterocosmic model. He substitutes for the view that a poem is an
imitation—"a copy"—of the real world the claim that each poem
is its own world, analogous to the ordinary world, but complete in
itself, and (in another term unprecedented before the eighteenth
century) "autonomous," that is, subject only to laws specific to its
individual cosmos.

In the 1920s the novelist and critic E. M. Forster asserted in parallel fashion that the poet's use of words has the power "to create . . . a world" that is governed by laws specific to itself, is complete in itself, is self-referential, and replaces the ordinary truth of correspondence to reality by the poetic truth of self-coherence. Reading the *Ancient Mariner,* for example,

we have entered a universe that only answers to its own laws, supports itself, internally coheres, and has a new standard of truth. Information is true if it is accurate. A poem is true if it hangs together. Information points to something else. A poem points to nothing but itself. . . . It is not this world, its laws are not the laws of science or logic, its conclusions not those of common sense.[6]

Here we have, then, within the shared perceptual paradigm of a work-in-being, two distinct ways of dealing with art. One deploys a model in which each work is a self-sufficient object that is contemplated for its own sake; the other deploys a model in which each work is a unique, coherent, and autonomous world. My concern is to show — cursorily, in the space available — that: (1) Both the contemplative and the heterocosmic models for art were first exploited in the eighteenth century; their novelty, however, was not in their conceptual content but in their application. For both models were imported into the criticism of the arts from theology, where they had been familiar though discrepant commonplaces in formulating the essential nature and activity of God. (2) Each model was at first brought to bear primarily on that art to which it was most plausibly applicable, but was later generalized to account for the other arts as well. (3) These two models, although diverse in their original formulations and distinctive features, nonetheless fostered similar assertions about the nature and criteria of works of art — assertions that constitute what I shall call the view of "art-as-such," and that have in large part dominated both the theory of art and the practice of artistic criticism from the 1920s to the present time.

THE CONTEMPLATION MODEL

The key terms "contemplation" and "disinterested" had been introduced into contexts that included reference to the arts as early as 1711, in the *Characteristics* of the Earl of Shaftesbury.[7]

The first full and systematic treatment of the fine arts exclusively in terms of the contemplation model, however, occurs in a short, densely written essay published in 1785 by a young German thinker, Karl Philipp Moritz. The essay was entitled "On the Unification of All the Fine Arts . . . under the Concept of the Complete-in-Itself" — that is, *des in sich selbst Vollendeten,* which is also translatable as "the perfected in itself." Moritz begins by rejecting the reigning attempts to define the arts as an imitation of nature that is subordinated to the end of giving pleasure to its audience. He sets up a basic opposition between useful objects, which are perceived merely as means to an end outside themselves, hence as "completed" only by achieving that external end, and beautiful works of art, which are perceived as wholes that are complete in themselves. He then proposes the following model for the way in which we perceive a work of art:

In the contemplation [*Betrachtung*] of the beautiful I roll its end back from me into the object itself; I contemplate it as something which is *completed,* not in me, but *in its own self,* which therefore constitutes a whole in itself and affords me pleasure *for its own sake* [*um sein selbst willen*]. . . . Since the beautiful object is valuable to me more for its own sake, [it] provides me with a higher and more disinterested [*uneigennützigeres*] pleasure than the merely useful object.[8]

The concept of the disinterested "contemplation of a beautiful work of art" thus involves a distinction between what is inside and what is outside the work; in its self-sufficiency, the contemplated object replaces what Moritz calls an "external purposefulness" with an "internal purposefulness" [*innere Zweckmässeigkeit*] of all its parts toward the achievement of the perfected whole. Hence the pleasure we experience in contemplating the work is merely supervenient upon an exclusive attention to the self-bounded whole, which is regarded, in Moritz's reiterated phrase, simply "for its own sake."[9]

Where did this complex of new terms for defining a work of art come from? Moritz himself provides the primary clue.

While its beauty draws our attention exclusively to itself . . . it makes us seem to lose ourselves in the beautiful object; and precisely this loss, this forgetfulness of self, is the highest degree of pure and disinterested pleasure which beauty grants us. In that moment we sacrifice [*opfern auf*] our individual confined being to a kind of higher being. Pleasure

in the beautiful must therefore come ever closer to disinterested *love,*
if it is to be genuine.[10]

The idiom of self-abandonment, self-loss, and the sacrifice of self
to a "higher being" is patently theological; most strikingly, it
assimilates the "pure" pleasure in the selfless contemplation of a
work of art to a "distinterested *love.*"

In such a passage, as Martha Woodmansee has pointed out,
Moritz has translocated into discourse about art the religious terminology of the Quietist creed in which he had been brought up;
for in Quietism the primary emphasis—as Moritz himself described it in his autobiographical novel, *Anton Reiser*—had been
on "the total annihilation of all so-called selfhood" in "a totally
disinterested [*uninteressierte*] love of God," which is "pure" only
if it is totally unalloyed by "self-love."[11] In a larger historical purview, however, this concept of the contemplation of a self-sufficient object as the manifestation of selfless love turns out to be a
long footnote to Plato. In the *Symposium* Diotima describes to
Socrates the ascent of human love from the beauty of sensible
objects through ever-higher stages, to culminate in the contemplation of the supersensible Idea of Ideas, which is "beauty absolute, separate, simple, and everlasting," and constitutes also the
absolute good. The *summum bonum*—"that life above all others
which men should live"—consists in this "contemplation of
beauty absolute . . . divine beauty . . . pure and clear and unalloyed," which is viewed not with the bodily eye but "with the eye
of the mind." In the *Philebus,* Plato stressed the feature of *autar-
kia,* or self-sufficiency, of this divine object of contemplation:
such a being "always everywhere and in all things has the most
perfect sufficiency, and is never in need of anything else."[12] Self-
sufficiency is also the prime attribute of the Absolute of Plotinus,
whose beauty is "perfect in its purity," and who in his perfection
is "wholly self-suffing," "self-closed," "autonomous," and "most
utterly without need." The apex and terminus of all human love,
Plotinus says, in passages that became central references for religious contemplatives and are echoed both in Moritz's Quietism
and in his aesthetics, is to "contemplate" this "Absolute Beauty"
in a "perfect surrender" of the self which is "the soul's peace,"
since in such contemplation alone there is "no movement . . . no
passion, no outlooking desire," but only "perfect stillness."[13]

In the theology of divers Church Fathers, the Absolute Beauty of Plato and Plotinus, impersonal, indifferent, and self-bounded, was merged, very incongruously, with the personal, loving, just, and often angry God of the Old and New Testament. And with this concept of the biblical Deity as the perfection of both beauty and goodness came the correlative concept that the highest human good is to contemplate this self-sufficient God with a selfless love, not for our sake but purely for His sake. Especially relevant for the Western Church are the views of St. Augustine, who converted the pagan *eros* doctrine into the doctrine of Christian *caritas* which dominated much of Western theology. Augustine deploys an opposition between *uti* and *frui*, "to use" and "to enjoy," to establish two sharply distinct kinds of love: to love something for its use, as means to an end outside itself [*propter aliud*], and to love something in a pure enjoyment [*fruitio*] of it as its own end, and for its own sake. The first class comprehends all the good and beautiful things in the sensible world, whether natural or works of the human arts; all these are to be loved only as means to the end of the supreme beauty and goodness which is God. The second constitutes a unique class: God alone is to be loved with a pure enjoyment, *gratis* (free of profit to the self), and *propter se ipsam* (for His own sake). In this life, such a love manifests itself at its highest in the enjoyment of the supreme beauty in a *visio Dei*, although not with the physical eye, but with the eye of the mind; only in God's own Kingdom will we be capable of that "enjoyment of contemplation [*fructum contemplationis*]" that "will be our reward itself, . . . when we enjoy completely [*perfruamur*] His goodness and beauty."[14]

The Platonic and Augustinian doctrines of a love that terminates in the selfless contemplation and enjoyment of an object of ultimate beauty and value, not for its use but as an end in itself, and for its own sake, constitute both the contemplation model and the distinctive vocabulary of Moritz's theory of art. The difference, to be sure, is a radical one: The Platonic Absolute, and Augustine's God, have been displaced by a human product, the self-sufficient work of art, and the organ of contemplation, the eye of the mind, has become the physical eye. Yet even today, phrases such as "an art lover" and "an amateur of art" serve as indexes to the origins of modern concepts of art in the philosophy and theology of earthly and heavenly love.

The main conduit, however, from the ancient doctrines of self-less contemplation of an otherworldly object to modern aesthetic theory was not Moritz (whose writings have until recently been inadequately heeded) but Immanuel Kant. In his *Critique of Judgment,* published in 1790, five years after Moritz's seminal essay, Kant develops a complex account of how the experience of a distinctive aesthetic perception is "possible," in terms of an interplay of the faculties that the mind brings to all its experience. He simply takes for granted, however, what it is that constitutes the normative aesthetic perception of an object (in his phrase, "the pure judgment of taste") whose possibility he sets out to explain; and the features of aesthetic perception that Kant takes for granted coincide with the contemplation model and the philosophical idiom already established by Moritz. Thus for Kant the pure judgment of taste "combines delight or aversion immediately with the mere *contemplation* [*blossen Betrachtung*] of the object irrespective of its use or any end." This judgment "is the one and only disinterested [*uninteressiertes*] and *free* delight," in that it is "purely contemplative [*bloss kontemplativ*]," hence without desire, indifferent "to the real existence of the object," and totally independent of reference to the "external" ends of utility, pleasingness, or moral good. The object contemplated, Kant says, is therefore experienced as "purposeful without a purpose," and "pleases for its own sake [*für sich selbst gefallt*]."[15]

THE WORK AS A WORLD

Three years after his essay of 1785, Moritz, in "The Formative Imitation of the Beautiful," turned from the topic of how we contemplate a completed work of art to "the question, how a thing must be created [*beschaffen*] in order not to need to be useful"; in his answer, he introduces a new order of concepts. In bringing a work of art into being, the "formative artist" does not imitate the sensible reality of nature; instead, he "imitates" the creative power by which nature produces this reality. (For this transformed sense of the ancient phrase "to imitate nature" Moritz uses as synonyms *nachstreben, wetteifern, nacherschaffen:* to "strive after," "vie with," "create in the manner of" nature.) The "formative power" of the artist, penetrating to the "inner being" and internal relations of creative nature, dissolves the sensible particulars of reality into "appearance," in order "to form and create" what nature has left unrealized "into a self-governing [*eigenmächtig*], self-sufficient whole." In this way the "active power" of the artist

creates [*schafft*] its own world, in which nothing isolated any longer has a place, but every thing is, in its own way, a self-sufficient whole [*ein für sich bestehendes Ganze*].[16]

Two years later Kant also turned his attention to the mental processes of the artist that brings into being a work that will satisfy the criteria he has already established by reference to the contemplation model. He introduces a similar concept:

The imagination (as a productive faculty of cognition) is a powerful agent for the creation [*Schaffung*], as it were, of a second nature out of the material supplied to it by actual nature.... We even use it to remodel experience, always following, no doubt, laws that are based on analogy, but still also following principles which have a higher seat in reason... with the result that the material can... be worked up by us into something else — namely, what surpasses nature.[17]

The radical metaphor in both Moritz and Kant is "create," and, as applied to art in the eighteenth century, this concept has three dimensions of application: the artist is a creator; his creative power resides in a mental faculty, usually identified as the imagination; and the resulting work of art constitutes a new creation — "its own world" or "a second nature." My concern in this paper is with the exploration of the third aspect, the concept that the work of art is its own world. Before turning to this topic, I want to note two important differences between the contemplation model and the creation model as applied to art.

First, although both models originate in views about God, they are based on very divergent concepts of the divine Being which it has been a formidable challenge for theologians to reconcile. The contemplation model, derived from pagan metaphysics, posits a self-bounded and self-sufficient Deity, totally unconcerned for anything beyond Himself, who is to be loved and contemplated entirely for His own sake. The heterocosmic model, on the contrary, posits the God of Genesis, who in a totally other-oriented act wills the creation of a world out of nothing, and outside the limits of His own being. (In Moritz God's creative power has in turn been delegated to a principle, a *natura naturans*, that is active within created nature itself.) In the former theory, God Himself is the prototype for the self-sufficient work of art that demands disinterested contemplation. In the creation theory, it is not the work of art but the artist, or creative "genius," who is god-like (for example, in his freedom from the constitution and laws of this world, and in his power of radical innovation, or "original-ity"); the work of art is an analogue to God's created world; and the "creative imagination" tends to displace the faculty of reason as the nearest human approximation to the processes of divinity.

Second, in contemplation theory the visual arts, and painting above all, had been the exemplary form. The contemplation of Absolute Beauty by the "eye of the mind," from Plato on, had been based on express analogy with visual perception by the bodily eye.[18] When translated from its other-worldly to a this-worldly form, the representative instances of contemplation be-came the arts accessible to the eye; only gradually were the cate-gories of the contemplation model expanded to other arts, but perforce in an attenuated form. Even in the present century con-templation theorists tend to advert to painting as the exemplary art. We can understand why. We confront a painting on a wall, sharply demarcated from its surroundings by a material frame and taken in by a glance of the eye. It seems on the face of it plausible to claim that the painting is contemplated as a self-bounded object that is entirely constituted by its components and their internal relations. Such categories, however, become much less plausible when applied to the art of poetry, in which the ver-bal medium signifies many nonvisual elements, and especially when applied to a long narrative form, such as *The Iliad* or *Para-dise Lost,* which is read intermittently and in which the narrative evolves in time.

Even in painting, the representational elements, with their seeming reference to things existing outside the frame, have been something of an embarrassment to proponents of aesthetic con-templation. They have focused instead on the elusive, nonrepre-sentational feature of a painting which they call its "beauty," and which Kant, following Shaftesbury, interchanged with the even more elusive term "form." For example, in his influential little book *Art* (1914), Clive Bell posited that "form," or "significant form," is "the essential quality" of the fine arts, and asserted that "the contemplation of pure form...leads to a...complete detachment from the concerns of life," and also that "the formal significance of any material thing is the significance of that thing considered as an end in itself," not "as a means to practical ends" in "the world of human business and passion." Bell in turn grades the various arts according to the "purity" of their independence from external reference; at the bottom of this scale is literature, which "is never pure" because "most of it is concerned, to some extent, with facts and ideas."[19] It is precisely the art of literature, however, that was central and exemplary for the alternative theory that a work of art is a created thing that constitutes its own world.

The antecedents of heterocosmic theory emerged in critics of literature who, beginning in the late fifteenth century, reversed the traditional comparison of God the creator to a human artisan by making the portentous comparison of the literary artisan to God the creator—with the cautious qualification, however, that while God created this world *ex nihilo,* a poet makes his own world by reworking the materials of God's prior creation.[20] In the sixteenth century the partial parallel between the poet's making and God's creating, with the corollary parallel between God's created world and the poem as "an other nature" or "a second world," occurred frequently enough to be almost a standard topos in literary criticism.[21] But through the seventeenth century this analogy functioned primarily as a topic of praise, designed to defend poetry against its detractors by assigning it a quasi-divine status.[22] Sir Philip Sidney's *Apologie for Poetry* (c. 1583) is typical. His express aim in introducing this concept is to confound the derogators who have "throwne downe [poetrie] to so ridiculous an estimation." To do so, he traces the etymology of "poet" to the Greek verb *poiein,* "to make," and suggests that the poet's making is parallel to the creative fiat of God in Genesis. While all other arts and sciences have "the workes of Nature" for their "principall object...onely the Poet...dooth growe in effect another nature." For "the heavenly Maker of that maker...set him beyond and over all the workes of that second nature, which in nothing hee sheweth so much as in Poetrie, when with the force of

a divine breath he bringeth things forth far surpassing her doo-
ings." But having, as he says, attributed to the poet "so un-
matched a praise as the Etimologie of his names will grant," Sidney goes on to "a more ordinary opening" of his subject, which
consists in grounding his critical theory on the standard definition
of a poem as an imitation designed for external ends:

Poesie therefore is an arte of imitation, for so Aristotle termeth it in his
word *Mimesis* . . . to speake metaphorically, a speaking picture: with this
end, to teach and delight.[23]

Not until the eighteenth century was the divine analogy converted from a topic of laudation into a principle of critical theory,
for only then was the concept that a poem is its own world exploited so as to qualify, then to displace, the concept that a poem
is credible imitation of the existing world. The process begins
with Addison's defense, in 1712, of "the fairy way of writing"—
defined as the presentation of supernatural beings such as
"fairies, witches, magicians, demons, and departed spirits"—
against men of "philosophical dispositions" who object that such
poetry "has not probability enough to affect the imagination."[24]
Addison's counterclaim, expanding on a suggestion by Sir Philip
Sidney, is that in reading about such poetic beings, who are entirely the product of the poet's "invention" and "imagination,"
"we are led, as it were, into a new creation, and see the persons
and manners of another species!" The allegorical personification
of abstract concepts also "has something in it like creation." In
both its nonrealistic and allegorical components, then, poetry

has not only the whole circle of nature for its province but makes new
worlds of its own, shows us persons who are not to be found in being,
and represents even the faculties of the soul, with her several virtues and
vices, in a sensible shape and character.[25]

After Addison, limited claims that the supernatural and allegorical elements in poetry are not imitations of this world, since
they constitute a world of their own, became common among
English defenders of such deviations from reality in Ovid, Spenser, Shakespeare, and Milton. For the development of the heterocosmic model beyond this restricted application we must turn, as

we did for the development of the contemplation model, to German philosophers; first, to Alexander Baumgarten. In 1735 Baumgarten, only twenty-one years of age, published his master's thesis, *Philosophical Reflections on Poetry*. The radical nature of this forty-page essay is veiled by its terse and awkward Latin, its outmoded philosophical terminology, and its deductive procedure for establishing the distinctive features and criteria of poetry. Baumgarten writes in the method and idiom of "rational philosophy," in the lineage of Descartes, Spinoza, and above all Leibniz — a mode rigorously systematized by Christian Wolff. This philosophy had claimed that the faculty of reason, which employs a deductive logic, is the sole mode for achieving a kind of knowledge that is "perfect," in the sense that it is necessarily true; it had, accordingly, relegated the factual and merely contingent knowledge achievable through sense perception to the status of "an inferior cognition." Baumgarten undertakes to show that the systematic study of poetry has its proper place in philosophy, in that a poem provides a mode of knowledge that possesses its own kind of "perfection" — a perfection specific to sensory discourse, which can be validated by criteria that are counterparts of the criteria by which we validate the logical process for achieving intellectual perfection, or "truth."[26]

Baumgarten sets out from the definition: "By poem we mean a perfect sensate discourse." He begins, that is, with the achieved poem-in-being; takes the approach that it is to be analyzed as a distinctive mode of language, or "discourse"; and sets up as its essential attribute that it is a language of sensory representations which is so developed as to exploit to the full (that is, "perfectly") its "sensate" or nonlogical potentialities. He explains that this perfection of its possibilities applies to all three aspects of a poem: the objects that the words represent, the specific "inter-relationships" of these objects, and the "articulate sounds" that constitute the verbal medium itself (pars. 6-11). Baumgarten goes on, with a great show of rigor, to deduce as the "consequences" of this definition all the distinctive features of a poem. Throughout he cites classical critics and rhetoricians, Horace's *Ars Poetica* above all, but his process of reasoning and his overall conclusions are very different from Horace's pragmatic recourse to the poet-maker's ruling aim to achieve effects on an audience. For Baumgarten's reasoning is controlled throughout by his undertaking to show that a poem yields valid knowledge, but that since this is sensuous as opposed to conceptual knowledge, its features are derivable by systematic parallel and opposition to the features of logical reasoning. Thus, the elements of logical discourse in philosophy are "conceptually" clear and "distinct," but the representations in poetry are clear in a specifically sensuous way, and are not distinct, but "confused" (that is, fused together, without distinction between essence and accidents). As a consequence, however, the elements of poetry, unlike those of logic, are "vivid" and "lively." Logic is abstract and general, but poetry is determinately particular, individual, specific. Logical concepts are simple and signify essences, but poetic representations are qualitatively rich, abundant, imagistic, and constitute concrete wholes. And as distinguished from rational or philosophic discourse, the sensate language of poetry is densely figurative, and above all metaphorical; it also exploits the pleasurably sensuous appeal of rhythm and meter.

Such conclusions seem to make Baumgarten a Continental Formalist, and even more a New Critic, *avant la lettre* — by some two hundred years. And with good methodological reason. Both Formalists and New Critics, like Baumgarten, take as their premise that poetry is to be dealt with as a distinctive mode of language and — on the assumption that uses of language fall into a bipolar distribution — these theorists proceed, as does Baumgarten, to establish the distinguishing features of poetry, or of literature in general, by systematic opposition to what are held to be the standard features of "practical," or "logical," or "scientific" language. The parallel is especially manifest in John Crowe Ransom who, in a fashion similar to Baumgarten, proposes that poetry is a mode of language that conveys a "kind of knowledge" antithetic to the knowledge provided by science, which is "only the cognitive department of our animal life." And science and works of art, he claims, "between them...exhaust the possibilities of formal cognition."[27] Hence, by Ransom's dialectic of contraries, the scientist interests himself "strictly in the universals," but "the artist interests himself entirely in individuals"; science abstracts, but poetry is "knowledge by images, reporting the fulness or particularity of nature." "Science gratifies a rational or practical impulse and exhibits the minimum of perception," as opposed to poetry, which exploits "many technical devices for the sake of increasing the volume of the percipienda or sensibilia." Among these devices are meter, a patent fictionality, and figurative language, especially "the climactic figure, which is the metaphor"; all these features, by "inviting perceptual attention," serve to weaken "the tyranny of science over the senses."[28] And in a fusion of contemplative and heterocosmic concepts that is frequent in recent critics, Ransom asserts that when "we contemplate object as object," under "the form of art," we do so not as in science, "for a set of practical values," but in order to know the object

for its own sake, and conceive it as having its own existence; this is the knowledge . . . which Schopenhauer praised as "knowledge without desire." . . . The knowledge attained there [i.e., "in the poem, or the painting"], and recorded, is a new kind of knowledge, the world in which it is set is a new world.[29]

Two centuries earlier Baumgarten had introduced the same radical metaphor of a poem-as-world into his logic of poetic knowledge, and had explored its implications beyond any preceding critic. He was able to do so because he had conveniently at hand the account of God's procedure in creating this world in the *Theodicea* of the philosopher whom he hails as "the illustrious Leibniz" (par. 22). In summary: Leibniz held that God at the creation had in his understanding an infinite number of model worlds, each of which is a "possible" world. Each possible world, however, is a "compossible" world; that is, it consists only of those essences and relations of things which are capable of coexisting, by virtue of the fact that they are mutually consistent. The universal necessities of logic, based on the Principle of Contradiction, apply to the entire array of possible worlds. The factual and contingent truths that apply to the existents, relations, and events within a possible world, however, are based on an alternative principle that Leibniz calls "the Principle of Sufficient Reason." And the specific modes in which this Principle manifests itself are not universal, but relative to the constitution of each model world. As Leibniz put it, with reference to the individual things and laws of order that constitute any possible world:

As there are an infinity of possible worlds, there are also an infinity of laws, certain ones appropriate to one; others, to another, and each possible individual of any world involves in its concept the laws of its world.[30]

The world in which we ourselves live was realized only because God's excellence entailed that, from these alternative models, He bring into existence this world as the best of all possible (which is to say, *com*possible) worlds.

Baumgarten converts Leibniz's cosmogony into poetics by distinguishing between two types of "fictions" in representations of characters, objects, and events. The first type he calls "true fictions" in that, though nonhistorical, they are possible in "the real world in which we find ourselves." The second type are fabulous and mythical elements that violate both the constitution and the causal order of the real world. Justifiable poetic instances of this type, which are necessary to some kinds of poems, he labels "heterocosmic fictions," in the sense that they are capable of coexisting in some other "possible" world. He rejects from poetry only a third class of fictions that he calls "utopian," in the literal sense of belonging "no place"; that is, either because they are logically "self-contradictory," or because they are "mutually inconsistent," such fictions are "absolutely impossible," since they cannot have a place within the coherent constitution of any possible world whatever. And for acceptable "heterocosmic fictions," the justifying criterion is not their "truth" of correspondence to the nature of the real world but a purely internal compossibility, or self-consistency (pars. 51-59).

Baumgarten takes a crucial step when he turns from heterocosmic fictions, or the nonrealistic elements in some poems, to what he calls the "method," or overall principle which determines the "interconnection," or "co-ordination," in "the succession of representations" within any poem whatever; for in this context he extends the heterocosmic analogue to apply to the ordonnance of all works of poetry:

> We observed a little while ago that the poet is like a maker or a creator [*quasi factorem sive creatorem esse*]. So the poem ought to be like a world [*quasi mundus*]. Hence by analogy whatever is evident to the philosophers concerning the real world, the same ought to be thought of a poem. (Par. 68)

What is evident to the philosophers about the real world, it turns out, is that Leibniz's Principle of Sufficient Reason determines the sequence and interconnections of its elements, together with the assurance that the ultimate "rule" of our mundane order is that "things in the world follow one another for disclosing the glory of the Creator." By analogy, each poetic other-world has its own inherent principle which determines the order and relations of its representations. Baumgarten calls this principle its "theme" [*thema*], and defines a theme as "that whose representation contains the sufficient reason of other representations supplied in the discourse, but which does not have its own sufficient reason in them." The consequence for poetics is that all the elements of a valid poem will either be "determined through the theme," or else "will be connected with it." "Therefore, they will be connected among themselves. Therefore, they follow each other in order, like causes and effects." And the "general rule" for the "method" that orders any poem is that "poetic representations are to follow each other in such a way that the theme is progressively represented in an extensively clearer way" (pars. 66-71).

In sum, what emerges from Baumgarten's parallel-in-opposition between rational logic and what in his later *Aesthetica* he called "esthetico-logic," the "logic of sensuous thinking," is a view that has become familiar in modern criticism. A poem provides sensuous knowledge of its own poetic world — a world governed by laws analogous to causal laws in our world but specific to itself; a world whose "poetic" truth and probability does not consist in a correspondence to actual world but in the internal coherence of its elements; and a world that is not ordered to an end external to itself but by an internal finality whereby all its elements are subordinate to the progressive revelation of its particular theme.

In his *Aesthetica* of 1750, Baumgarten altered and generalized his definition of a poem as the perfection of sensuous discourse to apply to other arts, and for the first time identified this achieved perfection as beauty: "The aesthetic end is the perfection of sensuous cognition, as such [*qua talis*]; this is beauty" (par. 14). He also applies the term "a new world" [*novus mundus*], passingly, to the realm of nonrealistic fictions into which we are introduced, not only by a writer "whether in verse or prose" but also by "a painter or a sculptor, etc." (par. 592).[31] As in his *Reflections on Poetry*, however, all of Baumgarten's specific analyses of artistic other-worlds are applied only to works of literature and, in considering these, he supplements his earlier work with a larger number of topics derived from classical theories of rhetoric.

In the Swiss-German critics and collaborators Bodmer and Breitinger, a resort to the heterocosmic model effected similar revisions in the standard concepts of the nature and criteria of a poem. Both these critics set out from the reigning premise that a poem is an "imitation of nature," so designed by the poet-maker as to please and be morally useful to the reader. Both were also passionate defenders of Milton's *Paradise Lost* (which Bodmer had translated into German) against detractors such as Voltaire and Gottsched, who had decried Milton's supernatural beings and events, together with his allegory of Sin and Death, as "improbable," in that they do not correspond to the experienced world; their defense of such nonrealistic elements forced Bodmer and Breitinger into a radical modification of their initial premise.

Bodmer's book *The Marvelous in Poetry. . . in a Defense of "Paradise Lost"* appeared in 1740, five years after Baumgarten's *Reflections on Poetry*. Bodmer expressly follows Addison's lead in treating nonnatural invention as "a new creation" that "makes new worlds." He elaborates this suggestive analogue, however, as had Baumgarten, by recourse to the theory of God's creative procedure proposed by Leibniz — "Leibniz," as Breitinger eulogized him, "the great world-sage of our Germany."[32] "The task of the poet," says Bodmer, "is to imitate the powers of Nature in bringing over the possible into the condition of reality." "Every poet who imagines something possible as real . . . imitates Nature and creation." Bodmer, by sleight of words, thereby converts an imitation theory into a creation theory of poetry, in which the poetic world is not a reflection but an analogue of the world that God has brought into being. As he also says:

This mode of creation is the chief work of poetry, which by this very fact distinguishes itself from the writings of historians and natural scientists, in that it always prefers to take the material of its imitation from the possible world rather than from the actual world.[33]

In his *Critische Dichtkunst,* published that same year, Breitinger is even more explicit and detailed in his conversion of poetic imitation into a version of Leibnizian cosmogony. "All the arts," he says, "consist in a skillful imitation of Nature, for the general profit and pleasure of men." But Nature is only one of many possible worlds.

Nature — or rather the Creator, who works in and through Nature — has from all possible world-structures chosen the present one to bring over into the condition of reality because it was, to his infallible insight, the best of all possible worlds.

Hence, in addition to the present world, "there need to be count-less possible worlds, in which there obtain other inter-relations and connections of things, other laws of Nature and motion . . . even productions and beings of entirely new and strange kinds." It is precisely these innumerable other worlds which provide the poet with

the model and materials for his imitation. . . . Since he is capable not only of imitating Nature in the actual, but also in the possible, the power of his art extends as far as the powers of Nature itself. . . . [In-deed] the imitation of Nature in the possible is the chief work that is specific to poetry.[34]

Correlatively to their distinction between the existing world and the poetic world, Bodmer and Breitinger introduce the dis-tinction between "rational truth," which is a truth of correspon-dence to this world, and "poetic truth," which is a truth of inner coherence, in accordance with whatever mode of sufficient rea-son governs the compossible world that constitutes a poem. "The poet," Bodmer answers a critic who, as he puts it, seeks "poetry in ontosophy," "troubles himself not at all with rational truth [*das Wahre des Verstandes*]," but only with "poetic truth [*das poe-tische Wahre*]."

This poetic truth is not without a certain reason and order; it has for the imagination and the senses its sufficient ground, it has no internal con-tradiction, and one part of it is grounded in the other. . . . For our part, we will look for metaphysics among the teachers of metaphysics, but demand from poets nothing more than poetry; in this we shall be satis-fied with the probability and reason that lies in its coherence with itself.[35]

Breitinger, like Bodmer, sets up a distinction between "histori-cal" or "rational truth" and "poetic" or "imaginative truth," then goes on to analyze—as had Baumgarten, but in much greater detail—the internal organization of a poem in a way that paral-lels Leibniz's view of the empirical order of the existing world:

I regard the poet as a wise creator of a new ideal world or of a new inter-relation [*zusammenhang*] of things, who not only has the right and the power to impart probability to those things which do not exist, but also possesses so much understanding that, in order to achieve his dominant intention [*Absicht*], he binds to one another his individual intentions in such a way that one must always serve as a means to the others, but all together must provide a means to the dominant intention. Accordingly, in this poetic world, as in the actual world, all things must be grounded in one another according to time and place, and the concordance of these toward a single end [*Zwecke*] constitutes precisely the perfection of the whole.[36]

As in Baumgarten, the inference drawn from the heterocosmic model is that the prime criterion of "perfection" in a poem is the interdependence and consistency of its elements, and the subordination of all the elements to an internal end.

One other important point. It is clear that like Baumgarten, the Swiss critics, who had adduced the concept of a poem as its own world in order to justify the invention of nonrealistic characters and events, extended the analogue to the overall organization of all well-contrived poems. As Breitinger explicitly says in *Critische Dichtkunst*:

What is poetic invention [*Dichten*] other than to form in the imagination new concepts and ideas of which the originals are to be sought not in the actual world, but in some other possible world-structure? Every single well-invented poem is therefore to be regarded in no other way than as the history of an other possible world. In this respect the poet alone deserves the name of *poietes,* that is, of a creator.[37]

And Bodmer in 1741 extended the heterocosmic model from poems to a work of prose fiction, Cervantes's *Don Quixote*:

The author, as the father and creator [of his characters], has determined and ordered them and all their destiny; not, however, without a distinct plan of inter-related intentions, which conduct his work to its primary end.[38]

If we turn again to Karl Philipp Moritz's essay of 1788, "The Formative Imitation of the Beautiful," we find two important innovations upon the views of these earlier theorists:

1) For Bodmer and Breitinger, as for Baumgarten, the exemplary heterocosmic art had been literature. That is, they introduced the concept of the poem as its own world in order to account for and justify deviations from the experienced world in the components and ordonnance of works of literary art, and especially in the persons, events, and organization of extended

narrative forms. Moritz, however, specifically expands the hetero-cosmic analogue to apply to the arts of music, sculpture, and painting, as well as literature.[39]

2) In Moritz, the conception of a work of art as a self-sufficient and self-governing world is stripped of its residual references to the imitation of nature and to the ends of effecting pleasure and moral utility;[40] as a result, the heterocosmic model falls into coincidence with the contemplation model, in terms of which the work of art is apprehended disinterestedly, entirely for its own sake. Moritz in fact adverted to the analogue of creation, we remember, precisely in order to explain how a work gets produced which "does not need to be useful." The "formative genius" himself, it turns out, can create his beautiful work only at a time when, by "annulling every trace of self-interest," his "restless activity gives place to quiet contemplation." The consequence that Moritz draws from his claim that the artist, emulating creative nature, "creates his own world" is specifically that this artistic otherworld is to be apprehended with a "*calm contemplation . . . as a single great whole . . .* in which all relationship stops," because "the genuine work of art . . . complete in itself, has the end and intention [*den Endzweck und die Absicht*] of its being solely in itself." The beautiful object thus requires that it "be contemplated and perceived, just in the same way in which it is produced, purely for its own sake."[41]

ART AS SUCH

In mid nineteenth-century France, the contemplation and hetero-cosmic models were often conjoined in the loose-boundaried movement known by its catchword, "Art for Art's Sake." In this movement the original theological context of these models re-emerged, in a displaced form, to constitute a religion of art and a morality of life for art's sake. Flaubert wrote in 1857, "Life is a thing so hideous that the only way to endure it is to escape it. And one escapes it by living in art."[42] And Flaubert, in employing the analogue between divine and artistic creation, also adopted the ancient theological notion that God is both transcendent and immanent, both concealed and revealed in His created world, when he said about the literary heterocosm:

An author in his book must be like God in the universe, present everywhere and visible nowhere. Art being a second Nature, the creator of that Nature must behave similarly. In all its atoms, in all its aspects, let there be sensed a hidden, infinite passivity.[43]

"Poetry," said Baudelaire, "is that in which there is more of reality, it is that which is not completely true except in *an other world.*" The creative imagination "has taught man the moral sense of color, contour, of sound and perfume."

It decomposes the entire creation and . . . creates a new world, it produces the sensation of the new. As it has created the world (one can indeed say this, I believe, even in a religious sense), it is just that it should govern its world. . . . The imagination is the queen of the true, and the *possible* is one of the provinces of the true.[44]

In a poem, furthermore, any requirements of "teaching," "truth," and "morality" are "heresies," for poetry "has no end except itself; it cannot have any other end."[45] Poetry, Mallarmé likewise asserts, is "close to creating." But for Mallarmé, to create a poem is to unrealize and abolish the natural objects that are its materials; hence, "Equivalent to creation: the notion of an object, escaping, which fails to appear."[46] Baudelaire's concept of "la poésie pure" (independent of an external end, or of awareness of an audience, or of the passions of the poet) and Mallarmé's concept of "l'oeuvre pure" (not needing a reader, and in which the poet "disappears," leaving the textual work "anonyme et parfait")[47] are both patently a reincarnation of the self-sufficient Deity of a Platonized Christianity—existing in the purity and perfection of a total lack of reference to, or concern for, anything outside itself—in the mode of being of a sacred work of art.

The claim that a work of art is a world created by the artist, which at the time of its origin had been felt to verge on blasphemy, has in our time become a commonplace of critical discourse. It is not surprising that Vladimir Nabokov, a fervent advocate of the autonomy of art, opened his lectures on the novel at Cornell with the premise that

the work of art is invariably the creation of a new world, so that the first thing we should do is to study that new world as closely as possible, approaching it as something brand new, having no obvious connections with the world we already know.[48]

It is something of a surprise, however, to find a critic of the opposite persuasion, the Marxist Georg Lukács, also asserting that

every work of art must present a circumscribed, self-contained and complete context with its own *immediately* self-evident movement and structure.... Thus every significant work of art creates its "own world."
Characters, situations, actions, etc. in each have a unique quality unlike
that in any other work of art and entirely distinct from anything in
everyday reality. The greater the artist ... the more pregnantly his fictional "world" emerges through all the details of a work.

It turns out, however, that by endowing its "exemplary men and
situations" with "the greatest possible richness of the objective
conditions of life," the great bourgeois novelist in fact "makes his
'own world' emerge as the reflection of life in its total motion, as
process and totality" — a "reflection," that is, of the alienation,
contradictions, and progressive evolution of bourgeois society.[49]
In both Nabokov and Lukács the exemplary heterocosmic art
remains, as it had been originally, literary narrative; but Wassily
Kandinsky indicates how all-inclusive the scope of the analogue
has become by applying it not only to paintings, but to nonrepre-
sentational paintings:

Painting is a thundering collision of different worlds, intended to create
a new world in, and from, the struggle with one another, a new world
which is the work of art.... The creation of works of art is the creation
of the world.[50]

I shall end by turning back to the two twentieth-century theorists with whom I introduced the topic of the poem-as-world in
order to stress this point: the heterocosmic model, despite its differences from the contemplation model in its theological prototype, and in the particular art to which it was initially applied,
eventuated in the same philosophical idiom — the idiom of art-as-
such — for specifying the defining features and primary criteria
for a work of art. Thus A. C. Bradley, from his premise that a
poem is "a world by itself, independent, complete, autonomous,"
educes the philosophical consequences that the experience of a
poem "is an end in itself," with an "intrinsic value" that excludes
reference to "ulterior ends"; that the purely "poetic worth" of a
poem "is to be judged entirely from within"; hence, that "it
makes no direct appeal to [the] feelings, desires, and purposes" of

ordinary life, "but speaks only to contemplative imagination."[51] Bradley's title is "Poetry for Poetry's Sake," and he explicitly undertakes to rid the earlier French doctrine of the extravagance of its claim that "Art is the whole or supreme end of human life." He nonetheless guards the self-bounded integrity of a poem by prohibitions against such "heresies" as "the heresy of the separable substance" (that is, of a paraphrasable content), as well as against reference to the "emotions and conditions" of the poet himself, which "are poetically irrelevant."[52]

E. M. Forster similarly entitled one of his essays "Art for Art's Sake," and he described the world of a poem as subject only "to its own laws" and to a standard of truth that is not one of external reference but of internal consistency: it "supports itself, internally coheres." "A poem is absolute. . . . It causes us to suspend our ordinary judgments." The sole analogue to the self-sufficing "internal" order and harmony of a work of art, he says, is "the divine order, the mystic harmony, which according to all religions is available for those who can contemplate it." And in opposition to "the demand that literature should express personality," Forster contends that "during the poem nothing exists but the poem. . . . It becomes anonymous," on the basis of the theological concept that "to forget its Creator is one of the functions of a Creation."[53] In Bradley's essay of 1901, and Forster's essays of the 1920s, we patently move from the theory of Art for Art's Sake to the premises and categories that were to recur in the New Criticism, in its view, as Cleanth Brooks put it, that, as opposed to propositional assertions about the world, the "coherence" of a poem consists in "the unification of attitudes into a hierarchy subordinated to a total and governing attitude," which in its unity constitutes "a simulacrum of reality,"[54] and also in its zealous defense of the boundaries of the autonomous and self-contained poem by quasi-theological prohibitions (in the lineage of Poe, Baudelaire, and Bradley) against the heresy of paraphrase, the intentional fallacy, and the affective fallacy.

By identifying their theological origins, I do not mean to derogate the practical value of the contemplation and heterocosmic models for art. Once adapted to aesthetics and criticism, what matters is not their provenience but their profitability when put to work in clarifying the features both of a work of art and of our experience of that work. Both these models have amply demon-strated their profitability for the applied criticism of literature and the other arts. Their focus on the aesthetic object as such, especially in the last half-century, has greatly enlarged our reper-tory of terms and distinctions for analyzing a work of art as con-stituted by distinctive elements, ordered into coherence by inter-nal relations, and made integral by subordination to an internal end. But to suggest the limits of the view of art-as-such—for as in all theories of art, the sharpness of its focus imposes limitations on its scope and adequacy—let me put this question. Why should the claim—radically opposed to all traditional views about the nature and value of art—that a work is to be contemplated for its own sake as a self-sufficient entity, severed from all relations to its human author, to its human audience, and to the world of human life and concerns, serve as the very ground for attributing to art its supreme human value?

The appeal of this view, I suggest, is not primarily empirical, for it accords only with selective aspects of our full experience of great works of art. Its primary appeal consists rather in its pro-found metaphysical and theological pathos. It is the same pathos that empowers the concept, which has endured from Plato through the Christian centuries, that perfection and ultimate value inhere solely in a metaphysical absolute or deity who is purely otherworldly, serenely integral, self-sufficient and self-bounded, and for those reasons, to be contemplated and revered above everything in the fragmented, incoherent, and conflict-ridden world in which we find ourselves. The attraction that many of us feel to the theory of art-as-such, if I am not mistaken, is the attraction that it shares with this concept, and with its fre-quent complement: that even in his seemingly other-oriented act of creation, the inscrutable deity brought into being a world that he then left to its own destiny, remaining himself—as James Joyce, echoing Flaubert, put it in describing "the mystery of esthetic like that of material creation"—remaining himself "invis-ible, refined out of existence, indifferent, paring his finger-nails."[55]

NOTES

1. See Paul Oskar Kristeller, "The Modern System of the Arts," *Journal of the History of Ideas* 12 (1951): 496-527; 13 (1952): 17-46.

2. Friedrich Schelling, *System des transcendentalen Idealismus, Sämtliche Werke* (Stuttgart und Augsburg, 1858), III: 349.

3. T. E. Hulme, *Speculations: Essays on Humanism and the Philosophy of Art,* ed. Herbert Read (London, 1924), p. 136.

4. Jerome Stolnitz, *Aesthetics and Philosophy of Art Criticism* (Cambridge, Mass., 1960), pp. 35, 209, 211.

5. A. C. Bradley, "Poetry for Poetry's Sake," *Oxford Lectures on Poetry* (London, 1950), pp. 5-6.

6. E. M. Forster, "Anonymity: An Enquiry," *Two Cheers for Democracy* (New York, 1951), pp. 81-82.

7. See Jerome Stolnitz, "On the Significance of Lord Shaftesbury in Modern Aesthetic Theory," *Philosophical Quarterly* 2 (1961): 97-113; and "On the Origins of 'Aesthetic Disinterestedness,'" *Journal of Aesthetic and Art Criticism* 20 (1961-62): 131-143. For the history of the concepts of "contemplation" and "disinterestedness," before and after Shaftesbury, see M. H. Abrams, "Kant and the Theology of Art," *Notre Dame English Journal* (1981): 75-106.

8. K. P. Moritz, *Schriften zur Asthetik und Poetik,* ed. Hans Joachim Schrimpf (Tübingen, 1962), p. 3. The emphases are Moritz's.

9. Ibid., pp. 6-8.

10. Ibid., p. 5. The emphasis on "love" is Moritz's.

11. Martha Woodmansee, "The Origin of the Doctrine of Literary Autonomy," a paper delivered at the International Association for Philosophy and Literature, Orono, Maine, May 9, 1980. See the first chapter of Moritz's *Anton Reiser.*

12. The Dialogues of Plato, translated by B. Jowett, *Symposium,* 210-212; *Philebus,* 59-60, 67.

13. Plotinus, *Enneads,* translated by Stephen MacKenna, revised by B. S. Page (London, 1956), pp. 380, 400-401, 619-620; 61-63; 409, 622-624.

14. See K. Svoboda, *L'Esthétique de St. Augustin et ses sources* (Brno, 1933), pp. 102ff. The relevant comments by Augustine on the distinction between love for use and love for enjoyment are conveniently collected in Anders Nygren, *Agape and Eros,* translated by Philip S. Watson (London, 1953), pp. 349-446, footnotes. See also Abrams, "Kant and the Theology of Art," in note 7, above.

Jacques Maritain's theory of the fine arts is of interest because it reintegrates the contemplation of a work of art with the theological concept of the loving contemplation of God which earlier theorists had used as the model for developing a purely secular view of aesthetic experience. The work of art, says Maritain, "of its very nature and precisely as beautiful . . . stirs desire and produces love," in an ecstasy which the soul experiences in its fullness only "when it is absorbed . . . by the beauty of

God." And on the express analogy of Scholastic views about contemplation of the divine wisdom, he declares that works of fine art are "disinterested, desired for themselves." A work is not made "in order that one may use it as a means, but in order that one may enjoy it as an end," and the "mode of being" of works of art "is contemplative . . . they aim at producing an intellectual delight, that is to say, a kind of contemplation" (*Art and Scholasticism and the Frontiers of Poetry,* trans. Joseph W. Evans [New York, 1962], pp. 23-37).

15. *Kant's Critique of Aesthetic Judgment,* translated by James Creed Meredith (Oxford, 1911), pp. 43, 48-49, 69, 90; the emphases are Kant's. Where I have altered Meredith's translation, I have also inserted the German phrases.

16. Moritz, *Schriften zur Ästhetik und Poetik,* pp. 71, 73-74.

17. Kant, *Critique of Aesthetic Judgment,* p. 176.

18. In *Phaedrus* 250, for example, Plato says, in his account of the soul's journey to the realm of forms: "But of beauty, I repeat again that we saw her there shining in company with the celestial forms; and coming to earth we find her here too, shining in clearness through the clearest aperture of sense. For sight is the most piercing of our bodily senses. . . . This is the privilege of beauty, that being the loveliest she is also the most palpable to sight."

19. Clive Bell, *Art* (New York: Capricorn Books, 1958), pp. 54-55, 107.

20. On the sharp distinction between God's creation "out of nothing" and the poet's creation from preexisting matter, see E. N. Tigerstedt, "The Poet as Creator: Origins of a Metaphor," *Comparative Literature Studies* 5 (1968): 455-488. Giovanni Capriano, in his *Della vera poetica* (1555) seems unique in his time by claiming that "the true poets must invent their poetry out of nothing" [*di nulla fingere la lor' poesia*]; he does not, however, use the verb *creare,* which was a theological term reserved uniquely for a power of God. Capriano is cited by Bernard Weinberg, *A History of Literary Criticism in the Italian Renaissance,* 2 vols. (Chicago, 1963), II: 733.

Probably the earliest clear statement of the analog between the poet's activity and God's relativity is by Cristoforo Landino who, in the "Proemio" to his *Commentary on Dante* (1481), said that the poet's feigning "is half-way between 'creating' [*creare*] which is proper only for God . . . and 'making' [*fare*], which applies to men when they compose with matter and form in any art [i.e., craft]. . . . Although the feigning [*figmento*] of the poet is not entirely out of nothing, it nevertheless departs from making and comes very near to creating." For similar passages elsewhere in Landino, see Tigerstedt, pp. 458-459.

21. See Tigerstedt; also M. H. Abrams, *The Mirror and the Lamp* (New York, 1953), pp. 272-275, and notes, pp. 380-381.

22. Leonardo da Vinci in turn adapted to painting the parallel between "the painter's mind" and "the divine mind"—with passing but undeveloped allusions to the painter as a "creator" and to aspects of his work as "a creation"—in order to raise his own disparaged art over all

other arts, including poetry. See Martin Kemp, "From 'Mimesis' to 'Fantasia'... in the Visual Arts," *Viator* 8 (1970): 347-398.

23. Sir Philip Sidney, *An Apologie for Poetry*, in *Elizabethan Critical Essays*, ed. G. Gregory Smith, 2 vols. (London, 1904), I: 155-158. A parallel distinction between theoretical and laudatory aims is apparent in J. C. Scaliger's influential *Poetices* (1561): "The basis of all poetry is imitation," although imitation "is not the end of poetry, but is intermediate to the end" of giving "instruction in pleasurable form." It is specifically in the attempt to elevate poetry over oratory and history that Scaliger makes the later claim that it excels "those other arts" in that while they "represent things just as they are... the poet depicts another sort of nature," and thus "transforms himself almost into a second God." For the poet, in making "images of things which are not" as well as more beautiful images "of those things which are," exceeds the historian and seems "like another God, to produce the things themselves [*res ipsas... velut alter deus condere*]" (F. M. Padelford, *Select Translations from J. C. Scaliger's Poetics* [New York, 1905], pp. 2, 7-8). I have altered a few of Padelford's English phrases to bring them closer to the Latin original.

24. Addison, *Spectator* 419. Addison had in mind the claims by empiricists such as Thomas Hobbes that, since a poem is "an imitation of humane life," the criterion of truth eliminates such elements as "impenetrable Armors, Inchanted Castles... flying Horses." For, "the Resemblance of truth is the utmost limit of Poeticall Liberty.... Beyond the actual works of nature a Poet may now go, but beyond the conceived possibility of nature, never." Hobbes, "Answer to Davenant's Preface to *Gondibert*," (1650) in *Critical Essays of the Seventeenth Century*, ed. J. E. Spingarn, 3 vols. (Oxford, 1908), II: 61-62. See Abrams, "Truth and the Poetic Marvelous," in *The Mirror and the Lamp*, pp. 265-268.

25. *Spectator* 419 and 421. In lauding the poet as one who invents "another nature," Sidney had already exemplified this power by reference to the poet's ability to bring forth "formes such as never were in Nature, as the Heroes, Demigods, Cyclops, Furies, and such like."

26. Baumgarten's *Reflections on Poetry*, translated by Karl Aschenbrenner and William B. Holther (Berkeley and Los Angeles, 1954), par. 115. In par. 116, Baumgarten goes on to apply the term "aesthetic" to "the science of perception" (which includes poetry in its scope), as distinguished from the noetic science of things that are "known by the superior faculty as the object of logic."

27. John Crowe Ransom, *The World's Body* (New York, 1938), pp. x, 205.

28. Ibid., pp. 206, 156-158, 130-133.

29. Ibid., pp. 44-45.

30. Leibniz to Arnaud, May 1686, in Leibniz, *Discourse on Metaphysics*, translated by George R. Montgomery (La Salle, Ill., 1947), pp. 108-109.

31. For Baumgarten's treatment in the *Aesthetica* of "heterocosmic

fiction" as the creation of a "possible" new world, whose "heterocosmic truth" and "heterocosmic probability" are a matter of internal noncontradiction and coherence, see, e.g., pars. 441, 475, 511-538, 598-599.

Georg Friedrich Meier, in his *Anfangsgründe aller schönen Wissenschaften* (1754), which is in large part an exposition of Baumgarten, declares that the "probability" of "heterocosmic fictions" such as fables are grounded "primarily on the fact that its inventor creates [*schaft*] a new world.... He draws the attention of his listener entirely to the coherence [*Zusammenhang*] that he has newly created. The listener so to speak forgets the present world... and gets involved in an entirely new inter-connection and order of things, and so must hold to be probable everything which is possible and grounded in the new order. These fictions are the ones in which a fine mind [*schöner Geist*] demonstrates his creative powers, or 'esprit créateur'...." (Part I, par. 107)

32. Johann Jacob Breitinger, *Critische Dichtkunst* (1740), facsimile, ed. Wolfgang Bender, 2 vols. (Stuttgart, 1966), I: 273.

33. Johann Jacob Bodmer, *Critische Abhandlung von dem Wunderbaren in der Poesie* (1740), facsimile, ed. Wolfgang Bender (Stuttgart, 1966), pp. 165-166, 32.

34. Breitinger, *Critische Dichtkunst*, I: 7, 54-57. It is noteworthy that in his "Formative Imitation of the Beautiful," written forty-five years later, Moritz also modeled his view of poetic creation on the creative power that God has delegated to a formative principle that operates within the natural world; see above.

35. Bodmer, *Von dem Wunderbaren*, pp. 47, 49. See also pp. 144-145.

36. Breitinger, *Critische Dichtkunst*, I: 425-426. See also I: 270-278, 286-290. Breitinger explains that creative Nature, as Leibniz has shown, is constrained to bring into being the best of all possible worlds, and that since the concept of what is best entails the greatest possible diversity of existents, our world necessarily contains many degrees of imperfection. Relieved of God's constraint, however, the poet is able to bring over into being a world that is more perfect in its individual elements than our best of possible worlds (I: 273-274).

37. Ibid., I: 59-60. Breitinger repeats this assertion in I: 271.

38. Bodmer, *Critische Betrachtungen über die poetischen Gemälde der Dichter* (Zurich, 1741), p. 543.

39. Moritz, *Schriften zur Ästhetik*, pp. 73-75.

40. See, e.g., Breitinger's exposition of the poet's rendering of the nature that he imitates so as to enhance its moral qualities and effects; *Critische Dichtkunst*, I: 282-290.

41. Moritz, *Schriften zur Ästhetik*, pp. 80, 83, 85-86. The emphases are Moritz's.

42. 18 May 1857, in Gustave Flaubert, *Correspondance* (Paris, 1926 ff.), IV: 182.

43. 9 Dec. 1852, in *The Letters of Gustave Flaubert, 1830-1857,* translated by Francis Steegmuller (Cambridge, Mass., 1980), p. 173.

See also 18 March 1857, p. 230: "The artist in his work must be like God in his creation — invisible and all-powerful: he must be everywhere felt but never seen."

The basic text for this concept of God's relation to His created world is Paul's Epistle to the Romans, 1.20, which was the subject of endless comment and expansion by biblical commentators: "For the invisible things of Him from the creation of the world are clearly seen, being understood by the things that are made, even His eternal power and Godhead...." In the 1790s, Friedrich Schlegel transferred this concept to the literary creator, as a ground for the mode of "Romantic irony": the literary artist, "visibly invisible," is both "objective" and "subjective" in his work; he establishes the illusion that his creation is a self-sufficient world, yet displays his own characteristics in that work, and is free to manifest his arbitrary power over that work. See Alfred Edwin Lussky, *Tieck's Romantic Irony* (Chapel Hill, 1932), Chap. II; and M. H. Abrams, *The Mirror and the Lamp,* pp. 237-241.

44. *Oeuvres complètes de Baudelaire,* ed. Y. G. Le Dantec and Claude Pichois (Bibliothèque de la Pléiade, 1963), pp. 637, 1037-1038. The emphases are Baudelaire's.

45. "Notes nouvelles sur Edgar Poe," in *Oeuvres complètes de Charles Baudelaire,* ed. F. F. Gautier and Y. G. Le Dantec (Paris, 1933), X: 29-30.

In Oscar Wilde's "The Critic as Artist" (191), Ernest proposes that "it is the function of Literature to create, from the rough material of actual existence, a new world that will be more marvelous, more enduring, and more true than the world that common eyes look upon." If made by a great artist, "this new world ... will be a thing so complete and perfect that there will be nothing left for the critic to do." To which Gilbert responds by adroitly transferring the creative analogue from the artist to the critic, and the concept of autonomy from the work of art to the work of criticism: "Criticism is, in fact, both creative and independent.... Nay, more, I would say that the highest Criticism ... is in its way more creative than creation, as it ... is, in fact, its own reason for existing, and, as the Greeks would put it, in itself, and to itself, an end." *The Artist as Critic: Critical Writings of Oscar Wilde,* ed. Richard Ellman (New York, 1968-69), pp. 363-365.

46. *Oeuvres complètes de Stephane Mallarmé,* ed. Henri Mondor and G. Jean-Aubry (Bibliothèque de la Pléiade, 1961), pp. 400, 647.

47. Ibid., pp. 366-367, 372.

48. Vladimir Nabokov, *Lectures on Literature,* ed. Fredson Bowers (New York and London, 1980), p. 1.

49. Georg Lukács, *Writer and Critic and Other Essays,* translated by Arthur D. Kahn (New York, 1971), pp. 35-40.

50. Wassily Kandinsky, "Reminiscences," in *Modern Artists on Art,* ed. Robert L. Herbert (Englewood Cliffs, N.J., 1964), p. 35.

51. Bradley, *Oxford Lectures on Poetry,* pp. 4-5, 7.

52. Ibid., pp. 17, 29.

53. Forster, *Two Cheers for Democracy,* pp. 82, 91-92, 85. R. G. Collingwood exemplifies the merging of the contemplative and heterocosmic models by a philosopher rather than a critic of art. "In art the mind has an object which it contemplates." But the object contemplated "is an imaginary object," created by the act of contemplation. "To imagine an object . . . is to be wholly indifferent to its reality," and the coherence of the imagined, hence simply contemplated, object "is a merely internal coherence . . . self-contained." Then, in a latter-day instance of the aesthetic application of a Leibnizian concept—this time, however, of Leibniz's concept of the monad:

Every work of art as such, as an object of imagination, is a world wholly self-contained, a complete universe which has nothing outside it . . . [and is] imaginatively contemplated. . . . Every work of art is a monad, a windowless and self-contained universe which . . . indeed is nothing but a vision or perspective of the universe, and of a universe which is just itself. . . . Whatever is in it must have arisen from the creative act which constitutes it.

Outlines of a Philosophy of Art (London, 1925), pp. 10-24, 76.

54. Cleanth Brooks, "The Heresy of Paraphrase," *The Well Wrought Urn* (New York, 1947), pp. 189, 194. Also Austin Warren, *Rage for Order* (Chicago, 1948), pp. v-vi: The poet's "final creation" is "a kind of world or cosmos; a concretely languaged, synoptically felt world, an ikon or image of the 'real world.'"

55. James Joyce, *A Portrait of the Artist as a Young Man,* in *The Portable James Joyce,* ed. Harry Levin (New York, 1947), p. 482.

III
THE AESTHETICS AND POLITICS OF
LANDSCAPE IN THE
EIGHTEENTH CENTURY

Carole Fabricant

In the eighteenth century, the aesthetic contemplation and appreciation of landscape assumed a significance it never had before. Poems, travel accounts, and garden treatises all stressed the role of landscape as a stimulator of the imagination and a provider of gratification for the senses: as an entity that could, in Stephen Switzer's words, "yield Satisfaction to the Eye of the Beholder" and "Entertain the Sight every Moment."[1] It is characteristic of the age that Addison chose to compare Milton's descriptions of Hell and Paradise on the basis of which one charmed the reader more, concluding that "they are both, perhaps, equally perfect in their Kind, but in the one the Brimstone and Sulphur are not so refreshing to the Imagination, as the Beds of Flowers, and the Wilderness of Sweets in the other."[2] Religious and doctrinal considerations diminished in importance as a landscape's ability to be "refreshing to the Imagination" became an increasingly significant criterion in the course of the eighteenth century. This concern with the aesthetic and sensuous properties of the landscape represented a distinct shift in emphasis from the pre-

49

ceding century, when topography was regularly, as a matter of habit, moralized. An obvious example is Denham's *Cooper's Hill*, where the physical features of an actual landscape are transformed into a symbolic panorama demonstrating, among other things, the evils of civil war and the need for a balanced polity. The poet's eye is very much in evidence, but what it gets from the landscape is not continuous entertainment or aesthetic delight but moral and political edification. When, for example, "[His] eye descending from the Hill, surveys / Where *Thames* amongst the wanton vallies strays," the river is seen to be "Hasting to pay his tribute to the Sea, / Like mortal life to meet Eternity" (159-160; 163-164).[3]

This is not to say that the moralizing of landscape disappeared in the eighteenth century. We need only think of Pope's *Windsor-Forest,* with its translation of the royal forest into a revived Eden whose groves are "At once the Monarch's and the Muse's Seats" (2), or Thomson's depiction of the "all-instructing page" of "Nature's volume," testifying to the glory of God's works ("Summer," 192-193), in order to recognize a thread of continuity between seventeenth- and eighteenth-century modes of perceiving the landscape.[4] Nevertheless, a distinct change is apparent. Thus in his *Lectures on Architecture* (1734), Robert Morris could associate the seclusion of a summer house with the act of philosophic and spiritual meditation—"It is HERE in the *cooler Hours* of Reflection, a Man might retire, to contemplate the important *Themes* of *Human Life*"—even as his primary emphasis is on a very different kind of contemplation: "Every Sprig of *Grass* may afford a multitude of fine Thoughts, to employ the Imagination; and by a Genius turn'd to *microscopical* Speculations, a Way is open'd to entertain the Fancy with unbounded Reflections."[5] Despite continuing statements recommending the use of rustic retreats for religious meditation, there was in fact widespread abandonment of the latter practice. As John Dixon Hunt notes: "...landowners [in the eighteenth century] sought to employ others to do their meditation for them. Charles Hamilton advertised for a hermit at Paine's Hill in Surrey and built him a hermitage where his contract required him to remain for seven years. ...Most vacancies had to be filled with stuffed dummies that gave the right emblematic effect at twenty yards."[6] Clearly what was important was not the actual meditation but the *appearance*

of it, the aesthetic effect it had on the (properly stationed) spectator. In this respect the situation was characteristic of the period's
treatment of landscape, which, despite recurring claims of "natu-
ralness" and simplicity, involved various, at times elaborate,
forms of optical illusion and deception (more usually and kindly
termed artful management and creative invention). Dummy her-
mits were obviously the relatives of sham castles (such as Ralph
Allen's, built to be distantly visible from his townhouse in Bath),
false façades, such as that of Wood's Queen Square, also in Bath,
and the fake ruins that became an increasingly popular part of
picturesque landscapes.[7]

The simultaneous continuity with and shift away from earlier
attitudes toward the world of external nature may be seen in the
fact that, while eighteenth-century depictions of landscape often
paid explicit homage to those of the preceding century by quoting
passages from them, these allusions were generally invoked as a
means of investing the later accounts with an aura of authority or
"official" sanction without, however, necessarily bringing to bear
the network of assumptions and values that originally informed
the passages. Both Defoe and the anonymous author of the mid-
century "Epistolary Description of the Late Mr. Pope's House and
Gardens at Twickenham," for example, cite Denham's lines on
the Thames, "Though deep, yet clear, though gentle, yet not
dull, / Strong without rage, without ore-flowing full" (191-192),
in the course of their own respective descriptions of Twickenham
and the Thames Valley. In each case, however, the cited passage
comes across as a somewhat mechanical "tag," an official and
expected tribute paid to literary convention rather than a deeply
felt assertion of the land's emblematic function. In *Cooper's Hill*,
the lines are preceded by the poet's wish that he could make the
Thames "My great example, as it is my theme!" (190), and lay the
groundwork for Denham's noted expression of *concordia discors*,
put forth as a combined religious, metaphysical, and political
principle. "An Epistolary Description of the Late Mr. Pope's
House," however, although it elsewhere exploits the purely visual
and aesthetic implications of *concordia discors*, gives no recognition to the river's emblematic significance, using Denham's lines
merely as a convenient bridge between two passages exalting the
beauties and elegancies of Pope's villa: "Twickenham is a delightful Village, situated about a North Country Mile above *Rich-*

mond, on the opposite Side of the River. Mr. *Pope's* House stands in the South-west End of the Village; the Area of the Ground is a gentle Declivity most agreeably sloping to the *Thames,* which here exactly answers *Denham's* inimitable Description of it."[8] We might note the way in which lines basically descriptive of what might be termed the Thames' moral qualities (i.e., its depth, gentleness, and strength) have become entirely visualized, rendered part of an ethically neutral, pictorial scene. Defoe likewise de-moralizes Denham's description, citing it as a seemingly gratuitous conclusion to his observation on the Thames' aesthetic attractions, while "viewing the beautiful prospect of the river, and of the meadows, on the banks of the river."[9] The lines are in fact not particularly appropriate to the occasion, for they have little to do with Defoe's main concerns here (after quoting the lines, he immediately drops the subject of the Thames and turns his entire attention to his travel itinerary). I am not arguing that the moral and philosophic principles underlying Denham's topographical descriptions no longer possessed any relevance for the eighteenth century; my point, rather, is that we cannot automatically assume such a relevance simply on the basis of allusions to or echoes from the past. In all such cases, the specific context must be examined in order to detect possible differences in nuance and meaning. In broader terms, I am suggesting that the obvious continuities between seventeenth- and eighteenth-century conceptions of landscape were accompanied by less obvious, but no less significant, *dis*continuities in the manner of perceiving and interpreting the natural world.

The new emphasis on a specifically aesthetic consideration of landscape was part and parcel of the historical movement noted by M. H. Abrams in his discussion in this volume: a movement, spanning the era from Addison to Kant, characterized by unprecedented interest in the arts and typified by the 1750 publication of Baumgarten's *Aesthetica.* Moreover, the growth of interest in aesthetic issues during the eighteenth century was clearly related to contemporary developments in philosophical thought and scientific ideas—in Lockean epistemology and the rise of empiricism, in associationist theories and the emphasis on subjective mental responses, in Newtonian optics and the resulting preoccupation with matters of light and color, along with new interest in the act of perception itself. These developments fit easily into a history of ideas framework — indeed, rather *too* easily, considering the abundance of abstractions they have produced. Too often ignored in (would-be) explanations of the rise of aesthetics in the eighteenth century are its links to contemporary social and economic, in the broadest sense political, realities: for example, to the changed and changing shape of English society in the years following the Glorious Revolution. In his attempt to counter this general neglect, Robert C. Holub associates the rise of aesthetics with such historical phenomena as the rise to power of the middle class, the decline of the patronage system combined with the artist's growing dependence on the marketplace, and the objectification of the work of art as a commodity consummable on an individual basis.[10] Unfortunately, Holub's brief discussion is long on theory while short on specific facts and precisely analyzed connections. Nevertheless, his essay makes several pertinent observations about the relation between aesthetics and society during the period with which we are concerned here. The aesthetics of landscape, for example, was very much tied up with the "business" as well as the pleasure of garden design — with the conspicuous consumerism of wealthy estate owners, willing to pay large sums to transform their property into works of art that were at the same time salable commodities. Raymond Williams, in his discussion of the rise of an agrarian capitalist class in the early part of the century and its inevitable effect on the way the land was perceived and reshaped, and John Barrell, in (for one) his analysis of the Claudian structure of eighteenth-century landscape in terms of its socioeconomic as well as epistemological implications, have laid the most significant groundwork for a study of the interconnections between the aesthetics and the politics of landscape in this period.[11]

It is not my intention in this essay to present a carefully worked out analysis of the aesthetics of landscape in terms of the class structure of eighteenth-century English society, or in relation to particular aspects of England's social and economic system. Rather, I wish to suggest, in a somewhat informal and unsystematic manner, a few ways in which the aesthetics of landscape fulfilled important ideological functions, serving to conceal as well as to reveal existing historical realities, and indirectly illuminating certain contradictions inherent in eighteenth-century society. In this regard, it possessed similarities with earlier treatments of landscape, which also played an important ideological role by alternately interpreting and mystifying the relationship between man and the external world, between the rulers and the ruled in human society. A work like *Cooper's Hill*, for example, may *seem* to be quite open about its political dimension in that it deals with questions of power and kingship, but in fact its entire thrust is to present a cosmic and moral statement that claims to transcend politics to the extent that the latter are inevitably tainted by partisanship and subjectivity, by the limitation that necessarily accompanies an argument for one particular side as opposed to another. As James Turner puts it in his examination of "The Politics of Landscape" in the mid-seventeenth century, "[*Topographia*] is well suited to the emotive politics of the *ancien regime,* for it allows the old order to seem permanent, orderly and universally agreeable.... *Topographia* turns subjective values into apparent facts."[12]

The aesthetic treatment of landscape in the eighteenth century, via an altered set of priorities and a somewhat different vocabulary, performed a similar function in naturalizing and thereby legitimating man-made, hence provisional, structures and systems. It, no less than its seventeenth-century counterpart, grew out of, and reflected, the politics of landscape. By the latter term I am not thinking primarily of such explicit examples as Pope's revived Eden, where "Rich Industry sits smiling on the Plains, / And Peace and Plenty tell, a STUART reigns" (*Windsor-Forest,* 41-42), or Addison's homage to the Goddess Liberty in his verse epistle *A Letter from Italy,* where Liberty's sensuous and visual attractions — "Profuse of bliss, and pregnant with delight!" (120) — concretely attest to England's superior political attributes: "'Tis Liberty that crowns *Britannia's* Isle, / And makes her barren rocks and her bleak mountains smile" (139-140).[13] Rather, I have in mind examples like those from the essays on "The Pleasures of the Imagination" in the *Spectator,* where Addison, eschewing the explicitly political message of his poem, presents other "landscapes of liberty" that focus upon epistemological and aesthetic matters:

The Mind of Man naturally hates every thing that looks like a Restraint upon it, and is apt to fancy it self under a sort of Confinement, when the Sight is pent up in a narrow Compass, and shortned on every side by the Neighbourhood of Walls or Mountains. On the contrary, a spacious

Horison is an Image of Liberty, where the Eye has Room to range abroad, to expatiate at large on the Immensity of its Views, and to lose it self amidst the Variety of Objects that offer themselves to its Observation. Such wide and undetermined Prospects are as pleasing to the Fancy, as the Speculations of Eternity or Infinitude are to the Understanding.[14]

Here the concept of liberty is psychologized and aestheticized, seemingly divorced from questions of governmental systems, but this passage from the *Spectator* reflects the politics of landscape no less than (although of course differently from) the passage in *A Letter from Italy*. The liberty of the eye, its freedom to range over wide expanses of terrain, relies upon the existence of other liberties more readily associated with the "goddess" Addison celebrates in verse. The eye's ability to "expatiate at large" and to "lose it self" amidst nature's diversity (we might be reminded of the "interminable meads / And vast savannas, where the wandering eye, / Unfixt, is in a verdant ocean lost," described in Thomson's "Summer" [691-693]) represents a very different situation from the far steadier, more disciplined concentration of Denham, whose occasionally "wandring eye," although it may threaten at moments to betray his "fixt thoughts" (112), never strays beyond the carefully constructed topographical framework of the poem, which is also to say the set boundaries of a particular kind of didactic vision.

Significantly, Addison's insistence upon the unfettered eye is immediately preceded by a celebration of the virtues of vastness and magnificence, especially as linked to seemingly boundless prospects: "By *Greatness,* I do not only mean the Bulk of any single Object, but the Largeness of a whole View, considered as one entire Piece. Such are the Prospects of an open Champian Country, a vast uncultivated Desart, of huge Heaps of Mountains, high Rocks and Precipices, or a wide Expanse of Waters, where we are not struck with the Novelty or Beauty of the Sight, but with that rude kind of Magnificence which appears in many of these stupendous Works of Nature." Addison, the well-to-do exponent of middle-class culture, combines the grandeur and majesty normally linked to a traditional aristocracy with the liberty and mobility more congenial to the nouveaux riches — to an expanding, prosperous capitalist class in the process of moving up into the world of (partly by appropriating portions of the landscape once exclusively owned by) the aesthetically cultivated, landed gentleman.

Prospects, even when (as in this case) not depicted didactically, possessed important ideological and symbolic overtones, due largely to the prospect viewer's lofty position and his consequent relationship to all objects within his scope of vision: a relationship epitomized in Arthur Young's assertion, after mounting a hill near Raby Castle, "You there command the whole, from the castle on one side to the hills beyond the farm house on the other."[15] William Gilpin takes Young's assertion a step further when, in the process of vicariously scaling the highest peak in Lebanon with the aid of Volney's travel account, he cites the latter's exultant description upon attaining the summit: "There on every side you see an horizon almost without bounds.... You seem to command the whole world."[16] It is clear why mountain peaks and other promontories were central features of an aristocratic landscape — and later, important features of the landscape toured and described by those who aspired to replace the nobility in the newly emerging social order. From such heights the eighteenth-century spectator, like a lord overseeing his creation, was able to "command" a view of the country stretching out beneath him and thereby exert control over it in much the same way that the aristocratic class (at least through the seventeenth century) ruled over those on the lower rungs of the social hierarchy. Addison in his essays shows that he is duly impressed with prospects and aware of the power they can confer upon the viewer: describing the "Man of a Polite Imagination," for example, he contends that such a person "often feels a greater Satisfaction in the Prospect of Fields and Meadows, than another does in the Possession. It gives him, indeed, a kind of Property in every thing he sees, and makes the most rude uncultivated Parts of Nature administer to his Pleasures."[17]

(The terms are very much those of the eighteenth century rather than of an earlier period; they underscore the economic aspect of control and identify power with the gratification of appetites rather than with the assertion of hierarchic order.) At the same time, we should keep in mind Addison's fascination with the idea of the spectator's sensuous and visual abandon to nature's seemingly infinite variety. This paradoxical coexistence of assertion of control over one's surroundings and one's loss of control, a temporary dissolution of self occasioned by acts of aesthetic surrender and release, characterizes much of the writings on landscape in the eighteenth century. It is interesting that a work like *The Seasons,* which contains some of the period's most conservative and traditional expressions of an aristocratic landscape, featuring a "commanding" prospect of the countryside below and conveying an image of hierarchic subordination, at the same time contains extreme examples of the eye's diffuse wanderings and its loss of mastery amidst the bewildering multiplicity and variousness of the natural world. (I will return to this matter at the end of my essay.)

The landscape Addison draws, however, while giving prospects their due and suggesting their connection with the sublime, deemphasizes their link to privileged positions of ascendancy and eminence. Addison stresses not the aspect of height but breadth, the "Room to range abroad," viewing prospects in light of his famous triad, "*Greatness, Novelty,* and *Beauty.*" There is to some extent a "horizontalizing" of the landscape in his writings; although "huge Heaps of Mountains" and "high Rocks and Precipices" appear in the description, they are set alongside the "vast uncultivated Desart" and the "wide Expanse of Water," differing from but aesthetically equal to the latter, and so become one more feature of the prospect rather than being privileged vantage points, towering over other parts of the terrain, from which the prospect becomes visible.[18] We see this again and again in Addison's (and his contemporaries') landscape depictions: a partial leveling process whereby mountains were, at least to some degree, cut down to size (thus placed within reach of those with no inherent claims to inhabiting or overseeing an aristocratic landscape), absorbed into the community of separate but equally entertaining topographical shapes, even as the dimension of "Greatness" and "Magnificence" was reaffirmed. In this respect Addison's physical landscapes bear similarities to the "social landscape" depicted in the De Coverley papers, where the composition of the Spectator Club presents a broad panorama of contemporary society with its various ranks and classes, and where the virtues of Sir Roger De Coverley, a baronet "of antient Descent" who espouses traditional Tory aristocratic values, blend into, and are qualified by, the middle-class virtues of Sir Andrew Freeport, "a Merchant of great Eminence in the City of *London.*"[19] (We might note here how "eminence" is associated not with the high-born gentleman but with the low-born though prosperous business-man.) I am arguing here, in short, that what Ronald Paulson calls the "Whig fiction" governing the portrayal of the Spectator Club governs also Addison's treatment of landscape[20] — although, as my references to Thomson and others indicate, I am in the final analysis talking about structures of feeling and perception widespread throughout the period and not limited to any one particular party.

An interesting gloss, for example, on Addison's protest against the eye's being "shortned on every side" by neighboring moun-tains — one that suggests it cannot be viewed simply in terms of Whiggish resistance to obstructions to individual freedom and mobility — is provided by Defoe, in recounting a return visit to Chatsworth, the Duke of Devonshire's estate: "Under this front lye the gardens exquisitely fine, and, to make a clear vista or prospect beyond into the flat country, towards Hardwick, another seat of the same owner, the duke, to whom what others thought impossible, was not only made practicable, but easy, removed, and perfectly carried away a great mountain that stood in the way, and which interrupted the prospect."[21] Addison's com-plaint, in other words, was part of a general demystification of once symbolically rich features of the landscape such as moun-tains, whereby the latter were divested of their privileged status and became one object among many in the natural world which were vulnerable to the spectator's restless eye and to the estate owner's desire for visual and territorial expansion. They became objects that could be moved about — and removed — at will, given sufficient amounts of money and proper instruments of demoli-tion. As Humphry Repton observed in relation to Blaise Castle (in Gloucestershire): "all improvements must depend on the axe, and tho' fully aware of the common objection to cutting down trees, yet, it is only by a bold use of that instrument that the won-ders of Blaise Castle can be properly displayed."[22] The "common objection" notwithstanding, many throughout the century acted in keeping with Repton's advice to make "bold use" of the axe in order to eliminate obstacles in one's path of vision — in this case, tall trees that hid the opposite woods. Concealing an attractive wood or interrupting a prospect were things the eighteenth-century spectator was not willing to permit even nature to do; her secretive, obfuscating ways were deemed in need of sometimes considerable correction (even though, paradoxically, landscape designers themselves were in the habit of concealing things from view or interrupting a vista in order to diversify the scene or create an element of surprise). It is easy, especially in the twentieth century, to take this attitude toward nature for granted, to view it as "natural" and inevitable. But in fact it is a peculiar, historically determined mode of perception that can view features of the landscape as mere obstructions, things that "stand in the way" (one is compelled to ask, what does it mean for trees to "stand in the way" of a forest, or for a mountain to "stand in the way" of a prospect?). It is ironic that an age that so soundly rejected topiary regularly indulged in far more radical, if less visually obvious, forms of reshaping the land in conformance to human design.

Much of this reshaping was done in order to satisfy the eye's demand for variety, novelty, and sense of motion. The high premium placed on these three elements in connection with landscape is explained by Addison's further comments in his *Spectator* 412. Recommending "whatever is *new* or *uncommon*" as a much-needed escape from being "conversant with one Sett of Objects, and tired out with so many repeated Shows of the same Things," Addison asserts:

It serves us for a kind of Refreshment, and takes off from that Satiety we are apt to complain of in our usual and ordinary Entertainments. . . . It is this that recommends Variety, where the Mind is every Instant called off to something new, and the Attention not suffered to dwell too long, and waste it self on any particular Object. . . . For this reason there is nothing that more enlivens a Prospect than Rivers, Jetteaus, or Falls of Water, where the Scene is perpetually shifting, and entertaining the Sight every Moment with something that is new. We are quickly tired with looking upon Hills and Valleys, where every thing continues fixt and settled in the same Place and Posture, but find our Thoughts a little agitated and relieved at the sight of such Objects as are ever in Motion, and sliding away from beneath the Eye of the Beholder.[23]

There is an interesting mixture of bourgeois and libertine sentiment underlying these remarks. The strictures against "wasting" one's attention on a particular object, combined with the sense of energy generated by the emphasis upon motion and change, lend support to the middle-class denigration of idleness and unprofitableness, and to its exaltation of industry, enterprise, and thrift. At the same time, the insistence on newness and continual relief from the "Satiety" that is apt to accompany "usual and ordinary Entertainments" suggests a teasing indulgence in thoughts of an implicitly sexual promiscuity and sensual experimentation which are more readily associated with an aristocratic-libertine ethic. (We might note that Addison, in this same paragraph, exuberantly praises "the opening of the Spring, when [Groves, Fields, and Meadows] are all new and fresh, with their first Gloss upon them, and not yet too much accustomed and familiar to the Eye"—a statement reminiscent of the Restoration rake's preference for young virgins over old mistresses.) The bourgeois ideology that strongly supported the institution of marriage was able at the same time to tolerate flirtations with less formalized and more pleasurable activities for men, provided that these were rendered "innocent" and safe (vis-à-vis the status quo) by being transferred from the social arena to the natural landscape.

The determination that things "perpetually shifting" and "ever in Motion" are of higher aesthetic worth than things "fixt and settled" is not based on any objective or universally agreed upon standard of values, or on any inherent virtues possessed by these two sets of objects. There is no necessary connection between incessant movement and beauty, or between stability and ugliness. The preference for one over the other in any given period is determined as much by perceptions about the nature of society and man's place in it as by contemporary epistemological assumptions and philosophical or scientific ideas (e.g., Newtonian optics). The ideological context and implications of Addison's aesthetic criteria, of his enthusiasm for variety and novelty, are evident from Defoe's comments in his preface to *A Tour through the Whole Island of Great Britain*:

As the work it self is a description of the most flourishing and opulent country in the world, so there is a flowing variety of materials; all the particulars are fruitful of instructing and diverting objects.

If novelty pleases, here is the present state of the country describ'd, the improvement, as well in culture, as in commerce, the encrease of people, and employment for them: Also here you have an account of the encrease of buildings, as well in great cities and towns, as in the new seats and dwellings of the nobility and gentry; also the encrease of wealth, in many eminent particulars.

. . . the face of things so often alters, and the situation of affairs in this great British Empire gives such new turns, even to nature it self, that there is matter of new observation every day presented to the traveller's eye.[24]

Here Defoe in a sense translates Addison's aesthetic discourse into social and, especially, economic terms, while at the same time retaining the concern for visual gratification. Defoe's formulation makes it clear that the fascination with new, ever-changing, multivaried beauties in one's physical surroundings derives its special force and character, its peculiar relevance—for the first half of the eighteenth century in particular—from optimistic faith in a new age of capitalist enterprise and expansion, from visions of continuous economic growth, invention, and unending prosperity, often linked, as in this case, to expressions of patriotic fervor (Defoe ends his preface, "and thus posterity will be continually adding; every age will find an encrease of glory. And may it do so, till Great Britain as much exceeds the finest country in Europe, as that country now fancies they exceed her"). Thomson, a man with very different politics from Defoe's, likewise depicts a multivaried, motion-filled landscape, continuously presenting "matter of new observation" to the spectator's eye, which is similarly linked to a glowingly patriotic vision of "Happy Britannia! where the Queen of Arts, / Inspiring vigour, Liberty, abroad / Walks unconfined even to thy farthest cots, / And scatters plenty with unsparing hand" ("Summer," 1442-1446).[25] We might also note that Pope, for all his Tory conservatism and his official opposition to the new class of financial speculators, himself invested substantially in the South Sea Company on the basis that "tis Ignominious (in this Age of Hope and Golden Mountains) not to Venture,"[26] and poetically embodied this attitude in his sanguinely expansionist and nationalistic portrayal of the English landscape in the *Epistle to Burlington*: "Let his plantations stretch from down to down, / First shade a Country, and then raise a Town. / ... Bid Harbors open, public Ways extend, / Bid Temples, worthier of the God, ascend" (189-190; 197-198). In this epistle too we can see how a land filled with pleasing diversity and change was dependent for its meaning and its very sustenance on a broader political and economic context (even though in Pope's verse the connection is a good deal more mystified than in Defoe's account).

There is, of course, the obverse side of the coin: In light of the importance accorded to novelty, variety, and movement (the growing interest in theories of the sublime in the later part of the period brought to the fore other aesthetic categories, but these three continued to function prominently as components of the beautiful and the picturesque), certain aspects of both the natural and the human landscape were automatically devalued by the eighteenth-century spectator, either viewed by him with contempt or else overlooked by him entirely. Particularly obvious and telling examples were the habitats and the environs of the poor. When Mrs. Piozzi, for example, traveled through Lyons and its surroundings in 1784, she recorded her enthusiastic approval of the scenery—"Here is no tedious uniformity to fatigue the eye, nor rugged asperities to disgust it; but ceaseless variety of colouring among the plants, while the caerulean willow, the yellow walnut, the gloomy beech, and silver theophrastus, seem scattered by the open hand of lavish Nature of a landscape of respectable extent"—but interrupted her exuberant testimonial in order to note with disgust: "Every town that should adorn these lovely plains, however, exhibits, upon a nearer approach, misery; the more mortifying, as it is less expected by a spectator, who requires at least some days experience to convince him that the squallid scenes of wretchedness and dirt in which he is obliged to pass the night, will prove more than equivalent to the pleasures he has enjoyed in the day-time, derived from an appearance of elegance and wealth."[27] Here the unmistakable signs of poverty are viewed not as social and economic ills but as intolerable eyesores. Their visual offensiveness to the spectator is at least partly due to their inability to provide the refreshing novelty and the "ceaseless variety" associated with a landscape of "elegance and wealth." The same can be said for most of the (relatively few) descriptions of the habitats of the poor during this period, including those written from a far more socially enlightened perspective than Mrs. Piozzi's. We might think, for example, of Swift's characterization of the impoverished areas he observed on a trip through Tipperary: "a bare face of nature, without houses or plantations; filthy cabins, miserable, tattered, half-starved creatures, scarce in human shape . . . a bog of fifteen miles round; every meadow a slough, and every hill a mixture of rock, heath, and marsh."[28]

Now it is obvious that we needn't have recourse to sophisticated aesthetic theories of the day to understand why such scenes would have been deemed wholly unappealing to contemporaries: poor in every way. Nevertheless, it is significant that the scenes would have been rejected — would have "failed" — even if measured solely according to the aesthetic criteria applied regularly to landscapes by Addison and others. Given the bleakness and the relentlessness of the poor's existence, the tedium of their daily labors, and the grotesque fixity of their lives resulting from their entrapment in a web of circumstances beyond their control, it is not surprising that their landscapes would have lacked appeal for the cultivated spectator, accustomed as he was to surrounding himself with scenery capable of offering constant relief from "so many repeated Shows of the same Things." To be sure, there were those who attempted to find such relief amidst the environs of the destitute — to aesthetically redeem the latter, as it were — though few could sustain such a sleight of eye for very long. When Resta Patching comes upon a village of poor people on his travels through Britain, his first response is to assimilate the scene to contemporary landscape theory by ignoring its dismal content in favor of its abstract form: the cottages of the poor, "scatter'd in an irregular Manner," evoke associations with the picturesque and are thus seen to create "a most Romantic Scene." But as soon as Patching considers the actual details of his surroundings the illusion bursts, and he is forced to confront what is before him: "The Inhabitants appear'd so poor and wretched, the Land about them so barren and stony, so unshelter'd from Wind and Weather, and so remov'd from the Comforts and even Necessaries of Life; that reflecting on the Difference of Condition between the People here, and those who with equal Industry live in rich and populous Cities, affected me with Pity for their hard Lot!" So disturbing are the realities that obtrude on his vision that he must seek escape by retreating, not this time into formal abstractions, but into philosophical reflections on the beneficent if inexplicable workings of Providence and a vindication of the rightness of things as they are. He then apologizes to the reader for his "moralizing Transition," but it is difficult not to feel that he is really apologizing for having forced on his readers such dismal and aesthetically unrewarding sights — for having "suffered [the Attention] to dwell too long" on discomforting aspects of the landscape. We can almost hear an audible sigh of relief as Patching, resuming his journey, tells us that for a long time thereafter, except for the mountains in the distance, "We travelled on without any thing to attract our particular Attention."[29]

In this connection it is interesting to note that the typical eighteenth-century spectator was proficient in the art of what might be called "scene-hopping," usually placing himself in a situation where he could view many different angles and features of the landscape while neither his mind nor his eye would have to "waste it self on any particular Object." Mounting "Grongar Hill," for example, John Dyer stops to rest on a flower bed "While stray'd my eyes o'er Towy's flood, / Over mead, and over wood, / From house to house, from hill to hill, / 'Till Contemplation had her fill." Upon gaining the mountain's brow, he looks out over a landscape that will never "tire the view":

> The fountain's fall, the river's flow,
> The woody vallies, warm and low;
> The windy summit, wild and high,
> Roughly rushing on the sky!
> The pleasant seat, the ruin'd tow'r,
> The naked rock, the shady bow'r;
> The town and village, dome and farm,
> Each give each a double charm, . . . [30]

Horace Walpole's description of Hagley Park reveals a similar mode of observation: "such lawns, such wood, rills, cascades, and a thickness of verdure quite to the summit of the hill, and commanding such a vale of towns and meadows, and woods extending quite to the Black Mountains in Wales. . . . Then there is a scene of a small lake with cascades falling down such a Parnassus! . . . and there is such a fairy dale . . . and there is a hermitage, so exactly like those in Sadeler's prints . . . and there is such a pretty well under a wood . . . and there is such a wood without the park, enjoying such a prospect!"[31] In both cases we encounter a visual restlessness and lack of concentration, a somewhat distracted wandering of the eye, legitimized as a submission to nature's seemingly infinite variety and breadth. While contemporary epistemological and aesthetic theories can be invoked to help explain this phenomenon, we should not overlook its ideological dimension insofar as it manifests a habit of mind and eye that militates against a close, steady focus on any particular object in one's surroundings and that provides a perspective from which certain objects can be passed over altogether, or at best glimpsed only fleetingly and relegated to the periphery of both vision and consciousness. It is this kind of perspective Goldsmith was indirectly commenting on when, in his prefatory remarks to *The Deserted Village* addressed to Sir Joshua Reynolds, he noted, "I know you will object (and indeed several of our best and wisest friends concur in the opinion) that the depopulation [*The Deserted Village*] deplores *is no where to be seen,* and the disorders it laments are only to be found in the poet's own imagination. To this I can scarce make any other answer than that I sincerely believe what I have written."[32] (Italics mine.) Within the context of the eighteenth-century spectator society, to be rendered invisible ("no where to be seen") was tantamount to being consigned to oblivion—in effect, to ontological extinction.

Thus the aesthetics of landscape during this period was as much dependent upon what was *not* seen as on what was. The common practice of viewing the landscape through what Thomson (for one) variously termed the "mind's creative eye" ("Autumn," 1016), the "philosophic eye" ("Autumn," 1133), and the "imagination's vivid eye" ("Spring," 459) sanctioned a kind of vision that could avoid seeing—supposedly by "transcending"— much of what actually existed in the landscape. The much-discussed analogy between landscape and painting during the century performed a similar function by providing the poet, landscape designer, and spectator alike with a definite "frame" in every sense (a framework of values, a frame of reference) which comprehended within its bounds certain kinds of objects, arranged in particular configurations, while it exiled others to a precarious and nebulous existence beyond the frame, where things became not only invisible but in a very real sense inconceivable as well. Architectural as well as landscape design during this period had the effect of relegating features in the environment to a realm of invisibility. Mark Girouard, noting several "revolutionary" innovations in country house life beginning in the Restoration period (e.g., the ejection of servants from the main hall and the invention of backstairs, with closets and servants' rooms often attached to them) explains their far-reaching consequences on both the social and the aesthetic levels: "The gentry walking up the stairs no longer met their last night's faeces coming down them. Servants no longer bedded down in the drawing room, or outside their master's door or in a truckle bed at his feet. They became, if not invisible, very much less visible."[33] The lower orders as well as all other distasteful matters were, in short, effectively removed from view (i.e., from the view of those who made up the privileged spectator class). E. P. Thompson sheds additional light on the growing separation between the classes in eighteenth-century England and its inevitable impact on aspects of visibility. Discussing what he interprets as an absentee system of "paternalism" during this period, he observes:

Physically [the gentry] withdrew increasingly from face-to-face relations with the people in village or town. The rage for deer parks and the threat of poachers led to the closure of rights of way across their parks and their encirclement with high palings or walls; landscape gardening, with ornamental waters and fish ponds, menageries and valuable statuary, accentuated their secretion and the defenses of their grounds.... If the great were withdrawn so much, within their parks and mansions, from public view, it follows that the plebs, in many of their activities, were withdrawn also from them.[34]

Goldsmith indirectly attests to this loss of visibility (on both sides) in his poem, *The Traveller,* in passages like the following:

> Though poor the peasant's hut, his feasts though small,
> He sees his little lot the lot of all;
> Sees no contiguous palace rear its head
> To shame the meanness of his humble shed;
> No costly lord the sumptuous banquet deal
> To make him loath his vegetable meal;
> But calm, and bred in ignorance and toil,
> Each wish contracting, fits him to the soil.   (177-184)

The poet's romanticized depiction of peasant life indicates that its harsh realities are concealed from his view. The poet interprets them through layers of social and political myth, which is to say that he doesn't really *see* them at all. (Significantly, the poem is subtitled "A Prospect of Society," with the poet himself assuming the stance of the typical prospect viewer as, "plac'd on high above the storm's career," he "Look[s] downward where an hundred realms appear" [33-34].) At the same time, Goldsmith makes a telling point about the restricted visibility of the class represented by the peasant, who "sees his little lot, the lot of all," since "no contiguous palace rears its head / To shame the meanness of his humble shed." The absence of such "palaces" from his purview points to the growing division between the classes and the corresponding separation of their respective landscapes.

The absence, however, is an expression of political need even more than it is a statement of historical fact. The peasant's restricted sight is in a sense necessary to maintain the status quo: There is no telling what resentments he might come to harbor, and what actions he might be moved to take, if he could view things within a broader perspective and thus perceive economic and social disparities—the stark contrast in living conditions between the haves and the have-nots. The distinctly unsettling ramifications of such a visual perspective are suggested by Robert Bloomfield's description of another peasant's situation in his poem, *The Farmer's Boy*: "Wealth flows around him, fashion lordly reigns, / Yet poverty is his, and mental pains." Bloomfield (himself a member of the labouring class) imagines the peasant's pained soliloquy; " 'Whence comes this change, ungracious, irksome, cold? / Whence the new grandeur that mine eyes behold? / The wid'ning distance which I daily see, / Has Wealth done this? . . . then wealth's a foe to me; / Foe to our rights; . . ."[35] It was to avert just such rebellious—hence potentially dangerous—thoughts and feelings that Goldsmith and other poets of the middle and latter part of the century placed the rural poor they described in carefully circumscribed habitats, safely shielded from the visual mockery (and provocation) of contiguous splendors and permitted a view limited to their own immediate environs. To put it another way, Goldsmith's peasant is put—and kept—in his place by virtue of his (both physically enforced and artistically depicted) exclusion from the class of Augustan spectators. Unlike the latter, his eyes, along with his feet, are glued to a single spot; his sight, in contrast to Addison's privileged spectator, is "pent up in a narrow Compass," and although he lives in the very midst of "the wide Fields of Nature," his sight is prevented from "wander[ing] up and down without Confinement."[36] Prospects and vistas that allow the perception of variety and contrast are unavailable to Goldsmith's peasant, who lacks both money and the mobility—the freedom to range over different kinds of landscape—that goes with it. Such views are *no where to be seen by him,* in an ironic counterpart to the situation where certain things are "no where to be seen" by his social superiors, with the crucial distinction that the element of choice exists in the one instance whereas it is absent in the other.

A large part of the aesthetics as well as the politics of landscape in the eighteenth century may be understood in light of these different modes and levels of perception, or, to put it another way, of varying degrees of blindness, some enforced by social and economic conditions, others freely chosen for purposes of personal enjoyment; some coercively established, others self-imposed in order to ensure a comforting world view. In his *Essay on Man,* Pope draws a picture of a Chain of Seeing as well as a Chain of Being:

> Far as Creation's ample range extends,
> The scale of sensual, mental pow'rs ascends:
> Mark how it mounts, to Man's imperial race,
> From the green myriads in the peopled grass:
> What modes of sight betwixt each wide extreme,
> The mole's dim curtain, and the lynx's beam. . . .   (I, 207-212)

If we were to translate this ostensibly natural, cosmic hierarchy into social or political terms, Goldsmith's peasant would be seen to occupy a position similar to Pope's "mole" insofar as scope of vision is concerned; his "dim curtain," even more than the mole's, helps sustain a hierarchy of ascending and descending powers. Bloomfield's peasant, while confirming the existence of this hierarchy on an economic level, implicitly casts doubt on the universality (if not the reality) of the visual gap supposedly characterizing the distance between the highest and lowest rungs of the ladder, since he himself does not seem to be trapped by limited perception and comprehension — *he* does not assume "his little lot the lot of all." His words suggest that Pope's and Goldsmith's visual hierarchy may be more wishful thinking or ideological projection than actual fact. Yet even Bloomfield's peasant can ultimately do little more than testify to the growing remoteness ("the wid'ning distance") between his own mode of existence and that of his social betters.

Addison examines the question of perceptual differences from a more Whiggish, hence less obviously elitist, standpoint than Pope. Eschewing the fixed hierarchies and the vertical landscape supporting Pope's scale of powers, he invokes the premises of Lockean epistemology in setting forth seemingly democratic and egalitarian theories about the act of perception: theories peculiarly appropriate to the class origins of his readers and well adapted to their need for an ideology that allowed all men, regardless of birth or rank, equal access to the aesthetic riches of nature. At the same time, Addison's exposition addresses its readers' need for an ideology that would distinguish between the haves and the have-nots, between men of superior wealth, taste, and judgment and men lacking these possessions, so that his description of "The Pleasures of the Imagination" in the final analysis serves to reinforce and legitimize existing social and economic hierarchies. The schizophrenic, or at least paradoxical, nature of Addison's aesthetic principles parallels that characterizing Locke's theories, particularly his political and economic ones, which begin with essentially egalitarian or liberal-democratic assumptions about the natural individual right to property, each man's right to his own labor, and the existence of free and equal beings in the state of nature, and end with a defense of monopoly capitalism and class division. As C. B. Macpherson puts it, "Starting from the traditional assumption that the earth and its fruits had originally been given to mankind for their common use, [Locke] has turned the tables on all who derived from his assumption theories which were restrictive of capitalist appropriation. . . . He also justifies, as natural, a class differential in rights and in rationality, and by doing so provides a positive moral basis for capitalist society."[37]

In "The Pleasures of the Imagination" we see what is in certain ways the aesthetic equivalent of Locke's political theory. Addison begins by emphasizing the primacy of sight ("Our Sight is the most perfect and most delightful of all our Senses") and arguing for the mechanistic operations of the external world upon the passive eye: "Besides, the Pleasures of the Imagination have this Advantage, above those of the Understanding, that they are more obvious, and more easie to be acquired. It is but opening the Eye, and the Scene enters. The Colours paint themselves on the Fancy, with very little Attention of Thought or Application of Mind in the Beholder."[38] If imaginative pleasures require "but opening the Eye, and the Scene enters," then such pleasures are freely and immediately available to all men (at least to all those not afflicted with blindness), without regard to social class, economic status, or intellectual capability. Yet in the very next paragraph, Addison in effect contradicts this viewpoint even as he tacitly claims to be merely extending its meaning. Speaking of "A Man of a Polite Imagination," he declares that such a person "is let into a great many Pleasures that the Vulgar are not capable of receiving . . . he looks upon the World, as it were, in another Light, and discovers in it a Multitude of Charms, that conceal themselves from the generality of Mankind." Nature, then, is not at all as promiscuous and universally accessible as suggested earlier. Her "Charms" are reserved for a privileged few, those who know how to view things in a superior light and who are therefore elevated above "the Vulgar." This group of *Spectator* papers makes it increasingly clear that to truly "see" a landscape one must possess capabilities at once inborn and cultivated through proper training. As Addison explains the matter in a literary context:

For, to have a true Relish, and form a right Judgment of a Description, a Man should be born with a good Imagination. . . . The Fancy must be warm, to retain the Print of those Images it hath received from outward Objects; and the Judgment discerning, to know what Expressions are most proper to cloath and adorn them to the best Advantage. A Man who is deficient in either of these Respects, tho' he may receive the general Notion of a Description, can never see distinctly all its particular Beauties: As a Person, with a weak Sight, may have the confused Prospect of a Place that lies before him, without entering into its several Parts, or discerning the variety of its Colours in their full Glory and Perfection.[39]

Thus Addison, despite his empirical and egalitarian premises, in the end affirms a hierarchic Chain of Seeing (and Nonseeing) similar to Pope's and Goldsmith's, one that justifies social distinctions by converting them into epistemological, aesthetic, even biological categories. In this respect, Addison's treatment of the perceiver is paralleled by his treatment of the object of perception, which first appears as an all-inclusive, exceedingly varied and diversified landscape but which finally emerges as a highly select and restricted area, a landscape of wealth and privilege — explicitly revealed as such in moments, for example, when Addison examines how "a whole Estate [may] be thrown into a kind of Garden by frequent Plantations, that may turn as much to the

Profit, as the Pleasure of the Owner" and how "a Man might make a pretty Landskip of his own Possessions."[40] In passages like these Addison gives his readers lessons in how the economically appropriated and the financially lucrative can be turned into—or be seen in terms of—the aesthetically satisfying.

So ingrained was this habit of thought and vision throughout the century, among men of varying political and class outlooks, that Arthur Young, in his travels through France and Italy, could survey the countryside (in this case in the Alps, near Chambery) and declare, "In several places the view is picturesque and pleasing: enclosures seem hung against the mountain sides as a picture is suspended to the wall of a room."[41] The simile Young uses is of course perfect for his age, providing the ultimate aesthetic sanction for economic enclosure by assimilating the latter into the pictorial tradition of eighteenth-century landscape. Later Young's observation of an enclosed countryside elicits the following description: "All hill and dale tossed about with so much wildness that the features are bold enough for the irregularity of a forest scene, and yet withal softened and melted down by culture and habitation to be eminently beautiful."[42] Here a profitable economic system is seen to possess transforming and redemptive powers vis-à-vis the land, powers similar to those associated with the creative imagination in Romantic ideology. The assumed links between natural beauty and economic prosperity are expressed in similar ways throughout Defoe's *Tour*. Describing, for example, the houses and gardens of the wealthy along the Thames in Middlesex and Surrey, Defoe exclaims, "Take them in a remote view, the fine seats shine among the trees as jewels shine in a rich coronet; in a near sight they are meer pictures and paintings; at a distance they are all nature, near hand all art," and he concludes, "In a word, nothing can be more beautiful; here is a plain and pleasant country, a rich fertile soil, cultivated and enclosed to the utmost perfection of husbandry, then bespangled with villages; those villages filled with these houses, and the houses surrounded with gardens, walks, vistas, avenues, representing all the beauties of building, and all the pleasures of planting: It is impossible to view these countries from any rising ground and not be ravish'd with the delightful prospect."[43] All of the preceding examples, whatever their specific differences, describe a similar process: the transformation and reorganization of the land in conformance to man's will, for the purpose of gratifying his earthly desires, coupled with the description of economic activities presented in aesthetic terms.

I would like to conclude by suggesting a major change that occurred in the attitude toward landscape in the Romantic period. It is impossible to assign a definite date to this change. In the final decade of the century Humphry Repton, in obvious continuity with earlier ways of viewing the land (however much he may have departed from the specific practices of his predecessors with regard to garden design), could assert that "where man resides, Nature must be conquered by Art, and it is only the ostentation of her triumph, and not her victory, that ought never to offend the correct Eye of Taste."[44] But the 1790s were also the period in which Wordsworth began writing his joyous psalms to nature — psalms affirming a reciprocal rather than a power relationship between man and his landscape ("Fair scenes, erewhile, I taught, a happy child, / The echoes of your rocks my carols wild") and celebrating a variety and transformation created by nature itself rather than imposed by human design: "How pleasant, as the sun declines, to view / The spacious landscape change in form and hue!" (*An Evening Walk*, 13-14; 98-99).[45] (Such natural changes are regularly observed in *The Seasons* as well, of course, but there they are linked to the changes brought about by "the power of cultivation," "the sons of art; / And trade," and an omnipotent Britannia who, overlooking what appears to be a simple, pastoral scene, "sees / Her solid grandeur rise" ["Summer," 1436; 1457-1458; 423-424].) For Pope's Lord Peterborough, who "tames the Genius of the stubborn Plain, / Almost as quickly, as he conquer'd Spain" (*Imit. Hor.*, Sat. *II, i,* 131-132), and for Cowper's militant spectator, whose roving eye "posted on this speculative height, / Exults in its command" (*The Task*, I: 288-290),[46] Wordsworth substitutes a solitary country dweller revealed in moments "When nature had subdued him to herself" ("Lines Left upon a Seat in a Yew-Tree," 38). This aspect of man's submission to rather than dominance over nature was, as we have seen, adumbrated in passages throughout eighteenth-century writings which described the eye's loss of control when encountering the diverse beauties of the landscape. (The aspect

of man's *merging* with nature, equally significant for Wordsworth's poetry, is, however, absent from his predecessors' works,
which consistently affirm the *separation* between man and his
external environment.) We can view these earlier passages, from
one perspective, as a titillating flirtation with surrender on the
part of men who were (or at least who felt themselves to be) very
much in control, and who could therefore afford to express a
momentary sense of powerlessness in certain well-defined, carefully circumscribed situations. The act of giving themselves over
to something beyond them was a "risk" they could dare to take
because in actuality it did not entail any genuine risk at all.
When, for example, Pope described the experience of "los[ing]
your eyes upon the glimmering of the Waters under the wood, &
your ears in the constant dashing of the waves," it was specifically
within the boundaries of a highly structured and controlled environment, one wholly subject to human design and supervision
(Lord Digby's gardens at Sherborne).[47]

There were, however, several aesthetic documents of the eighteenth century which reflected a rather different sensibility—
which embodied a mode of feeling and perception that in certain
respects anticipated the Romantic era. (See Harold Bloom's discussion of Collins's "Ode to Fear," which points to examples of
daemonic poetry and the Romantic Sublime in the mid-eighteenth century.) The best-known and most important of these
documents is Burke's *Philosophical Enquiry into the Origin of
Our Ideas of the Sublime and Beautiful,* which characterizes the
sublime as a natural force by its very definition beyond man's
ability to control or exploit. The sublime was of course associated
throughout the period with greatness and grandeur, and was seen
to possess suprahuman attributes; nevertheless, as has already
been suggested in Addison's case, it was regularly brought down
to earth and "civilized" (if not exactly socialized), rendered in the
final analysis—contrary to the very essence of its nature—manageable, possessable, and useful in the sense of answering man's
needs. Because "Our Imagination loves to be filled with an
Object, or to graspe at any thing that is too big for its Capacity,"[48]
the sublime features of an Addisonian landscape tend to become
either items almost physically containable within the human
mind or else objects that serve to whet man's acquisitive appetites,

even though they remain "too big" to be completely appropriated by him.[49] In a related vein, Mrs. Piozzi expresses the wish to have her sublimity and tame it too: looking out of her cottage window in Bagni di Pisa, she claims to see "sublimity happily wedded with elegance, and majestick greatness enlivened, yet softened by taste."[50] Burke, however, will have nothing to do with such attempts at accommodation. Emphatically distinguishing between the beautiful and the sublime, he makes it clear that the latter can in no way be harmonized with things like elegance and refined taste: "In short, the ideas of the sublime and the beautiful stand on foundations so different, that it is hard, I had almost said impossible, to think of reconciling them in the same subject, without considerably lessening the effect of the one or the other upon the passions."[51] Implicitly countering Addison's contention that a man can make even "the most rude uncultivated Parts of Nature administer to his Pleasures," Burke argues:

Look at a man, or any other animal of prodigious strength, and what is your idea before reflection? Is it that this strength will be subservient to you, to your ease, to your pleasure, to your interest in any sense? No; the emotion you feel is, lest this enormous strength should be employed to the purposes of rapine and destruction. That power derives all its sublimity from the terror with which it is generally accompanied, will appear evidently from its effect in the very few cases, in which it may be possible to strip a considerable degree of strength of its ability to hurt. When you do this, you spoil it of every thing sublime, and it immediately becomes contemptible. An ox is a creature of vast strength; but he is an innocent creature, extremely serviceable, and not at all dangerous; for which reason the idea of an ox is by no means grand. A bull is strong too; but his strength is of another kind; often very destructive, seldom (at least amongst us) of any use in our business; the idea of a bull is therefore great, and it has frequently a place in sublime descriptions, and elevating comparisons.[52]

In directly opposing the sublime to the subservient, the safe, the self-gratifying, and the useful, and in removing the sublime from the realm of mental processes to the world of external objects having an objective reality of their own, Burke affirms the existence of powerful forces in nature ungovernable by man: forces alien to his laws, resistant to his will, and indifferent to his desires and needs. The sublime, in its aspect described above, remains impervious to human efforts at conquering, domesticating, and exploiting the natural environment.

This is not to deny the existence of other, even contrary strains in Burke's *Philosophical Enquiry*. Frances Ferguson's point (in her essay in this volume) that Burke's sublime, in the final analysis, guarantees and reinforces the claims of society is well taken — Burke was, after all, very much a man of his age, and therefore necessarily concerned that sublime forces should not remain wholly beyond the pale of human society, ready at any moment to unleash their savage fury and wreak havoc upon man's creations. At the same time, Burke throughout his life remained acutely sensitive (and in certain situations, sympathetic) to the existence of political forces "sublime" in their defiance of, and in their potential threat to, the status quo: forces capable of triumphing over the established order. As he noted in regard to the oppressed Irish Catholics, "But the Question is not, as the Hucksters of Ascendency think, of dealing with a credulous Mob, soon inflamed, soon extinguished. . . . The igneous fluid has its Lodging in a solid Mass. There are Persons amongst the Catholics of Ireland, of deep thought, keen sagacity, and sound Understanding; and those not a few. There are successions of them. If one is bought off, twenty will come on. . . . Do they think that such men can be cheated: — by their poor little transparent threads."[53] Man's (in this case in the guise of colonial England's) impulse to control and to subjugate is here seen to be as ineffectual in the face of a united political force as it is in the face of the *Enquiry's* raging bull. (In connection with the mob of the French Revolution, of course, this sublime force assumes decidedly negative and wholly destructive meanings.[54])

There is, moreover, a less political, more personal aspect to Burke's abiding preoccupation with and insistence on powers in the world not subject to human will and not moldable according to human design. Published shortly after his marriage to Jane Nugent in 1756, the *Philosophical Enquiry* reveals in part the sensibility of a bridegroom, of a man very much concerned with the joys of surrender and release, and very aware of the extent to which all pleasure, aesthetic as well as sexual, requires a relinquishing of control, a yielding up of oneself to wondrous and mysterious forces whose value lies precisely in their independence of man's mastering will. Although we find occasional expressions of what might be termed a traditional "masculine" perspective consistent with his new role as husband ("we love what submits to us"[55]), there is a more pervasively "feminine" note recorded throughout Burke's observations.[56] Even with respect to beautiful, loved objects, the relationship is not one defined by clear-cut domination; on the contrary, the act of submission is shown to be a two-way process, involving the lover as well as the loved object. After describing the physical manifestations of love, for example, Burke concludes: "beauty acts by relaxing the solids of the whole system. There are all the appearances of such a relaxation; and a relaxation somewhat below the natural tone seems to me to be the cause of all positive pleasure. Who is a stranger to that manner of expression so common in all times and in all countries, of being softened, relaxed, enervated, dissolved, melted away by pleasure?"[57] This emphasis on physical yielding and dissolution underlies Burke's aesthetic reflections and contributes to the impression he conveys of observing the world in an attitude of receptivity, from the perspective of a lover rather than of a proprietor or environmental engineer.

A half-century after the publication of Burke's *Philosophical Enquiry,* this stance was to become the predominant one as man's relationship to nature became defined by forms of ecstasy (literally, *ekstasis,* as in Keats's stepping outside himself to merge with the objects he addresses) and prophecy. Possessing a very different political consciousness and having a different economic relationship to the land they wrote about, the Romantic poets expressed an altered conception of power—no longer a power *over,* but rather a power *through, in conjunction with* outside forces of nature and divinity. We see in their writings an eye that views mountains, not as the sacred hieroglyphs of monarchy depicted by Denham, or as things to be appropriated or moved out of the way in order to achieve a desired prospect, but as a source of creative power and energy which man can submit to in reverence or unite with, through an act of Orphic transcendence. The typical eighteenth-century spectator, estate owner, or landscape designer, who identified himself with the "imperial" role characterized in Pope's *Epistle to Burlington* ("Back to his bounds their subject Sea command, / And roll obedient Rivers thro' the Land" [201-202]), would not have understood the kind of power Wordsworth celebrated through the example of "the infant Babe," who, although a "Frail creature . . . [and] helpless as frail," derives a very special—indeed, incomparable—strength from being "An inmate of this active universe":

> For feeling has to him imparted power
> That through the growing faculties of sense
> Doth like an agent of the one great Mind
> Create, creator and receiver both,
> Working but in alliance with the works
> Which it beholds. . . .   (*The Prelude,* II, 255-260)

NOTES

1. Switzer, *Iconographia Rustica,* 2d ed. (London, 1742), III: 5.

2. Addison and Steele, *The Spectator,* ed. Donald F. Bond, 5 vols. (Oxford: Clarendon Press, 1965), III: 567.

3. References to *Cooper's Hill* are to *The Potential Works of John Denham,* ed. Theodore Howard Banks (2d ed.; Hamden, Conn.: Archon Books, 1969).

4. I have used the following editions of Pope and Thomson: *The Twickenham Edition of the Poems of Alexander Pope,* ed. John Butt et al. (London: Methuen & Company, 1939-1961); and *James Thomson: Poetical Works,* ed. J. Logie Robertson (1908; New York: Oxford University Press, 1971).

5. *The Genius of the Place: The English Landscape Garden 1620-1820,* eds. John Dixon Hunt and Peter Willis (London: Paul Elek, 1975), pp. 234, 235.

6. Hunt, *The Figure in the Landscape: Poetry, Painting, and Gardening during the Eighteenth Century* (Baltimore: The Johns Hopkins University Press, 1976), p. 8.

7. Eric Rothstein's analysis of the "illusion of reality" and the "duplicity of form" characterizing later eighteenth-century fiction suggests that this treatment of landscape grew out of certain fundamental aesthetic and epistemological assumptions that helped shape *all* of the period's artistic endeavors. See *Systems of Order and Enquiry in Later Eighteenth-Century Fiction* (Berkeley, Los Angeles, and London: University of California Press, 1975), pp. 251-254.

8. *The Genius of the Place,* p. 248.

9. Defoe, *A Tour Through the Whole Island of Great Britain,* intro. G. D. H. Cole and D. C. Browning, 2 vols. (New York: Dutton [Everyman], 1962), I: 143-144.

10. Holub, "The Rise of Aesthetics in the Eighteenth Century," *Comparative Literature Studies* 15 (Sept. 1978): 278-280.

11. See Williams, *The Country and the City* (New York: Oxford Uni-

versity Press, 1973), esp. chapter 6; and Barrell, *The Idea of Landscape and the Sense of Place, 1730-1840: An Approach to the Poetry of John Clare* (Cambridge: At the University Press, 1972), chapter 1. Barrell's book in particular is indispensable reading for an understanding of eighteenth-century landscape theory and practice. Less impressive but also pertinent to the whole question of the ideological implications of (in this case exclusively pictorial) representations of landscape during this period is Barrell's more recent study, *The Dark Side of the Landscape: The Rural Poor in English Painting, 1730-1840* (New York: Cambridge University Press, 1980). In this connection see also Ann Bermingham, *The Ideology of Landscape: Gainsborough, Constable, and the English Rustic Tradition,* forthcoming from the University of California Press.

12. Turner, *The Politics of Landscape: Rural Scenery and Society in English Poetry 1630-1660* (Oxford: Basil Blackwell, 1979), p. 106.

13. The passage is cited from *The Works of Joseph Addison* (London, 1721).

14. *The Spectator,* III: 540-541.

15. Young, *A Six Months Tour Through the North of England,* 3 vols. (Dublin, 1770), II: 119.

16. Gilpin, *Observations. . . Relative Chiefly to Picturesque Beauty* (London: 1809), pp. 151-152.

17. *The Spectator,* III: 538.

18. See also Addison's comment, "Reading the *Iliad* is like travelling through a Country uninhabited, where the Fancy is entertained with a thousand Savage Prospects of vast Desarts, wide uncultivated Marshes, huge Forests, mis-shapen Rocks and Principices" (*The Spectator,* III: 564) — a description in which the balance seems to be tipped in favor of boundless expanse and sheer sense of space over vertical grandeur.

19. *The Spectator,* I: 7; 10.

20. Paulson, *The Fictions of Satire* (Baltimore: The Johns Hopkins University Press, 1967), pp. 211-216.

21. Defoe, *A Tour Through the Whole Island of Great Britain,* II: 175.

22. *The Genius of the Place,* pp. 362-363.

23. *The Spectator,* III: 541-542.

24. Defoe, *A Tour Through the Whole Island of Great Britain,* I: 1-2.

25. Thomson's technique of linking pastoral description to patriotic affirmation is discussed in Ralph Cohen, *The Unfolding of "The Seasons"* (Baltimore: The Johns Hopkins Press, 1970), esp. pp. 61-64, 100, 164-167. See also Cohen's article, "The Augustan Mode in English Poetry," *Eighteenth-Century Studies* 1 (Sept. 1967): 3-32, which (among other things) examines the prospect view in terms of spatial extension, as a poetic technique of "connecting patriotism with peace, plenty, and property" (p. 9).

26. *The Correspondence of Alexander Pope,* ed. George Sherburn, 5 vols. (Oxford: Clarendon Press, 1956), II: 33-34.

27. Piozzi, *Observations and Reflections Made in the Course of a*

Journey Through France, Italy, and Germany, ed. Herbert Barrows (Ann Arbor: University of Michigan Press, 1967), p. 15.

28. *The Correspondence of Jonathan Swift,* ed. Harold Williams, 5 vols. (Oxford: Clarendon Press, 1963-1969), IV: 34. For an extensive study of Swift's perception and treatment of his geographical environs, and the latter's inextricable connections to both his writings and his ideological outlook, see my book, *Swift's Landscape* (Baltimore: The Johns Hopkins University Press, 1982). Chapter 5 in particular deals with matters directly relevant to my discussion here.

29. Patching, *Four Topographical Letters* (London, 1757), pp. 24-25.

30. Dyer, *Poems* (London, 1761), pp. 10, 14. In this connection see Barrell's discussion of the passage from *The Seasons* ("Spring," 950-962) which describes the prospect from atop a hill in Hagley Park, as Lord Lyttelton's eye "excursive roams" after it is "snatched o'er hill and dale, and wood and lawn, / And verdant field, and darkening heath between, / And villages embosomed soft in trees" (*The Idea of Landscape and the Sense of Place,* pp. 17-20). Barrell explains this optical movement specifically in terms of the Claudian structure whereby "the eye is drawn immediately to the horizon, and registers the objects in the landscape only briefly and in passing," only at a later stage moving back over the landscape to examine its specific features in somewhat more detail.

31. *The Yale Edition of Horace Walpole's Correspondence,* ed. W. S. Lewis (New Haven: Yale University Press, 1973), vol. 35, pp. 148-149.

32. *The Collected Works of Oliver Goldsmith,* ed. Arthur Friedman, 5 vols. (Oxford: Clarendon Press, 1966), IV: 285. I have used this edition for subsequent references to Goldsmith's poetry.

33. Girouard, *Life in the English Country House: A Social and Architectural History* (New Haven: Yale University Press, 1978), p. 138.

34. Thompson, "Patrician Society, Plebeian Culture," *Journal of Social History* 7 (Summer 1974): 389, 390.

35. Bloomfield, *Collected Poems (1800-1822),* intro. Jonathan N. Lawson (Gainesville, Fla.: Scholars' Facsimiles & Reprints, 1971), p. 66.

36. *The Spectator,* III: 541, 549. Addison in these instances is talking about "the Mind of Man" in general, but as my paper demonstrates there is always a class differential implicit in even his most seemingly universal statements.

37. Macpherson, *The Political Theory of Possessive Individualism: Hobbes to Locke* (Oxford: Clarendon Press, 1962), p. 221.

38. *The Spectator,* III: 538.

39. Ibid., p. 561.

40. Ibid., pp. 551-552.

41. Young, *Travels in France and Italy,* intro. Thomas Okey (New York: Dutton [Everyman], 1934), p. 301.

42. Ibid., p. 303.

43. Defoe, *A Tour Through the Whole Island of Great Britain,* I: 167-168.

44. *The Genius of the Place,* p. 361.

45. References to Wordsworth's poetry are from *The Poetical Works of William Wordsworth,* ed. E. de Selincourt, Vol. I (Oxford: Clarendon Press, 1952); and *The Prelude, or Growth of a Poet's Mind,* 2d ed., ed. E. De Selincourt, rev. Helen Darbishire (Oxford: Clarendon Press, 1959). For a sensitive discussion of Wordsworth's treatment of landscape, also in terms of an intimacy between man and nature and a power paradoxically acquired through passivity and self-restraint, see Karl Kroeber, *Romantic Landscape Vision: Constable and Wordsworth* (Madison: University of Wisconsin Press, 1975), especially the observations about *Home at Grasmere* (pp. 117-131).

46. *The Poetical Works of William Cowper,* ed. Rev. George Gilfillan, 2 vols. (Edinburgh: James Nichol, 1854), I: 193.

47. *The Correspondence of Pope,* II: 238. Even in instances where this self-abandon occurred in less structured and less manageable environments (e.g., amidst nature's vastness) the spectator retained ultimate control through his imposition of aesthetic categories and judgments, which served to define and organize the scene, and to render it subject to his powers.

48. *The Spectator,* III: 540.

49. See also Addison's remark, in reference to "those wide Fields of *Ether,* that reach in height as far as from *Saturn* to the fixt Stars": "our Imagination finds its Capacity filled with so immense a Prospect, and puts it self upon the Stretch to comprehend it" (*The Spectator,* III: 575). This portrayal of the imagination as an expandable and contractible bodily organ much like a stomach is an apt expression of Addison's desire to (so to speak) have his sublimity and eat it too.

50. Piozzi, *Observations and Reflections Made in the Course of a Journey Through France, Italy, and Germany,* p. 183.

51. Burke, *A Philosophical Enquiry into the Origin of our Ideas of the Sublime and Beautiful* (2d ed., 1759; Menston, Eng.: The Scolar Press, 1970), p. 212.

52. Ibid., pp. 112-113.

53. *The Correspondence of Edmund Burke,* ed. Thomas H. Copeland et al., 10 vols. (Chicago: University of Chicago Press, 1958-1978), VII: 301.

54. In this regard see Ronald Paulson, *Representations of Revolution (1789-1820)* (New Haven and London: Yale University Press, 1983), pp. 66-73.

55. Burke, *A Philosophical Enquiry,* p. 212.

56. Isaac Kramnick presents a partly Freudian, partly ideological interpretation of the *Philosophical Enquiry* in *The Rage of Edmund Burke: Portrait of An Ambivalent Conservative* (New York: Basic Books, 1977), pp. 93-98. As he sees it, "The sublime is a package of masculine traits, the beautiful, feminine" (p. 94), and he then goes on to translate these categories into ideological terms: "The life-style of the bourgeoisie is inherently masculine, that of the tasteful and elegant aristocracy is inherently feminine" (p. 97). Kramnick's discussion is interest-

ing and suggestive, but it oversimplifies the meanings accorded to both
the beautiful and the sublime, and at moments turns the *Enquiry* into
ludicrous allegory: "For Burke the sublime is Will [Burke] and the beautiful Jane, and both are essential to peace and well-being" (p. 97).

57. Burke, *A Philosophical Enquiry,* pp. 287-288.

IV

DOCUMENTS OF SOCIAL CHANGE: PUBLICATIONS ABOUT THE SMALL HOUSE

Dora Wiebenson

One of the most important aesthetic documents of social change may be the house design, and one of the best mediums for the transmission of aesthetic concepts of the house may be the archetypical examples contained in publications about houses. It is my intention here to suggest a method by which this aesthetic medium — an almost purely visual source — can be used as a departure for speculation on probable development and change in social structure. The method will consist of a presentation of all major examples of this type in the eighteenth century. Whatever evidence appears will be determined as much as possible by the material itself.

According to a chronological chart showing all known editions of the small house publication up to 1800 (fig. 1), the publications fall into two major groups, the first beginning in 1747 and ending around 1770 and the second beginning around 1780 and extending well past our cut-off date of 1800 into the nineteenth century. With a few exceptions these publications appear only in France and England, the vast majority of them in English.

The earlier group of publications was preceded by several books; the first of these, the multivolume *Vitruvius Britannicus* by Colin Campbell (1676-1792) which began to appear in 1715, forms a link between late seventeenth-century works on views of large country estates and the later house publications.[1] The folio edition was devoted almost entirely to country houses; the style of the vast majority of the examples was related to that of the Palladium-inspired buildings of the seventeenth-century architect Inigo Jones. Campbell stated in the introduction to his work that he wished to promote a specifically British style of architecture — one that he maintained would be equal or superior to that of other countries. His was the first attempt in England to form a specific national architectural taste, an attempt that was begun, suitably, with a publication on the house, for, of all types of architecture, the house is the one that most closely reflects indigenous and national stylistic predilections.

The second of these early works is a study of model house plans and elevations which was included by the architect James Gibbs (1682-1754) in his *Book on Architecture,* published in 1728.[2] His study ranges from small to large houses, all of which are in the Palladian style. The volume suggests the later practical aims of house publications — the presentation of models for the improvement of the taste of the client unable to afford an architect, and the concern with economic expenditures. One senses in Gibbs's work the beginning of a broadening of the base of classical architecture to include all levels of society as well as a concern for the function of the designed building.

Robert Morris, the outstanding representative of those who offered abstracts of the simplest elements of house architecture for universal use, added a Palladian dimension that came to be associated with later house designs.[3] His *Lectures on Architecture,* published in 1734-35, is important for its contribution to the abstracting of the essentials of the Palladian style and also for its subsequent use by the amateur and builder of the small house.[4] The subtitle of his book, "Rules founded on Harmonick Arithmetical Proportions in Building designed as an Agreeable Entertainment for Gentlemen: and more particularly useful to all who make Architecture, or the Polite Arts their Study," leaves no doubt about Morris's intended readership. In addition to sections on the general principles of architecture and a discussion of spe-

cific villas and houses, intended to demonstrate universally applicable proportional systems, Morris's book includes extensive
descriptions of the type of setting for each house. These descriptions expand concepts of landscape theory, first popularized by
Addison, that are related to the later association of our house
publications with landscape design.

The one figure universally identified (and often credited) with
the stylistic reform with which the work of these architects is associated is Richard Boyle, Lord Burlington (1694-1753). Burlington exerted a major influence on artistic achievement in Britain
in the first half of the century.[5] For example, Campbell, who
hoped to promote his own career with *Vitruvius Britannicus,* was
successful for a short time when Burlington became his patron.
Morris—considered to be the theoretician for the architecture of
the Burlington circle—and almost all of the authors of our first
group of house publications were personally involved with Burlington. Only Gibbs was linked with the architectural and political groups to which Burlington was opposed: his adoption of this
style suggests the extent to which it had, very early in the century,
permeated British popular culture.

The first author of one of the house publications I wish to discuss is Daniel Garrett (d. 1753).[6] Garrett was a contemporary of
Burlington, and acted as his clerk and draftsman from the early
1720s when Burlington was forming his cultural program. Garrett's thin folio volume, *Designs and Estimates of Farm Houses
...,* was published in 1747. It is the first of the English illustrated
publications devoted specifically to houses, and Garrett was the
first architect to consider that the farmhouse merited architectural recognition. In this work Garrett developed a method of
presentation that would be adopted in later house publications:
each design is recorded in a plan and an elevation, the uses and
sizes of rooms are designated, and an estimate of prices is given
for all phases of the construction (fig. 2). Garrett voices what
would be the chief concern in these publications, whether the
house design should be based on practicality and utility or on
ornament. His opinion would seem to be firm: he stated in his
introduction that "Ornament, is rather a Profusion, than a useful
Branch [of architecture], but Convenience, above all, should be
the Builder's principal Care. . . . A Structure should be justly
composed, and appropriated to the Use it is intended for."[7] But

the clarity and symmetry of the organization of plans and elevations suggest that Garrett also intended to present examples of good architectural taste to a group of landowners who had been unable to acquire them previously. And although the structures were too elementary to be ornamented, the massing is that of the Palladian country house, a style consistently exemplified in this first group of publications.

The second author, Isaac Ware (c. 1707-1766), was certainly a member of Burlington's circle.[8] His *Complete Body of Architecture,* published in 1756, is one of the major architectural publications of the eighteenth century. In his preface Ware stated that he intended to collect all that was useful in the earlier works of others and to bring his study up to date with the addition of recent discoveries and improvements. He desired the publication to be a comprehensive treatise on architecture, to serve as an encyclopedia to the gentleman and builder, replacing other architectural publications.[9] But this was a selective universal work, for although Ware proposed that "the principal regard will be shown to what is necessary and useful," and although he began his work with a discussion of the principles of construction and ornament, he applied these principles not to public buildings but almost exclusively to country houses. Ware's work can be considered as an encyclopedic manual for the building of country houses from the small farmhouse to the large country estate: it contains information about construction, materials, site planning, garden design, and even drainage. Ware, like Garrett, considered design as well as utility to be important. He recommended that the "best instructions [for designing a country house with a farm for a person of independent means] should be taken from the *villas* of the antient *Romans.*"[10] Furthermore, in a statement surely related to contemporary garden theory, he proposed that "under the direction of a skillful architect, the barns, stable, and cow-houses, will rise like so many pavillions; and the very sheds will assist in the designs."[11] But the style of Ware's architecture, despite its professed relation to Roman classical architecture and to garden design, is based, like Garrett's, on Palladian architectural principles.

The third author, Robert Morris (c. 1702-1754), who was mentioned earlier, published *Rural Architecture* in 1750. It is a small book of farm designs that achieved several later editions, and that is very similar to Garrett's work. In it, one plate, of "An Ady-tum," was dedicated to Garrett,[12] and one plate, a design for a farmhouse, is almost identical to Garrett's designs, although Morris states that his work presents a group of designs to a hither-to neglected group of country dwellers—those who would like "a cottage, or plain little villa," now passed by unregarded, in favor of designs for palaces, and situated in an area where "so few *Persons,* residing in the *Country*...are capable of *Designing.*"[13] Like Garrett, Morris preferred plainness and utility to ornament and listed prices for each building, although he did not include a complete estimate of the costs.

But Morris was more concerned than Garrett with pure design: some of his plans are abstract studies in geometrical configura-tions, and functions are never assigned to the rooms, for Morris maintained that the individual owners would find specific uses for the spaces.[14] One structure that he maintained was designed originally as a bath is so removed from every normal function that Morris suggested several exotic ones: a synagogue, a mosque, a chapel, a dissecting room, an auction room, or even possibly a library (fig. 3).[15] Several of Morris's designs are intended to be garden structures (including the one dedicated to Garrett); their only function is to shelter the stroller.[16] The designs, perhaps just because of their abstract character, were taken up as models for housing by newly developing social groups, and Morris's work became very popular in the American colonies.

Morris is associated not only with the architects who were con-cerned with the initiation of a specific taste in architectural design, reflected in the architectural publications; he is also closely linked to the popularization of the resulting style by a group of men primarily involved in the writing of architectural handbooks. Of these men, one, known as William Halfpenny (d. 1755), who described himself as "architect and carpenter" on the title pages of some of his works, produced a number of books, including three on houses within as many years, and attempted to profit from what must have been a considerable demand for farmhouse publications.[17] Halfpenny sometimes collaborated with Morris, and in 1749 he acknowledged his debt to his col-league in his *New and Complete System of Architecture.*[18] Half-penny was also indebted to Garrett: he developed a series of books on farmhouses, several containing measurements and cost estimates similar to those in Garrett's work.[19] But Halfpenny did not restrict himself to farmhouses and, despite his claims of concern for convenience and utility,[20] he produced some designs, such as those for *Chinese and Gothic Architecture,* that reveal bizarre ornament and inexhaustible variety (fig. 4).[21] The closest prototypes to these designs are those for garden structures, which were often found in house publications as well as in Halfpenny's own works; it is not unlikely that many of the designs for houses may have been intended to appear as if they were garden structures on country estates.

Although it is doubtful that Halfpenny's extreme designs for the rural house were ever used as models for actual structures, the house publication type that he helped to popularize caught on quickly, and was taken up by authors established in the building trades who attempted to promote themselves by such works. Abraham Swan (fl. 1745-1768), a carpenter and joiner, published a book on houses, *A Collection of Designs in Architecture,* in 1757.[22] The work, a thick folio edition of small houses for middle-class "gentlemen of moderate Fortune,"[23] is both the most practical and pretentious of this group. (See fig. 5.) The farmhouse is not included, nor are complete dimensions or costs (only the size of the "best room" is considered), but the book reflects the nationalism and Palladian taste that can be associated with all these publications, for Swan patriotically announced that he intended his designs to demonstrate that *"England* is blest with as happy Geniuses as any Nation under Heaven."[24] Swan's work, like Morris's, became a major source book for American craftsmen and builders.

Swan's publication is the only one of this first group in which there is no reference to gardening. The relation of the ideal house designs to landscape design is continued in one late example: the *Gentleman and Farmer's Architect* (1764) by Timothy Lightoler (fl. 1757-1767), a carver.[25] It is a picture book containing general dimensions, but without estimates, preface, or descriptions of the plates. Like Halfpenny, Lightoler included not only farmhouses but also buildings in exotic styles and buildings that could be used for garden structures. In fact, he goes beyond Halfpenny in his emphasis on landscape, and his may be the first house publication in which structures designed entirely for a landscape setting—that is, "picturesque" architecture—appear (fig. 6).

There are two more publications from the late 1760s which belong to this group but which also indicate a new direction these publications would take: John Crunden's *Convenient and Ornamental Architecture* of 1767,[26] and Thomas Rawlins's *Familiar Architecture* of 1768.[27] Both men were associated with the building trades, produced designs in the Palladian taste, and represented themselves as architects. Of the two books, Crunden's (c. 1745-1835) is by far the most sophisticated, possibly because of his early training: he was assistant to a master builder, the father of the architect Henry Holland. Crunden's designs are close in style to the reduced Palladian examples of Garrett, and Crunden, like Garrett, includes in his book the functions of the rooms and their dimensions, although he does not include the cost estimates. Crunden introduced one new element to these publications: his book includes houses for all classes of people, and for both the town and the country. The subtitle of his work reads: ". . . consisting of original designs, for plans, elevations, and sections: beginning with the Farm House, and regularly ascending to the most grand and magnificent VILLA; calculated both for TOWN and COUNTRY, and to suit all Persons in every Station of Life." Crunden's intention may have been to publish a universal handbook on good house design. But whatever the purpose for which the book was intended, it achieved a wide reading public, going through six editions from 1767 to 1815.

Rawlins (fl. 1743-1780), a stone mason, must have had considerable ambition for social and professional advancement. He exhibited architectural designs at the Society of Artists in the 1760s and 1770s, and he later entered the competition for the design of the new Royal Exchange in Dublin. His work, a folio volume, is pretentious (even containing a list of subscribers). It is specifically intended, as was Swan's book, for "gentlemen" as well as tradesmen,[28] and includes buildings for estates and decoration for interiors. One triangular house recalls Morris's work. Only Rawlins's justification for the production of his book is new, perhaps suggesting professional developments that were just beginning to occur among the architects. He describes his book as being of assistance to the studies of the young architect, who is "hurried imperceptibly away with extatic Views of becoming great at Once,"[29] and admonishes: "let him study and make himself well acquainted with the necessary Conveniencies for the

Completion of small Buildings, before he aspires to Schemes of Palaces, which he may never probably have occasion to apply to Practice."[30]

Recent research indicates that, although many of these architects were associated with Burlington or with other aristocratic patrons devoted to establishing a national and Palladian taste, they also moved in an artistic circle that was actively opposed to dependence on this patronage and to the classicism it represented. These artists were concerned with experiment, eclecticism, and a close association with the immediate practical world in which they lived. Furthermore, they were involved in creating means, such as art schools, exhibitions, and state-supported academies, for raising the stature of artists, so that they could assume control of their profession and acquire a decision-making role in design.[31] Architects such as Isaac Ware played a prominent role in this movement of the 1730s and 1740s. Ware taught at Saint Martin's Lane Academy, an art school controlled by the artist rather than by the State or the patron. And architects such as Sir John Soane would continue the development of a professional tradition as architectural lecturers at the Royal Academy of Arts after its establishment in 1768.[32] These architects surely were allied with the artists in a desire for creative independence, and for a definition of their profession.

The modern concept of architecture as a profession was formed after about 1750, although it was not separated from the profession of builder-contractor-surveyor until the second quarter of the nineteenth century.[33] (The two major books of English professional architectural instruction of the eighteenth century, Ware's *Complete Body of Architecture* and Sir William Chambers's *Treatise on Civil Architecture*, both appeared in the 1750s; Chambers's work was published in 1756 and was intended to be the first volume of a projected two-volume work, the second volume of which would contain information on construction.) I suggest that the house publications played a major role in the development of this new professional stature. Already with Garrett's work the foundation for control by the architect of the design of all structures associated with a country estate is implied. In his book of farmhouse designs Garrett developed design standards that could be transmitted directly from architect to patron, eliminating the influence of the local builder-craftsman in design decisions. It is clear from the evidence of the house publications that architects were beginning to look elsewhere than to the State or the aristocracy for their commissions.

In a further move away from aristocratic and State control of the arts, which had been associated with the Palladian movement and with nationalistic anti-French sentiment, artists turned to the French rococo style for inspiration. Despite the pronounced national bias of the Palladian movement, architects also seem to have been considerably influenced by the French rococo style, at least in the designing of interiors such as those by Garrett and Ware (fig. 7).[34]

It is possible that the English house publications were influenced by French house publications. In fact, the ancestor of all house publications originated in France: the unpublished (until the twentieth century) study from the 1540s, by Sebastiano Serlio, of French and Italian house types for all classes of people (fig. 8).[35] By 1559 Jacques Androuet Du Cerceau had published a study of house types ranging from "economical" to elaborate in which he included descriptions of the buildings and a discussion of the materials used to construct them.[36] He later published a book on country houses which included many imaginative plans that were based in some cases on geometrical figures similar to those of the later English designs (fig. 9).

For our purposes the most important of the French publications was Pierre Le Muet's *Manière de bien bâtir pour toutes sortes de personnes,* which appeared in 1623.[37] This work, which included twenty-five designs for urban residences for all classes of people, complete with descriptions, sections on the construction of masonry and timber framing, and a discussion of measurements, was extremely popular for over a century. There were four French editions, the last appearing in the eighteenth century, and an English translation, published in 1675. In none of the later French works on houses was there a deeper commitment to architectural designs for the lower classes and to the study of an anonymous vernacular style (see fig. 10). The comprehensive and practical spirit behind the work dominated later English as well as French studies of the house.

In contrast to the English works of this period, however, French eighteenth-century house publications were largely encyclopedic studies in which all aspects of the house were discussed in considerable depth. In 1728 sixty designs for houses for all classes of people, produced by Gilles Tiercelet, were published, with additional illustrations and a comprehensive treatise on building construction that may have been provided by Charles Etienne Briseux.[38] The subtitle of this work, *L'Art de bien bâtir pour toutes sortes de personnes,* must consciously refer to Le Muet's work. The final edition of the earlier author's publication was put out by the publisher of the Tiercelet edition, probably at about the same date.[39] (It should be noted that Gibbs's *Book of Architecture* also appeared in 1728.)

Within fifteen years two comprehensive works on the design and construction of country houses were published in France. The first, by Jacques-François Blondel, published in 1736,[40] contained only elegant houses, though all elements of the furnishings, gardens, and so forth, were studied (despite the fact that he maintained his work contained buildings from the least to the most considerable consequence).[41] The second, by Briseux (who is associated with the Tiercelet work), was published in 1743.[42] It was concerned with designs for all classes of people, as well as with the techniques for building them. Briseux also included abstract, geometric designs among his house plans. The purpose of the work — to provide good, inexpensive house designs — is similar to that of the later English editions.[43]

No more French house publications appeared until the 1760s when the Briseux-Tiercelet work was reprinted, and when Jean François de Neufforge began to put out sets of designs of houses for all types of people, in which even the format recalls Le Muet (fig. 11).[44] But Neufforge was concerned — and this indicates the direction in which the second group of house publications would be moving — more with appearance and style than with practicality and construction. By the end of the decade Neufforge would also publish groups of designs of country houses, mainly villas, and, again, his work in this genre may predict the work of English authors of house publications in the 1780s, when the emphasis would be on stylistic variation and its application to all types of buildings.[45]

In contrast to the French works, English studies were focused on only a few architectural subjects and were written as handbooks for the builder or client, or as entertainment for the amateur, rather than as comprehensive reference works for the professional. Their authors often were only peripherally associated with the architectural profession. Almost all of the French books on domestic architecture, however, were associated with major French architects. These works reflect the secure and dominant position of the architect in France and his control of architectural design. Such stature had not yet been achieved by the English architect, but it was one to which he would surely aspire. Perhaps for this reason, among others, some of the English works that have been discussed can be associated with specific French publications. Le Muet's *Manière de bien bastir* may have had considerable influence on English house books. As we have seen, Ware gave examples from all ranges of house types and Crunden designed his work around examples of houses for all classes of people. Ware, who produced one of the two comprehensive eighteenth-century English treatises on architecture, surely based his work in part on the earlier comprehensive house publications of Tiercelet and Briseux (as the other comprehensive treatise, by Chambers, was surely inspired by the standard French *Cours d'architecture*[46]). Morris's early *Lectures on Architecture* may have been influenced in part by Tiercelet's work or by the French ambience that produced Jacques-François Blondel's work (brought out only three years after Morris's *Lectures* appeared). It is possible that Morris's disdain for assigning functions to the rooms of houses he designed derives from his opposition to the overly fastidious emphasis on "distribution" and "commodité" in French designs.[47] Even Colin Campbell's *Vitruvius Britannicus* is undoubtedly influenced by an earlier, professionally oriented French work: Jean Marot's seventeenth-century series of engravings of French architecture.[48]

With the exception of a few new editions and three or four works published belatedly in the 1780s which were still strongly influenced by Morris, Halfpenny, and Lightoler, the publications of the first group came to an end in 1768. For the following twelve years no new publications on designs for the house appeared in England. Oddly, this is the only type of architectural publication that is not continued during this period. Moreover, the publications that appear after 1780 reflect a new set of values and priorities, and they appear to be written for a new social class, which sought a special expression of its own character in new types of houses and even a new outlook on what constituted a house.

The causes for both the gap and the alterations in the material of these publications are uncertain.[49] It is generally assumed that the gap may have occurred because of the death of the first generation of authors and taste-makers, including Burlington, during the 1750s and 1760s, but this explanation does not take into account the discontinuation of the publication format or the alteration in the type of small house illustrated in the publications when they reappeared. An alternate and more complex solution may be related to economic and social developments. Poor interest rates and a depression may have put a temporary end to the opportunities for constructing a small house. The major social changes that had been developing earlier, such as the divisions of agrarian society into landowners, tenant farmers, and laborers, and into poor parish gentry and wealthy "county families," both occurring in the 1770s,[50] may have begun to be reflected by the 1780s in a change in aesthetic values toward the more personal and less intellectual concept of the picturesque as well as toward a desire for social reform. Moreover, during the 1780s the lowered interest rates, which resulted in building expansion and in innovation,[51] may have further encouraged a new social group whose aesthetic attitudes would be reflected in a new type of house publication. It is even possible that houses for the middle-class owner began to be designed in quantity by architects at this time, although it is not certain that the houses depicted in the publications were designed as models for the "poor gentry"—a new type of client—or for the even greater extension of the large landholders' estates (the publications of the second period often seem to be associated with condensing some estates), when both "beautifying" and "modernizing" of the property are undertaken.[52] (This is just the period when the concept of the urban villa begins, and when urban estate development on a large scale is undertaken.) But whatever the cause, after 1780 the publications were concerned not only with the farmhouse—or, in more practical publications, with the villa—but also with the cottage.

However, the first publication of this group, John Wood's *A Series of Plans for Cottages or Habitations of the Labourer* (1781), although it dealt exclusively with the new dwelling type, the cottage, still relied almost entirely on the format of the first group.[53] Wood included designs for rural, utilitarian buildings as well as dimensions, prices, and functions for the rooms (fig. 12). In fact, although Wood (1728-1781) represented the climax of the Palladian tradition in Bath, where he carried out his father's planning schemes for this sophisticated baroque town plan,[54] his publication was similar to Garrett's work on Palladian farmhouse designs, which was published one generation previously. The book contains dwellings intended to be built by landowners and occupied by their tenants. Wood's examples are basic, utilitarian, well constructed, and well designed; he includes amounts of materials, supplying unit prices for specific locations. There is no doubt of the relation of Wood's work to Garrett's. Even the format of both books, a slender folio, is similar.

The work thus appears to represent the extreme extension of Palladianism as a universal style, accessible to all. In fact, this is the first publication after Crunden's in which the need for urban housing is recognized, for the full title of the work states that designs could be "adapted as well to Towns as to the Country." However, the point of view is far from that of the original promoters of Palladianism, who were concerned only with the style of significant public and private monuments. Wood's book implied a new recognition of social groups and of social reform in this type of publication.

Wood's concern with cottages is surprising, for the cottage, which was the lowest type of habitation since no land was attached to it (though by tradition it shared a common with other cottages), was a structure associated with a class of people who had been omitted from architectural and even social consideration up to this time. This class was, to quote Wood, "the LABOURERS, [whose cottages] were become for the most part offensive both to decency and humanity; . . . the state of them and how far they might be rendered more comfortable to the poor inhabitants, was a matter worthy the attention of every man of property not only in the country, but in large villages, in towns, and in cities."[55] These were the same structures that had been hidden from sight in the vast estates designed from 1720 to 1780,[56] and concern for them indicates an entirely new attitude on the part of the architect—a concern with public welfare and with housing not only on country estates but also in urban centers, where the great estate developments had just begun.[57] Wood recognized this new class as possessing different needs and customs from his own. He noted that "in order to make myself master of the subject, it was necessary for me to feel as a cottager himself,"[58] and thus he interviewed cottagers to determine their needs. Wood also turned to the work of a reformer of cottage architecture, Nathaniel Kent (1737-1810), whose *Hints to Gentlemen of Landed Property*, the first agricultural book to include model plans for laborer's cottages (fig. 13), was published in 1775, only six years before the *Plans for Cottages*.[59] Both Kent and Wood recommended double cottages, raised floors, thick exterior walls, solid construction, and limited roof spans. In fact, the only major difference in the work of the two men is that while Kent recommended several acres of garden and grazing land for each cottage, Wood thought that a kitchen garden would be sufficient. Indeed, Wood's designs appear to be simply rearrangements of the elements of Kent's plans to form handsomely designed structures, in a reduced Palladian style.

One other transitional work of this period is also based on earlier publications. Written by James Peacock (1738?-1814) under the pseudonym of Jose MacPacke and published in 1785, it is an amusing and even malicious parody of the earlier house publications, especially Robert Morris's *Rural Architecture* and Thomas Rawlins's *Familiar Architecture*. Peacock was an architect who, like Wood, was concerned with social and economic questions. He was the author of several treatises of considerable interest to the history of social welfare.[60] In his book Peacock imitates Rawlins's earlier work: he assumes the profession of bricklayer's laborer (Rawlins was a mason), contrasts his lowly octavo with a folio edition (Rawlins's work was in folio),[61] and even exaggerates some of Rawlins's eccentricities of plan and measurement. And possibly in parody of Halfpenny, or in reference to Morris who did not assign functions to his rooms in his *Lectures on Architecture,* Peacock observed that his designs could be executed in any style and gave dimensions only to the "best or principle rooms,"[62] as Swan had done. Moreover, he supplied tables of proportions that carry to a ridiculous extreme the concept of refinement through the application of theories of proportions, which can be found in Morris's *Lectures*.[63] In imitation of another trend, just beginning to develop, he suggested that his designs could be used by "gentlemen of large fortune" to "erect little villages of this kind."[64] Peacock also pointed out the new direction that this group of publications would take, for his work consists of designs for smaller houses (even "small villas") scarcely larger than cottages, but intended for a client of limited means who has been a city dweller.

These two publications were transitional, marking the end of interest in the farmhouse type, the Palladian style, and even the copper plate engravings of the first group. The first house publication of the second group is John Plaw's *Rural Architecture,* which appeared in 1785. It was popular enough to be republished — with additions — five times by 1804. Plaw (c. 1745-1820), like many of the previous authors, was both an architect and a master builder, and he published several other handbooks.[65] In addition, he was a member and later a president of the Society of Artists, an affiliate of the new artistic movement. In his book, questions of utility, social conscience, economy, and practicality of construction are all abandoned; only *effect* is considered (fig. 14). Indeed Plaw's book is considered by Hussey to initiate a new concept of the house publication which was focused almost exclusively on picturesque architecture and omitted any real concern with social needs.[66] The amateur readership is indicated in the list of subscribers to the 1795 edition, which, however, also includes architects and tradesmen.

Plaw's work was followed by seven major publications up to 1800,[67] and then from 1800 to 1820 by a vast number of works, which must be seen as forming a distinct group. One of their chief attributes is the concept of the picturesque. By the end of the century the term picturesque (probably derived from the French term)[68] implied an association with landscape. Gilpin had already used the word "picturesque" in this context,[69] and by the 1770s he was advocating a picturesque arrangement of cottages on estates, an arrangement that he maintained could be achieved by a combination of architectural styles and the introduction of landscape views.[70]

Plaw's views of houses are the first to be placed within a landscape setting in a house publication. After this, almost without exception, the publications include landscape settings with the house illustrations. Although cost, construction methods, and room functions and dimensions may still be included (Plaw's book contains room functions and dimensions), and many of the designs are still symmetrical (not until the nineteenth century will asymmetry, the final step in the development of the picturesque architectural style, appear in these publications), the textures, styles, and shapes of the house in elevation, rather than the plan, dominate the publications. And a new technique — acqua-tint — is introduced, which permits textures to be indicated, a picturesque "effect" to be created, and is entirely opposed to the sharp copper engraved lines of the first group, in which the parts of the structure could be accurately scaled so that the designs could become models for actual buildings. As a result of the use of acqua-tint, France continued to have some influence on English publications. This process was invented in France in 1768 and brought to England in 1774.[71]

In addition, this new group of publications demonstrates an interest in the philosophy of Rousseau, who had stayed at Nuneham Courtenay during a visit to England between January 1766 and May 1767.[72] The book on gardens of his later French patron, the Marquis de Girardin, was translated and published in 1783, shortly after Rousseau's death.[73] The introductions to many of the house publications now began to reflect new, sentimental, Rousseauian attitudes on morality and the benefits of country living.

These publications, rather than the large, aristocrat-sponsored works such as Campbell's *Vitruvius Britannicus* which had been so influential to the style of the first group, established the content of many later architectural publications, and they even influenced the folio and double folio volumes of country house designs which were associated traditionally with aristocratic patronage and thus presumably would be unrelated to the philosophy of the small house books. For instance, George Richardson's double folio *New Designs in Architecture,* published in 1792 in both French and English, with a dedication to the Earl of Gainsborough and an impressive list of aristocratic subscribers, was similar in its format to the most elegant and costly of the publications associated with royal patronage. But Richardson (?-c. 1813), who was an engraver and drawing master as well as an architect, had no connection with the building trades.[74] The book's beautifully rendered and costly plates were produced in the new medium of acqua-tint (fig. 15). Richardson proposed, in his introduction, "to publish a series of useful and ornamental Designs in Architecture, beginning with buildings of the more simple form and construction, and advancing to the most complicated and adorned edifices."[75] Among these beautiful plates are illustrations of houses with thatched roofs, double cottages, a farm yard, park ornaments, villas, country seats, and two town mansions, all directly related to our house publications, with functions, dimensions, and building materials (in a short specification) all included. The book also devoted a very large section to interior elevations and Adamesque ornament that derive from other types of publications.

Richardson developed the ornamental rather than the functional aspect of domestic architecture in his book, but the authors of other large publications attempted a more balanced synthesis of the picturesque with social awareness. One year after Richardson's work appeared, Sir John Soane (1753-1837), who was the most prominent architect to be associated with this group, issued a book of designs in folio, including cottages for laborers (fig. 16), villas for persons of moderate fortune, and a few garden structures.[76] These designs were produced for the real uses and comforts of life, and in the introduction to his work Soane described in detail considerations of the conveniences for cottage dwellers that surely derive from Wood.[77] However, his specifications are scanty, and he includes among them such totally picturesque elements as tree trunks decorated with vines.

Concepts of "cottage" and "picturesque" developed quickly. By the late 1790s the term "cottage" was no longer used in its original sense as a building (hovel) without land attached, but was defined as a special style applied to residential design or to garden structures of picturesque design, such as lodges, gates, and garden pavilions on large estates. In 1798 James Malton (d. 1803), a self-proclaimed and nonpracticing architect who published views (without plans) of architecture, brought out *An Essay on British Cottage Architecture*.[78] In the long introduction to his work he developed a concept of the picturesque as it could be applied to the cottage (defined as a purely picturesque building type); the vocabulary of architecture was no longer based on classical ornament but on vernacular building elements such as diamond-paned windows, steep thatched roofs, ornamental brick corbelled chimneys, half-timber facades, and porches. Malton declared asymmetry to be a principle of picturesque architecture and, for the first time, he produced asymmetrical house designs in the small house publication (fig. 17). The main purpose of Malton's house designs was to demonstrate methods of designing by which the house could be related to the surrounding landscape. These were indeed romanticized re-creations of the laborer's cottages which were considered by Malton to be retreats for noblemen and gentlemen of taste also. Their original association with poverty and need had all but disappeared. The fact that Malton—an architectural draftsman, illustrator, and writer, not an architect—could contribute influentially to this genre points out the new concern of the architect with painterly effects.

By the very early years of the nineteenth century Richard Elsam (fl. 1808-1825), a quarrelsome minor architect,[79] wrote a rebuttal to Malton's work entitled *An Essay on Rural Architecture*. It was produced, according to the subscription list, mainly for people in the building trades. He urged his readers not to recall or return to the specific forms of the original cottage type. Instead, he recommended substituting the thatched cottage or retreat, small rural dwellings in the Gothic style, and country houses in the "modern *elegant* style" (fig. 18).[80] In this manner he encompassed the entire range of house types of three major social categories, and assigned a special style to each category. This was a transformation of the French type of encyclopedic presentation of house types; it was concerned with new categories of house types, in an untraditional, stylistic context—a stylistic transformation that had been implied, for instance, in the 1760s by Neufforge.

The development of styles, subdivisions of types, and the eventual absorption of the concept of the cottage into actual built residential house designs are events of the nineteenth century which lie beyond the scope of this essay. However, I cannot resist mentioning two of the most outstanding of the early nineteenth-century publications, both of which appeared in 1805. In them, almost all of the elements of the eighteenth-century publications discussed here were summed up. These books, *The Rural Architect* and *Designs for Cottages, Cottage Farms and Other Rural Buildings,* are both by Joseph Gandy (1771-1843), a pupil and assistant to Sir John Soane.[81] The basic geometrical forms of the first group were united with the picturesque vocabulary and landscape setting of the second group and both symmetrical and asymmetrical designs were used interchangeably (fig. 19). In these designs, the most remarkable characteristic is that the two totally contradictory styles—the picturesque and the reduced Palladian—are completely merged.

The blending of these two opposed methods of design was

made possible by pisé, the material used for the construction of the buildings. It is composed of a mixture of clays and earth, tamped in molds, that forms very substantial walls and permits structures to be erected without skilled labor and with minimum expense. The built forms were unornamented, restricted to basic geometric shapes. Pisé was popularized in France in the 1780s by François Cointeraux, who came to England in the 1790s to demonstrate his product.[82] Plaw mentioned this building material in his *Ferme Ornée* in 1795, possibly for the first time in an English publication.[83] In the same year it was considered seriously as a material for rural housing by the architect Henry Holland in a publication for the Board of Agriculture,[84] and for the first decade of the nineteenth century it was mentioned by authors of most of the house publications. Like thatch, it was a symbol of simplicity and the rural life, with the additional characteristic of permitting the designing of structures in basic geometric forms. But the material was probably never actually used except for those real cottages that were in fact habitations of the meanest and lowest class. Pisé, along with the sentimental associations, picturesque affectations, and extremes of the cottage style, was abandoned in the English house publication by the 1810s in favor of more substantial materials such as stone and brick, just as the ideal designs of the eighteenth-century books were replaced by permanent and practical models for building real houses.

NOTES

1. For Colin Campbell, see H. Colvin, *Biographical Dictionary of British Architects: 1600-1840* (London, 1978), pp. 182-185, with bibliography. (Hereafter referred to as *Dictionary.*) For Campbell's *Vitruvius Britannicus,* see T. P. Connor, "The Making of 'Vitruvius Britannicus,'" *Architectural History* XX (1977): 14-30. For alternate methods and objectives to the study of the eighteenth-century house publication, see bibliography listed in note 67, especially the article by G. Teyssot.
2. For James Gibbs, see Colvin, *Dictionary,* pp. 337-345.
3. For Robert Morris, see Colvin, *Dictionary,* pp. 558-559. In addition to *Rural Architecture* (London, 1750; reissued as *Select Architecture,* 1755, 1757), Morris published another house publication, *Architectural Remembrancer* (London, 1751; reissued as *Architecture Improved,* 1755, 1757). Morris's illustrations were included in Robert Say-

er's *Modern Builder's Assistant,* along with those of Halfpenny and Lightoler (see note 25 below).

4. R. Morris, *Lectures on Architecture* (London, 1734), pp. 184, 189.

5. For Richard Boyle, Lord Burlington, see Colvin, *Dictionary,* pp. 128-132, with bibliography.

6. For Daniel Garrett, see P. Leach, "The Architecture of Daniel Garrett," *Country Life,* CLVI, 12 Sept. 1974, pp. 694-697; 19 Sept. 1974, pp. 766-769; 26 Sept. 1974, pp. 834-837. Also see Colvin, *Dictionary,* pp. 332-334.

7. Garrett, *Designs and Estimates of Farm Houses...* (London, 1747; later eds. 1759, 1772), "Introduction," n. p. In addition, he stressed that his book contained designs for small farms without unnecessary space, which would be less costly to build and for which less rent could be charged.

8. For Isaac Ware, see Colvin, *Dictionary,* pp. 864-867.

9. Ware, *Complete Body of Architecture* (London, 1756; 2d ed. 1767), "Preface," n. p.

10. Ibid., p. 352. Ware may be recalling Robert Castell's *Villas of the Romans* (London, 1728), which was dedicated to Burlington.

11. Ibid., p. 353. His remarks may be related to the development of landscape garden theory at this point in time, especially to the work of Thomas Whately.

12. R. Morris, *Rural Architecture,* p. 2. For Morris, see note 3 above.

13. Ibid., unpaginated preface.

14. Ibid., unpaginated preface.

15. Ibid., pp. 7-8.

16. For instance, the design of a "Small Pleasure Room" (pl. L). Morris's description, "A Building of this Kind would be an Object seen at a Distance, and render it as well an Amusement to entertain the Fancy of others, as to those on the Spot, for a Variety of beautiful Hills, Vales, Landskips, &c. for the Pleasure of the Inhabitants, create a new Succession of pleasing Images and call forth the Beauty, Order, and Harmony of Nature, to decorate and enliven the Scene" (p. 8), foreshadows the work of Lightoler (see text, below).

17. For William Halfpenny ("*alias* Michael Hoare") and his publications, see Colvin, *Dictionary,* pp. 378-379, with bibliography.

18. Halfpenny, *New and Complete System of Architecture, delineated in a variety of plans and elevations of designs for convenient and decorated houses* (London, 1749; reissued 1759), unpaginated preface.

19. *Twelve Beautiful Designs for Farm Houses* (London, 1750; reissued 1759, 1774); *Six New Designs for Farm Houses,* Part I (London, 1751); *Six New Designs for Farm Houses,* Part II (London, 1751); *Thirteen New Designs for Farm Houses,* Part III (London, 1752). Parts I, II, and III of the *New Designs for Farm Houses* series were combined into *Useful Architecture in Twenty-One New Designs* (London, 1752) reissued 1755, 1760).

20. Halfpenny, *Select Architecture,* unpaginated preface: "more real

Beauty and Elegance appears in the due Symmetry and Harmony of a well-constructed Cottage, then can be found in the most exalted Palace."

21. William and John Halfpenny, *Chinese and Gothic Architecture* (London, 1752).

22. For Abraham Swan, see Colvin, *Dictionary,* p. 799.

23. Swan, *A Collection of Designs in Architecture* (London, 1757), "Preface," p. iii.

24. Ibid., p. vi.

25. For Timothy Lightoler, see Colvin, *Dictionary,* pp. 520-521. Lightoler was associated with Morris and Halfpenny in the publications of the *Modern Builder's Assistant,* published by Robert Sayer. However, the early date of 1742 for this work has been emended by Colvin, p. 379, n. 1, to 1757 (based on the fact that the printed date of MDCCVLII, which has been interpreted as MDCCXLI, is interpreted by Colvin as MDCCLVII).

26. For John Crunden, see Colvin, *Dictionary,* p. 242. An incomplete list of later editions of *Convenient and Ornamental Architecture* is 1785, 1788, 1791, and 1815.

27. For Thomas Rawlins, see Colvin, *Dictionary,* p. 672, who describes him as a "monumental mason." *Familiar Architecture* (London, 1768) was reissued in 1789 and 1795. Rawlins's essay, "Masonry of the Semicircular and Elliptical Arches, with practical Remarks," is appended to this work.

28. Rawlins, *Familiar Architecture,* title page.

29. Ibid., p. iii.

30. Ibid., p. viii.

31. For information on this artistic circle, see M. Girouard, "English Art and the Rococo," *Country Life* CXXXIX (13 Jan. 1966), pp. 58-61; (27 Jan. 1966), pp. 188-190; (3 Feb. 1966), pp. 224-227. Connections with Fielding, Hogarth, and Jonathan Tyers (owner of the Vauxhall), and Frederick, Prince of Wales, and Lords Lyttleton and Chesterfield are examined.

32. For lecturers at the Royal Academy, see Colvin, *Dictionary,* pp. 32-36. The Royal Society of Arts was founded in 1754. Its primary concern was the encouragement of industrial arts; architects exhibited there from 1760. The Royal Academy of Arts was founded in 1768, and provided for the appointment of a Professor of Architecture. Not until 1834 with the founding of the Institute of British Architects (chartered in 1837) was a strong professional architectural organization established.

33. See Colvin, *Dictionary,* "The Architectural Profession," pp. 26-41, on the development of architectural professionalism. Also see Frank Jenkins, *Architect and Patron* (London, 1961), pp. 67-119, for the broadening of patronage parallel with the development of exclusivism among architects; and Borrington Kaye, *The Development of the Architectural Profession in Britain* (London, 1960), Chapter IV, "The Status and Training of the Architect in the 17th and 18th Centuries,"

pp. 39-53; 56-61. For further information see J. Wilton-Ely, "The Rise of the Professional Architect in England," in *The Architect,* ed. S. Kostof (New York, 1977), pp. 180-208.

34. See Girouard, article cited in note 31 above, esp. p. 61.

35. For Serlio's book on houses, see Marco Rosci's fundamental study, *Il trattato di architettura di Sebastiano Serlio* (Milan, 1966), and its companion volume, S. Serlio, *Delle habitationi di tutti li gradi degli homini,* ed. Rosci (Milan, 1966); and, more recently, S. Serlio, *On Domestic Architecture, the Sixth Book,* ed. M. N. Rosenfeld (New York, 1978).

36. Jacques Androuet Du Cerceau, *Les Trois Livres d'architecture* (Paris, 1559, 1561, 1582), especially Book I. Book III, on villas, contains ideas concerning the relationship of villas to nature which will be developed by Antoine Le Pautre in his *Desseins de plusieurs palais...* (Paris, 1652?) (later published as *Les Oeuvres d'architecture d'Anthoine Le Pautre*), and which are peripherally related to the subject of this article.

37. Pierre Le Muet, *Manière de bien bâtir pour toutes sortes de personnes* (Paris, 1623; later French eds. in 1647, 1664, 1681, and 17--); and English transl., *The Art of Fair Building,* ed. Robert Pricke (London, 1675).

38. For the author of this publication, see W. Herrmann, "The Author of the Architecture Moderne," *Journal of the Society of Architectural Historians* (May 1959), pp. 60-62. J. F. Blondel, *Architecture Français.* Vol. I, book 2, part 2, p. 255, note a, says that Tiercelet took Le Muet's book as a model (Herrmann, p. 61).

39. The publisher of these editions was Jombert.

40. Jacques-François Blondel, *De la distribution des maisons de plaisance, et de la decoration des edifices en général,* 2 vols. (Paris, 1737-1738). See also R. Etlin, "'Les Dedans': Jacques-François Blondel and the System of the Home c. 1740," *Gazette des Beaux-Arts* XCI (April 1978): 137-147.

41. Blondel, *Distribution,* p. iij.

42. Charles Etienne Briseux, *L'Art de bâtir des maisons de campagne où l'on traite de leur distribution, de leur construction, & de leur décoration...,* 2 vols. (Paris, 1743; 2d ed., 1761).

43. Ibid., I: v. But see also Briseux's edition of Tiercelet's work: *Architecture moderne, ou l'art de bien bâtir pour toutes sortes de personnes, tant pour les maisons des particuliers que pour les palais...,* 2 vols. (Paris, 1728), I: ij r.

44. J. F. de Neufforge, *Recueil élémentaire d'architecture,* 9 vols. (Paris, 1757-1780). For information on this little-known architectural publisher, see A. Braham, *The Architecture of the French Enlightenment* (London, 1980), pp. 60-61.

45. Neufforge, Books III (1760), town houses including multiple dwellings; LV (1761), villas, pavilions, and maisons de plaisance; VII (1767), and Supplement (1780).

46. See text above.

47. Among the possible French influences, Morris refers specifically to the "Ten Kate" translation of Le Blond in 1732. Morris also cites Fréart de Chambray in *An Essay in Defence of Ancient Architecture* (London, 1728), pp. 34, 38, and 40. For the French attitude toward distribution, see Etlin, article cited in note 40 above.

48. Jean Marot, *L'Architecture française* (Le Grand Marot), Paris, before 1699: *Petit oeuvre d'architecture* (Le Petit Marot), Paris, between 1645 and 1660.

49. See, for instance, K. A. Esdaile, "The Small House and its Amenities in the Architectural Handbooks: 1749-1847," *Transactions of the Bibliographical Society* XV (1917-1919): 115; and E. L. Jones, *Agriculture and the Industrial Revolution* (New York, 1974), p. 73. Also see Girouard, article cited in note 31 above, p. 190.

50. W. J. Shelton, *English Hunger and Industrial Disorders* (New York, 1973), p. 65.

51. Ashton, *Economic Fluctuations in England 1700-1800* (London, 1959), p. 165.

52. J. W. Robinson, "Model Farm Building of the Age of Improvement," *Architectural History* XIX (1976): 17, where Robinson states that 1770-1815 is the age of the great improver landlords.

53. *A Series of Plans for Cottages or Habitations of the Labourer, either in Husbandry or the Mechanic Arts, adapted as well to Towns as to the Country.* For John Wood the younger, see Colvin, *Dictionary,* pp. 911-922.

54. Wood took his father's place at Bath after the death of the older man in 1754, and he added the Royal Crescent and the New Assembly Rooms, among other structures, to his father's uncompleted designs. Colvin, *Dictionary,* p. 911, states that Wood's work "represents the climax of the Palladian achievement in Bath."

55. Wood, *Plans,* p. 3.

56. On estate villages, see Mavis Batey, "Oliver Goldsmith: An Indictment of Landscape Gardening," in P. Willis, ed., *Furor Hortensis, Essays on the History of English Landscape Gardening in Memory of H. F. Clark* (Edinburgh, 1974), pp. 57-71. See also text, below.

57. See Summerson, *Georgian London* (Harmondsworth, 1962 rev.; 1st ed. 1945), pp. 163-176.

58. Wood, *Designs,* p. 3.

59. For Nathaniel Kent, see *Dictionary of National Biography* (London, 1892 ed.), XXXI: 22-23. Kent's contribution to our subject is in *Hints to Gentlemen of Landed Property* (London, 1775; 3d ed. 1793), "Reflections on the Great Importance of Cottages," pp. 228-258.

60. For James Peacock, see Colvin, *Dictionary,* p. 628.

61. Peacock, *OIKIΔIA, or, Nutshells: being ichnographic distributions for small villas; chiefly upon oeconomical principles. In seven classes with occasional Remarks* (London, 1785), p. 4.

62. Ibid., p. 7.

63. Ibid., pp. 20-24.

64. Ibid.

65. For John Plaw, see Colvin, pp. 642-643. Other Plaw handbooks are: *Ferme Ornée* (1795, 1813); and *Sketches for Country Houses* (1800, 1803). *Rural Architecture, or Designs from the Simple Cottage to the Decorated Villa*, which consisted mainly of villas in landscape settings, but also of a few cottages and a "farm house," with no explanatory preface and only brief plate descriptions, was reprinted in 1794, 1796, 1800, 1802, and 1804.

66. C. Hussey, *The Picturesque: Studies in a Point of View* (London, 1927), p. 216.

67. For further bibliography see E. Spiegel, *The English Farm House*, Ph. D. dissertation, Columbia University, 1960; C. W. Nachmann, "The Early English Cottage Book," *Marsyas XIV: 1968-1969*, pp. 67-76; S. Blutman, "Books of Designs for Country Houses: 1780-1815," *Architectural History* XI (1968): 25-33; M. McMordie, "Picturesque Pattern Books and pre-Victorian Designers," *Architectural History* XVIII (1975): 43-59; K. A. Esdaile, "The Small House and its Amenities in the Architectural Handbooks: 1749-1847," *Transactions of the Bibliographical Society* XV (1917-1919): 115-132; and G. Teyssot, "Cottages et Pittoresque: les origines du logement ouvrier en Angleterre," *Architecture/Mouvement/Continuité* XXVIII, no. 34 (1973): 26-37.

68. W. Templeman, *The Life and Works of William Gilpin* (Urbana, Ill., 1939), pp. 113-115.

69. Ibid., pp. 117-118, suggesting Gilpin was describing landscape in this sense by 1748, and that he used the word "picturesque" in 1752 (p. 129).

70. G. Darley, *Villages of Vision* (London, 1975), pp. 6-8; quoted from William Gilpin, *Observations on Several Parts of England, particularly the Mountains and Lakes of Cumberland and Westmoreland, relative chiefly to picturesque beauty, made in the year 1772* (London, 1808 3d ed.), I: 22. Gilpin contributed to the designing of the grounds of Nuneham, but only in 1830. Nuneham Courtenay was planned by Lord Harcourt from 1761. The second Lord Harcourt who succeeded to Nuneham Courtenay in 1777 was a friend of Rousseau's, and the French philosopher visited England and stayed at the estate in 1766.

71. See McMordie, article cited in note 67 above, p. 43. Paul Sandby was responsible for importing acqua-tint to England in 1774.

72. Rousseau was in England from January 1766-March 1767. William Mason designed Julie's Nature Garden (based on Rousseau's description in his Nouvelle Héloise) at Nuneham after 1777.

73. Girardin's book was brought out by Daniel Malthus, as *An Essay on Landscape; or, on the Means of Improving and Embellishing the Country round our Habitations* (London, 1783).

74. For George Richardson, see Colvin, *Dictionary*, pp. 687-688.

75. Richardson, *New Designs in Architecture* (London, 1792), "Introduction," p. i. Richardson also produced, among many other publications, *Original Designs for Country Seats or Villas*, in 1793, and

added the final two volumes to the Vitruvius Britannicus series in 1802-1808 and 1808-1810.

76. *Sketches in Architecture*, London, 1793. For Sir John Soane, see Colvin, *Dictionary*, pp. 765-772. Soane evidently underwent a change in attitude, for he notes in his Introduction (unpaginated): "Some years since, I published a collection of plans, elevations, and sections of buildings already executed, and chiefly on a large scale [*Designs in Architecture...,* 1778]; which work having been favorably received, I am thereby induced to offer another publication on the same subject, but on a smaller scale, consisting of cottages for the laborious and industrious part of the community, and of other buildings calculated for the real uses and comforts of life, and such as are within the reach of moderate fortunes."

77. Ibid. "In cottages the rooms are unavoidably small, few in number, and frequently crowded with inhabitants. Their ground floors should be raised at least three or four steps from the soil: they should be placed in the most open and airy situations, perfectly dry and warm, built with the best and most durable materials, and well supplied with good water." "As to estimates, however desirable, nothing certain can be advanced until the situation and local circumstances are known and considered."

78. For James Malton, see Colvin, pp. 535-536. In addition to his *An Essay on British Cottage Architecture: being an Attempt to Perpetuate on Principle, that Peculiar Mode of Building, which was originally the Effect of Chance,* 1798 (2nd ed., 1804), Malton also produced *Collection of Designs for Rural Retreats... principally in the Gothic and Castle Styles of Architecture,* London, 1802.

79. For Richard Elsam, see Colvin, *Dictionary*, pp. 292-293. In 1816 Elsam published *Hints for Improving the Condition of the Peasantry.*

80. Elsam, *An Essay on Rural Architecture* (London, 1803), p. 2.

81. For Joseph Gandy, see Colvin, *Dictionary*, pp. 328-329. *Designs for Cottages* is the more important of the two books; it contains a dedication to Thomas Hope, and includes an important introduction, room sizes, and the total price of the house.

82. For François Cointeraux, see P. Collins, *Concrete: The Vision of a New Architecture* (London, 1959), pp. 21-24.

83. J. Plaw, *Ferme Ornée* (London, 1759), "Advertisement," unpaginated.

84. H. Holland, "On Cottages," *Communications to the Board of Agriculture on Subjects Relative to Husbandry and Internal Improvement of the Country,* 7 vols. (London, 1797-1813), I, sect. ix, pp. 97-102.

FIGURES

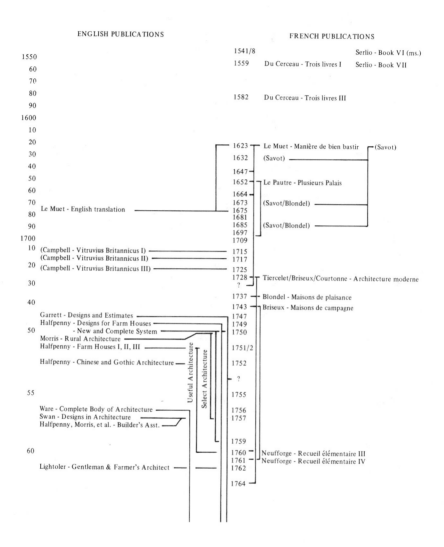

Fig. 1. Chronological Chart of House Publications.

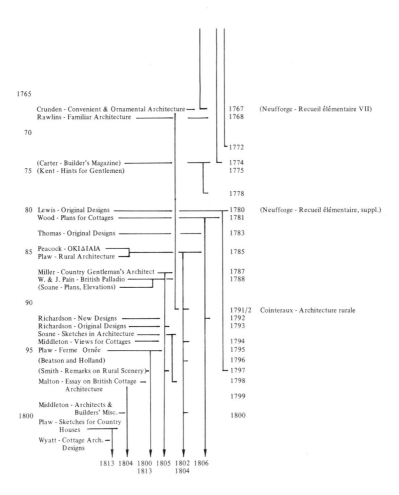

Fig. 1. Continued.

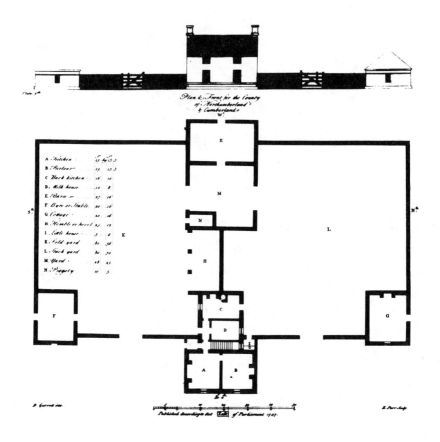

Fig. 2. D. Garrett, *Plans,* plate. 5.

Fig. 3. R. Morris, *Rural Architecture,* plate 47.

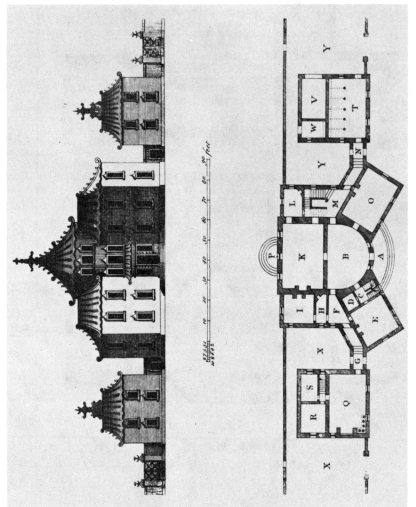

Fig. 4. W. Halfpenny, *Chinese and Gothic Architecture*, plate ix.

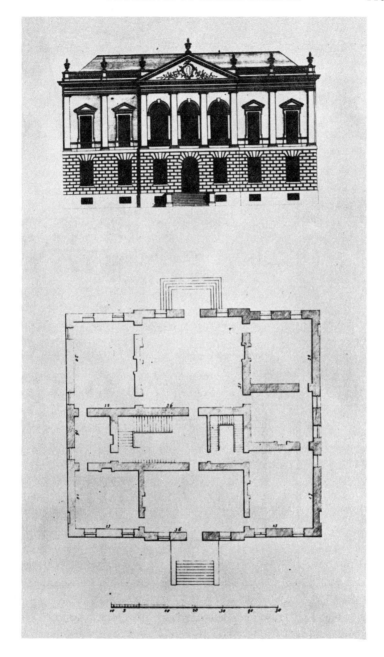

Fig. 5. A. Swan, *Collected Designs,* plate 22.

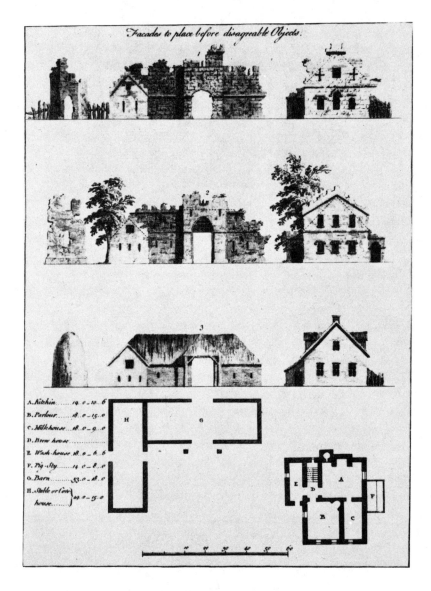

Fig. 6. T. Lightoler, *Gentleman... Architect,* plate 25.

Fig. 7. I. Ware, *Complete Body,* pp. 81-82 (design for ceiling of music room, Chesterfield House).

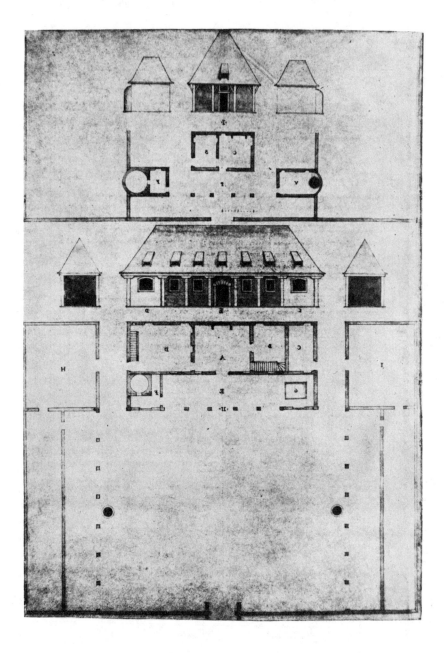

Fig. 8. S. Serlio, Book VI, plate 1 (from M. N. Rosenfeld, *Sebastiano Serlio on Domestic Architecture*).

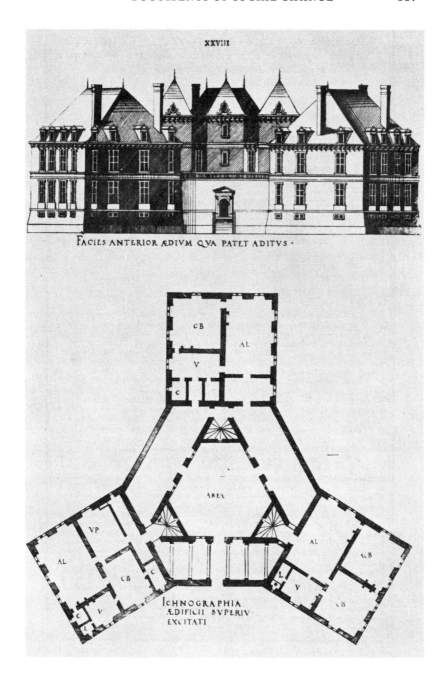

Fig. 9. J. Androuet Du Cerceau, *Trois Livres,* Book I, plate 28.

Distribution de la premiere place, ayant de Largeur 12 pieds, et de profondeur, depuis 21 pieds et demi à toute autre qui sera moindre que 25 pieds.

Plan du premier Estage

Plan du second Estage

Cour 5 p 6 · Puits · Passage 3 p · Salle 9 P · Lict · Chambre 12 P · Caue ·

Largeur 12 P · · Profondeur 21 P. · · Largeur 12 P · · Profondeur 21 P. ·

Pied · · · Rez de chaussée de la Rue

Thoises

En cette place premiere de douze pieds de largeur, sur vingt et vn pieds et demy de profondeur, la largeur se distribue en vne salle de 9 pieds, et vn passage de 3 pieds. la profondeur se diuise en la salle de quatorze pieds, et en vne cour de cinq pieds et demy de largeur; et le reste de la largeur sur toute cette profondeur, est employé en vn escalier qui aura 6 pieds en quarré, ou sous le rampant des marches sera fait le priué. Avn des angles de la cour, joignant la Salle, est le puys. Pour la descente de la caue, elle se fera au passage, par le moyen d'vne trappe, tant en cette figure comme aux suiuantes, iusques à la sixieme distributiõ de la 6.e place. Pour le regard du 2.e estage, la chambre occupera la largeur tant de la sale que du passage, et partant aura 12 pieds de largeur; et pour la profondeur, elle est reglée par celle de la Salle de dessous, qui est 14 pieds; le reste de ce plan ne differe point du I.er Et quant sur cette mesme largeur d'edifice, la profondeur se trouueroit entre 21 pieds et demy, et 25, les mesures de la largeur demeurant en leur entier, il faudroit distribuer le surplus de la profondeur en la cour, et en la sale, selon le desir de celuy qui bastiroit. Et auons trouué bon de declarer toutes les mesures des edifices, sur le discours particulier que nous auons fait de la structure d'vn chacun; encore que nous les eussions marquês par chiffres sur les plans, pour plus grande instruction de ceux qui sont moins exercez en la connoissance des plans. Et Pour le regard des hauteurs, le I.er estage aura 9 pi. sous soliues, depuis l'aire de la Salle, et l'epaiss.r du plancher, les soliues comprises aura 8 pou. qui sera plus que suffisam.t sur vne si petite largeur. Dont toute la hauteur sera de 9 pi. 8 pou. laquelle estant departie en 18 marches, ce sera 6 pou. 5 lignes 2 tiers pour la hauteur de chacune; laquelle distribution suiura aussi au second estage, lequel a 9 pieds de haut, come le I.er Le 3.e Estage à de hauteur 8 pi. sous soliues, et 8 pou. estant compris les soliues et plancher. Cette hauteur de 8 pi. et 8 pou. estant distribuée en 16 marches, nous donnera 6 pou. et demy de hauteur pour chacune, qui sont 2 tiers de ligne, de plus que les autres marches; et partant leur difference est come insensible. Au dessus seront greniers. Et d'autant que l'eschapée necessaire pour l'escalier est empeschée par la hauteur qu'il faut donner au priué, on descendra de la cour au priué, par deux marches, dont l'vne sera dans la cour, et l'autre dans le priué, ayant chacune 9 pouces de hauteur.

Fig. 10. P. Le Muet, *Manière de bien bâtir*, plate 1.

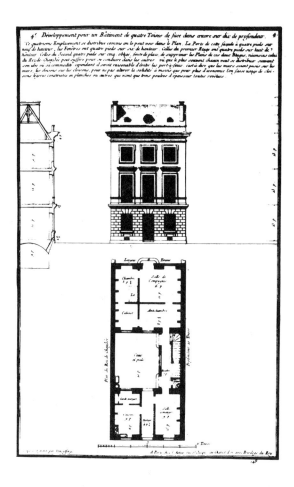

Fig. 11. J. F. de Neufforge, *Recueil,* vol. III, cah. 25, plate 1.

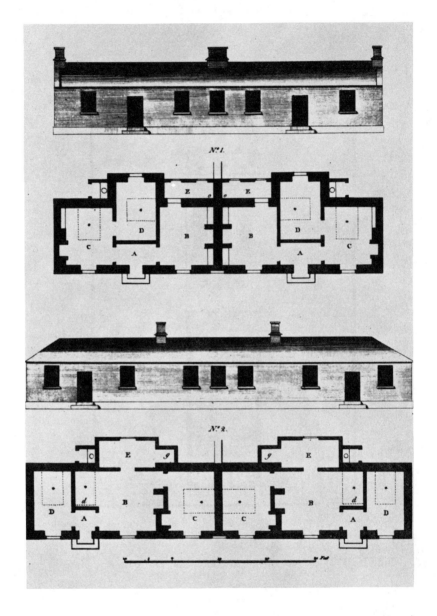

Fig. 12. J. Wood, *Plans...Cottages,* plate xvi.

Fig. 13. N. Kent, *Hints to Gentlemen*, folded plate before p. 247 (elevation).

Fig. 14. J. Plaw, *Rural Architecture*, plate 3.

Fig. 15. G. Richardson, *New Designs*, plate 2.

Fig. 16. J. Soane, *Sketches*, plate I.

Fig. 17. J. Malton, *British Cottage Architecture*, plate 4.

Fig. 18. R. Elsam, *Essay on Rural Architecture* (small house in style of modern cottage).

Fig. 19. J. Gandy, *Designs*, plate 21.

V

LEGISLATING THE SUBLIME

Frances Ferguson

As the monster recounts his history in *Frankenstein,* he recalls his chance encounter with Victor Frankenstein's younger brother William:

> At this time a slight sleep relieved me from the pain of reflection, which was disturbed by the approach of a beautiful child, who came running into the recess I had chosen with all the sportiveness of infancy. Suddenly, as I gazed on him, an idea seized me that this little creature was unprejudiced, and had lived too short a time to have imbibed a horror of deformity. If, therefore, I could seize him, and educate him as my companion and friend, I should not be desolate in this peopled earth.
>
> Urged by this impulse, I seized on the boy as he passed, and drew him towards me. As soon as he beheld my form, he placed his hands before his eyes, and uttered a shrill scream: I drew his hand forcibly from his face, and said, "Child, what is the meaning of this? I do not intend to hurt you; listen to me."
>
> He struggled violently; "Let me go," he cried; "monster! ugly wretch! you wish to eat me, and tear me to pieces—You are an ogre—Let me go, or I will tell my papa."
>
> "Boy, you will never see your father again; you must come with me."
>
> "Hideous monster! let me go; My papa is a Syndic—he is M. Frankenstein—he would punish you. You dare not keep me."[1]

The humor of the scenario in which the monster looks to William like some fairy-tale ogre, and in which William threatens

128

him with his father, fades as the monster describes the dénoue-
ment (which readers of the novel already know, of course, from
the letters exchanged between Elizabeth Lavenza and Victor):
the monster kills William upon learning that he is related to Victor Frankenstein. Whereas William invokes his father to claim
that his father *is* the law, the monster murders William to revenge
himself upon his (the monster's) father Victor for dereliction of
paternal duty. William, as part of the almost incredibly charmed
domestic circle of the Frankensteins, sees the law as an ally of the
stability of the home and the domestic affections; the monster,
however, outside of any domestic circle, acts the part of the ter-
rorist in asserting the superiority of his sheer physical force. The
gross inequality of the struggle between William and the monster
makes the monster's first attack on humanity (in the form of the
Frankenstein family) particularly shocking. For a creature who
has given expression to sensitive and generally benevolent reflections to pick on someone who is not nearly his own size makes the
violation of every code of civilized behavior all the more dramatic.

Although I shall return to *Frankenstein* later, because it treats
the sublime in a variety of interesting ways, suffice it to say here
that the confrontation between William and the monster is useful
for illuminating the opposing claims of the beautiful (which is on
the side of the domestic, amiable affections)² and the sublime
(which is on the side of power that inspires terror). The beautiful,
inasmuch as it represents the virtues of custom and civilized
behavior, is a near relation to the law that, of course, continually
functions to support the force of custom and civilization; the sublime, which is cut off from custom inasmuch as it is associated
with novelty and surprise, quite simply overruns the claims of
legality. In other words, the beautiful and the sublime, instead of
appearing as complements to one another, present themselves in
Frankenstein as irreconcilable antagonists.

Of course, the opposition between the beautiful and the sublime that we encounter in *Frankenstein* is a great deal starker
than either Burke or Kant had earlier presented it to be. Yet
Frankenstein, published in 1818, does not so much contradict
Burke's *Enquiry into the Origin of Our Ideas of the Sublime and
Beautiful* of 1757 or Kant's *Critique of Judgment* of 1790 as it
reflects the widespread influence of their prevailing logic. Moreover, the irreconcilable oppositions of *Frankenstein* make explicit

the contradictions that arise from attempting to bring the sublime under the legislation of what, for Burke, must be supposed
to be the commonality of experience for all men, and of what, for
Kant, is the guiding principle of all such commonality among
men—namely, the reason.

Let me turn first to Burke. As is well known, Burke in the
Enquiry adopts a position that subordinates man's role as a
rational creature to his being susceptible to the workings of external objects upon the senses. External objects operate on humans
through a purely physical mechanism, as Burke insists when he
explains how each of the five senses is affected by external stimuli.
Thus, he provides a variety of examples of what he calls the
"natural and mechanical causes of our passions"[3] that help to
explain why we respond as we do to certain sensations. And
although Burke traces the operations of external objects at least
partially to apparently psychological factors (such as expectation,
p. 110, or curiosity, which Burke describes as "the first and simplest emotion which we discover in the human mind," p. 31), it is
important to recognize that such emotions or psychological elements are nowhere seen by him as anything more than components of the mechanism through which the external stimuli act.
When we find rather elaborate accounts of the operations of such
conditions as darkness upon the human sense and mind, Burke's
practice is always to derive the mental reaction from the physical
rather than the reverse. In his painstakingly thorough physiological account, darkness, for example, turns out to act as an assault
upon the body that then transfers itself to the mind.

Some who allow darkness to be a cause of the sublime, would infer from
the dilation of the pupil, that a relaxation may be productive of the sublime as well as a convulsion; but they do not, I believe, consider, that
although the circular ring of the iris be in some sense a sphincter, which
may possibly be dilated by other sphincters of the body, that it is furnished with antagonist muscles, which are the radial fibres of the iris; no
sooner does the circular muscle begin to relax, than these fibres, want-
ing their counterpoise, are forcibly drawn back, and open the pupil to a
considerable wideness. But though we were not apprized of this, I believe that any one will find if he opens his eyes and makes an effort to see
in a dark place, that a very perceivable pain ensues. And I have heard
some ladies remark, that after having worked a long time upon a ground
of black, their eyes were so pained and weakened they could hardly see.
It may perhaps be objected to this theory of the mechanical effect of
darkness, that the ill effects of darkness or blackness seem rather mental

than corporeal; and I own it is true, that they do so; and so do all those that depend on the affections of the finer parts of our system. The ill effects of bad weather appear often no otherwise, than in a melancholy and dejection of spirits, though without doubt, in this case, the bodily organs suffer first, and the mind through these organs. (146-147)

One can well see why Kant should have found himself opposed to Burke's account of the sublime and the beautiful; such an extreme empiricism as Burke's purchases its lucidity at the price of the notion of human freedom, as all human action is described as a mechanical response to external stimuli. For it is a behaviorism that is a version of high formalism which can proclaim that "Our minds and bodies are so closely and intimately connected, that one is incapable of pain or pleasure without the other" (p. 133) and can cite as evidence for this assertion the "curious story of the celebrated physiognomist Campanella," who,

When he had a mind to penetrate into the inclinations of those he had to deal with, . . . composed his face, his gesture, and his whole body, as nearly as he could into the exact similitude of the person he intended to examine; and then carefully observed what turn of mind he seemed to acquire by this change. So that, says my author, he was able to enter into the dispositions and thoughts of people, as effectually as if he had been changed into the very man. (132-133)

While Burke's behavioristic schema may present a mechanical version of the operations of the human mind, it does enable him, however, to insist upon the similarity of the reactions of all men to the various types of experience that he examines. For in the course of outlining human reactions to various beautiful and sublime objects (or properties of them), Burke manages to construct what would appear to be an objective aesthetics — which obviously forestalls the possibility of an endless subjectivism in aesthetic matters that would preclude the possibility of our ever even discussing aesthetic judgments, much less agreeing on them. And, in a sense, one can discern Burke the political strategist even here in the thick of his aesthetic discussion as he tries to establish the basis for a legislation of taste by appealing to the uniformity and commonality of individual responses to aesthetic objects. Thus, Burke counters "those, who on a superficial view imagine, that there is so great a diversity of Tastes both in kind and degree, that nothing can be more indeterminate" (p. 13) by asserting that

"We do and we must suppose, that as the conformation of their organs are nearly, or altogether the same in all men, so the manner of perceiving external objects is in all men the same, or with little difference" (p. 13). While the Burkean account of the sublime and the beautiful may reduce men to machines, it does produce an implicit social compact among these human machines as it stresses the similarity, indeed the uniformity, of their responses. If men were not like one another already, nature would quickly make them so, for in this account the external object makes the man. The same external objects will, of course, quickly make men "become what they behold" and will make them become like one another in the process, so that one can see that the social compact for Burke emerges as a fact derived quite directly from nature.

Burke, of course, has to acknowledge differences in aesthetic judgments, but for him they arise merely "from the different kinds and degrees" of knowledge (p. 20) that the various judges possess. Thus, he can claim both that "So far as Taste is natural, it is nearly common to all" (p. 20) and that "the greater attention and habit [i.e., the cultivated taste] . . . will have the advantage" (p. 22); in short, he thereby acknowledges differences in aesthetic judgments and also renders them trivial by claiming that the variations in taste result merely from variations in the amount of exposure to the aesthetic stimuli. Taste, in other words, can be acquired in exactly the same way that muscles can—by exercise.

Now although Burke is seeking a standard of taste that will apply equally to all men, it would seem at first glance that only the beautiful would remain within the boundaries of the domestication inherent in Burke's rule-governed account of the sublime. After all, he describes the sublime as that "which in all things abhors mediocrity" (p. 81), and the sublime continually appears on the side of power and terror rather than of the law. Even though his account of the operation of all aesthetic properties stipulates that a human observer be the passive instrument of the external object, he repeatedly describes the sublime as rendering the mind especially passive before its force:

[The] astonishment [produced] by the sublime in nature is that state of soul, in which all its motions are suspended, with some degree of horror. In this case the mind is so entirely filled with its object, that it cannot entertain any other nor by consequence reason on that object which employs it. Hence arises the great power of the sublime, that far from being produced by them, it anticipates our reasonings, and hurries us on by an irresistible force. (57)

Yet while the sublime clearly represents what is humanly ungovernable, one rather peculiar aspect of Burke's account is that the effects of the sublime are seen as of particular social utility. This seems like something of a paradox, because of the thrust of many of his arguments. He has aligned the beautiful with what he calls "the passions which belong to society," because, he says, the passions "which belong to *generation* have their origin in gratification and *pleasures*" (p. 40). And he has suggested two different connections between the sublime and individuality or solitude. On the one hand, the sublime involves "passions belonging to the preservation of the individual"; on the other, when individuality is seen as "absolute and entire solitude," it is itself sublime—and thus a cause of positive pain. In fact, Burke avers that complete solitude is among the strongest notions of the sublime and that "Death itself is scarcely an idea of more terror" (p. 43). But the sublime ultimately becomes an instrument of society as it turns out that Providence (which for Burke seems merely the largest version of an external stimulus) employs the sublime notion of absolute solitude so that "we may discern [that we are creatures designed for society and] that an entire life of solitude contradicts the purposes of our being" (p. 43).

There are still other respects in which the sublime, though repeatedly set apart from the claims of society, nonetheless reinforces them. As we have observed earlier, the very insistence on all men agreeing to see certain things as sublime relies on social agreement rather than the rupture of it that the sublime seems to represent. Moreover, whereas Burke claims that "fear created the first gods" (cf. p. 70), the idea of God is a sublime idea with obvious social utility; the same divine providence that makes solitude sublime—that is, terrifying—therefore ensures the preservation of the social network. When Burke differentiates the amiable virtues from the admirable ones that "are of the sublimer kind" and "produce terror rather than love" (p. 110), he repeats his earlier association between power and sublimity (p. 67). We are in awe of such animals as wolves, because we are affected by strength which is *natural* power. The power which arises from institution in kings and commanders, has the same connection with terror. Sovereigns are frequently addressed with the title of dread majesty. (67)

Moreover, power is here conceived as awesome but also as a guarantor of society, because it fosters the work ethic. The chief benefit that Burke sees issuing from the sublime is that it prompts us to "exercise or labour," which is necessary to counteract the baleful effects of indolence: "Melancholy, dejection, despair, and often self-murder, is the consequence of the gloomy view we take of things in this relaxed state of body" (p. 135). In other words, the sublime contributes to our productivity in society, and the sublime is preferable to the beautiful inasmuch as it represents a labor theory of aesthetic value. Whereas Kant will later insist on the importance of detaching the aesthetic object from any thought of the labor that went into its production, Burke sees the aesthetic object as valuable not for the labor that produced it but for the labor it will produce. For Burke, heroes, though participating in the sublime, are almost incidentally important for their singularity. They are instead essentially important for the contribution their sublimity makes to civilized society; they make the world safe for society. And, in keeping with the logic that Burke earlier sketched out with regard to the basic uniformity and universality of taste, heroes provide not merely an example of superiority but an example of what any of us might become with the proper exercise of our capacities for overcoming what seem to us like dangers; as Burke says, "custom reconciles us to everything," and thus converts much of the domain of the terrifying, the sublime, to that of the amiable, the beautiful, the domestic, the available.[4]

There are numerous occasions in the *Enquiry* in which Burke suggests that the progression from the sublime to the beautiful which occurs under the pressure of habit is continually threatening a reversal — as when, in the example I cited earlier, the enterprise of embroidering on a black background is seen as testimony to the sublimity of darkness. Although Burke has gone to great pains to isolate and to distinguish from one another the positive properties that produce sublime and beautiful effects, such examples continually raise the possibility of movement between the two distinct areas of experience.

It should be stressed, however, that while Burke raises various cases of the sublime encroaching upon the beautiful, the greater threat in the *Enquiry* seems to be posed by the kind of gravitational pull that the beautiful and habit exercise on the sublime, thus robbing it of its vigor and force. For while he avers that "the sublime suffers less by being united to some of the qualities of beauty, than beauty does by being joined to greatness of quantity, or any other properties of the sublime," because "there is something so over-ruling in whatever inspires us with awe..., that nothing else can stand in their presence" (p. 157), habit and custom are constantly presented as eroding the liveliness of the sensations we had "In the morning of our days, when the senses [were] unworn and tender, when the whole man [was awake in every part], and the gloss of novelty fresh upon all the objects that [surrounded] us" (p. 25).

It is, however, when Burke introduces properties of sublimity which he allies with habit and custom that the sublime begins to appear particularly threatening—largely because habit and custom operate to obscure the nature of the threat. Thus, he speaks of infinity as a source of the sublime which "has a tendency to fill the mind with that sort of delightful horror, which is the most genuine effect, and truest test of the sublime" (p. 73). He then produces a series of examples of the mental and perceptual inertia that causes us to continue repeating an idea largely because we have frequently repeated it before, to continue to see objects whirling even after we sit down because we have been whirling about, and so forth.

The senses strongly affected in some one manner, cannot quickly change their tenor, or adapt themselves to other things.... This is the reason of an appearance very frequent in madmen; that they remain whole days and nights, sometimes whole years, in the constant repetition of some remark, some complaint, or song; which having struck powerfully on their disordered imagination, in the beginning of their phrensy, every repetition reinforces it with new strength; and the hurry of their spirits; unrestrained by the curb of reason, continues it to the end of their lives. (74)

The sublime notion of infinity, combined with habit, reveals the human mechanism completely at the mercy of external stimuli that cannot be expunged; the specter of the madman, moreover, is particularly terrifying because he is merely the most extreme version of the insistent force of the external in Burke's behaviorist model. Similarly, when Burke outlines how "excessive loudness" is "sufficient to overpower the soul" (p. 82) (and is, therefore, sublime), he offers an example of sublime noise that is accompanied by the social — and thus beautiful — passion for imitating (pp. 49-50).

The shouting of multitudes has a similar effect [—that of awaking a great and aweful sensation in the mind]; and by the sole strength of the sound, so amazes and confounds the imagination, that in this staggering, and hurry of the mind, the best established tempers can scarcely forbear being borne down, and joining in the common cry, and common resolution of the crowd. (82)

Although in the *Enquiry* Burke remains quite confident that the danger and pain that are the leading elements provoking sublime terror can be kept from pressing "too nearly" (p. 40), one can discern in these examples I have just cited the kind of sublimity that will later, in *Reflections on the Revolution in France* of 1790, seem threatening to Burke because of its apparent ungovernability. The madman and the mob merely have the reactions that Burke sees as universally probable in experiences of the sublime where the passions operate with "no assistance from our reasoning" (p. 92); but whereas Burke in 1757 almost always points beyond the individual being overcome by the sublime and toward the reassertion of individual autonomy, in the *Reflections* it would appear that individuality has been permanently sacrificed to the sublimity of the mob. Moreover, in the *Reflections* Burke seems particularly aggrieved to see the sublime functioning in an unanticipated direction; while the *Enquiry* had stressed the awe we feel in our contemplation of those who possess power and had emphasized the heroic as an example of the connections between the power of the hero and of the state that he represents, the *Reflections* suggests that the sublime category of obscurity has functioned in ways rather counter to Burke's view of the sublime and its bracing influence. The ungovernability of the mob turns out to represent rather too much sublimity for Burke's taste when that ungovernability ceases to contribute to the orderly functioning of a productive society. And the obscurity of sublimity seems to him to have been fulfilled too literally when those who legislate in France after the Revolution are men of whom one would have known nothing if the normal, that is, nonrevolutionary, course of events had been followed. They are new men, made overnight.[5] One difficulty that Burke has in accepting them as examples of legitimate power lies in the fact that in the *Enquiry* he has recognized the authority of fathers as sublime (while describing the love of mothers, "where the parental authority is almost melted down into the mother's fondness and indulgence," and the love of grandfathers, "in whom this authority is removed a degree from us," p. 111), but he has never hinted at the possibility that the sons—or any kinds of underling—might usurp the father's authority. Because Burke has derived the legitimacy of both aesthetic and political judgments from the external objects that produce them (i.e., nature), any major disruption in legitimate power is as unthinkable as a change in nature. Although the sublime, as that which masters us, would seem by definition the obverse of property, who would have thought that men of no property (handed down by lineal succession) could assume power and its accoutrements of sublimity?

One could argue that Burke's effort in the *Enquiry* is to reconcile man and nature; certainly that union seems a secure one as he outlines the ways in which nature operates on our senses and thus on our emotions and thoughts, and as he sees a providential design in the fitting between man and nature which enables each to function efficiently for the greater good of mankind. And if Burke's account continually suggests a resemblance between man and machine, he would seem to be ready to reply that God makes good machines. Moreover, it is significant that Burke everywhere implies that aesthetic judgments can be right or wrong, that is, objective, because such a position reveals his commitment to gauging judgment in terms of the objects which provoke it. Just as he continually describes the *properties* of external objects as commanding certain responses from us, so he later derives the authority of a government from its basis in *property*. Although men are all created the same for Burke, they become distinguished from one another precisely because of their external attachments, and political and aesthetic rights become the reflection of those external holdings. Ronald Paulson has very aptly noted the way in which Burke treats the French Revolution as an aesthetic phenomenon,[6] and I should only like to add a corollary to his observation: for Burke both government and aesthetics must ultimately be on a par with one another because both arise from versions of the notion of property. Property produces legitimate government for him, just as the properties of aesthetic objects command responses to their beauty or sublimity. The difficulty that appears with the French Revolution, however, is that the very possibility of a drastic change registers the unnaturalness of nature by laying bare the fact that the properties of things, as well as the property belonging to any particular group in power, do not necessarily compel assent. For Burke property creates (or ought to create) a legitimate power structure, and any social compact is an implied by-product of the relationship between persons and properties—merely a description of universal assent to an existing reality. For Kant, as for many other writers on the sublime, the relationship between the natural and the human does not begin in any confidence about the priority of the natural—or about the possibility of harnessing the threatening aspects of the natural to socially useful purposes.

Certainly, in *Frankenstein* nature and society are pitted against one another as radical alternatives, not as the ultimate reinforcements of one another that they are for Burke. Victor Frankenstein's researches into "natural philosophy" may be an attempt at human mastery of nature, but the union of man and nature that is presented in the form of the monster is monstrous largely because the novel repeatedly underscores the difficulty of reconciling these two terms. Thus, when Victor Frankenstein sees "the lightnings playing on the summit of Mont Blanc" (p. 70), the "noble war in the sky [elevates his] spirits" (p. 71) not merely because it is sublime but largely because its sublimity is useful as an anodyne: it enables him to forget the affront to the claims of society he committed in creating the monster who murdered his brother William. When the lightning in the sublime scene illuminates the figure of the monster, however, it is clear that the sublime is no longer a particularly strenuous version of pastoralism and the comforts of retreat that it might afford. For the figure in the landscape may be sublime in stature and strength, but he is primarily the assertion of the power of deprivation. As it is with Burke's shouting mob, so it is with Frankenstein's monster: while Burke and Victor Frankenstein have attempted to delimit the sublime and to see its legitimate purview in terms of the possession of strength, the mob and the monster are terrifying because their strength and their violence proceed from their dispossession. Thus, when the monster, having just murdered William, gazes on him and picks up his locket, he justifies his rage in terms of his disfranchisement:

I took it; it was a portrait of a most fovely woman [William's—and Victor's—mother]. In spite of my malignity, it softened and attracted me. For a few moments I gazed with delight on her dark eyes, fringed by deep lashes, and her lovely lips; but presently my rage returned: I remembered that I was for ever deprived of the delights that such beautiful creatures could bestow; and that she whose resemblance I contemplated would, in regarding me, have changed that air of divine benignity to one expressive of disgust and affright.

. . . I only wonder that at that moment, instead of venting my sensations in exclamations and agony, I did not rush among mankind, and perish in the attempt to destroy them. (139)

Even though the monster could be seen to act merely from envy in killing off members of the Frankenstein family (which has been marvelously capable of extending itself to include Elizabeth, Justine, and Clerval—all of whom are killed), an essentially political question forms the basis of his thinking. All of his comparisons between himself and Adam are designed to stress his standing as a natural man, due all the rights due any man, and, implicitly, to repudiate a determination of any individual's human worth in terms of anyone (such as family) or anything (such as property) outside of himself.

Kant, in emphasizing that judgments of taste must be pure, continually reinforces the monster's celebration of internally grounded human rights as he establishes the basis of judgments not *in* objects (which are external to us) but in ourselves. Moreover, he strives to preserve that autonomy in arguing that our aesthetic judgments must be disinterested, that is, uninfluenced by the sense that we have anything other than pleasure to gain. Man must not be forced into assenting to an aesthetic judgment by the opinions of others, nor must he be susceptible of being bought— in some way rewarded for judging as others would desire. And the lack of any reward beyond the judgment itself is the basis on which Kant establishes the connection between the aesthetic and the moral. Getting nothing *except oneself* thus becomes the sign of moral power, particularly with regard to the sublime, which compounds the virtuous autonomy of individual taste with a consciousness of our "supersensible destination."

In the pre-Critical *Observations on the Feeling of the Beautiful and Sublime* of 1763, Kant presents an almost Burkean series of categorizations of various things and kinds of people under the beautiful or the sublime. There he specifically sees aesthetic judgments as reflecting not merely moral characters but moral characters for entire societies.

The mental characters of people are most discernible by whatever in them is moral, on which account we will yet take under consideration their different feelings in respect to the sublime and beautiful from this point of view. [7]

It turns out, however, that the moral portraits of societies frequently suggest a total squandering of a consciousness of our "supersensible destination," as when Kant declares that

The Negroes of Africa have by nature no feeling that rises above the trifling. Mr. Hume challenges anyone to cite a single example in which a Negro has shown talents, and asserts that among the hundreds of thousands of blacks who are transported elsewhere from their countries, although many of them have even been set free, still not a single one was ever found who presented anything great in art or science or any other praiseworthy quality, even though among the whites some continually rise aloft from the lowest rabble, and through superior gifts earn respect in the world. . . . The religion of fetishes so widespread among them is perhaps a sort of idolatry that sinks as deeply into the trifling as appears to be possible in human nature. (110-111)

The moral of the passage is that the Negroes of Africa do not know what to do with freedom, but I cite this passage not to expose Kant's racism but rather to suggest the way in which the very notion of a society tends to be seen as a vitiating force upon the individual's morality and freedom. The ultimate problem with the Negroes of Africa, for Kant, is that they appear to him a particularly homogeneous society, that is, a society that does not produce individuals. By the time he wrote the *Observations*, Kant claimed that he was already indebted to Rousseau for having taught him respect for the masses, not just for solitary genius; [8] but what Kant was to proceed to do in the *Critique of Judgment* was to develop that respect for the masses more thoroughly—but always in the form of a respect for individuals and not their societies.

Kant's account of aesthetics in 1790[9] does not employ metaphors of legislation and government merely for decorative purposes, but his treatment of the sublime in particular constitutes an avowal of the rights of man because of the ways in which the grounds of legitimate judgment are explicitly located in the human and not in anything external to the human. In fact, it frequently appears that objects must be legitimated—by having their existences validated by the common assent of the individuals who perceive them. While Kant pays homage to Burke, by declaring that he "deserves to be regarded as the most important author who adopts this mode of treatment" (that is, "a merely empirical exposition of the sublime and beautiful," p. 118), he concludes by praising Burke's analyses as "psychological observations" that "afford rich material for the favorite investigations of empirical anthropology" (p. 119). And he then goes on to mount what is the crucial argument against Burke's empiricist aesthetics:

If . . . we place the satisfaction in the object altogether in the fact that it gratifies us by charm or emotion, we must not assume that any *other* man agrees with the aesthetical judgment which *we* pass, for as to these each one rightly consults his own individual sensibility. But in that case all censorship of taste would disappear, [unless] except indeed the example afforded by the accidental agreement of others in their judgments were regarded as *commanding* our assent; and this principle we should probably resist, and should appeal to the natural right of subjecting the judgment, which rests on the immediate feeling of our own well-being, to our own sense and not to that of any other man. (119)

It should be stressed that Kant's argument here has nothing to do with the notion that one may be held in thrall by an unworthy or inappropriate object. In fact, in the *Critique of Judgment* external objects—and especially the natural objects that arouse feelings of the sublime—are continually seen not really as objects but as pretexts for the aesthetic judgment. Thus, he goes so far as to argue that "we express ourselves incorrectly if we call any *object of nature* sublime. . . . All that we can say is that the object is fit for the presentation of a sublimity which can be found in the mind, for no sensible form can contain the sublime properly so-called" (pp. 83-84). What Kant's argument points to is the fact that Burke (or anyone else offering an empiricist aesthetic) can, finally, only expect to gain assent to his own judgments by invoking brute force or a variant of it, the civilized mob force of popular opinion, "What everyone thinks." Burke of course has almost admitted something of his own difficulty in the *Enquiry*; for even though he has based his claims to ground aesthetic legitimacy in the uniformity of the operations of the senses in all men, he has had to admit that the relative familiarity or novelty of certain experiences begins to erode that uniformity over the course of various individuals' lives. In other words, his grounding of aesthetic judgments in the uniformity of all men's senses can remain meaningful only if men never have any experiences at all or if they only have identical experiences throughout their lives. Otherwise, the claim of one man's judgment to assent from anyone else is an appropriation of a completely arbitrary, that is, accidental, kind.

Kant does not dismiss the workings of such accidental power as trivial. But he does, however, consistently expose the triviality of the claims it can legitimately make. Moreover, one of the curious features stemming from his efforts to beat back illegitimate claims about taste is that he spends a great deal more time with the beautiful than with the sublime, *even though* the sublime is everywhere credited with a moral superiority to the beautiful. Even when Kant provides his analytic specifically addressing the subject of the sublime, the beautiful gets more attention. The beautiful continually needs watching, because it can never be purified enough — for the very reason that it is allied with society. As he says,

Empirically the beautiful interests only in *society*. . . . A man abandoned by himself on a desert island would adorn neither his hut nor his person; nor would he seek for flowers, still less would he grow plants, in order to adorn himself therewith. It is only in society that it occurs to him to be, not merely a man, but a refined man after his kind (the beginning of civilization). (139)

For while Kant seeks to establish the importance of disinterestedness in our aesthetic judgments, of judging without sacrificing one's free judgment to external pressures, the question that haunts the *Critique of Judgment* is whether or not social existence renders such disinterestedness an empty and purely theoretical notion. The beautiful is a mixed, or radically compromised, cate-

gory in part because of the very fact that it includes objects created by men, so that a question of power can be raised the
moment the viewer of the artifact recognizes it as testimony to the
intention of another human being. Kant's concern for the tensions between society and aesthetic freedom of disinterestedness
may suggest, moreover, the force of a rather puzzling example of
deception that he provides:

> What is more highly praised by poets than the bewitching and beautiful
> note of the nightingale in a lonely copse on a still summer evening by the
> light of the moon? And yet we have instances of a merry host, where no
> such songster was to be found, deceiving to their great contentment the
> guests who were staying with him to enjoy the country air by hiding in a
> bush a mischievous boy who knew how to produce this sound exactly like
> nature (by means of a reed or a tube in his mouth). But as soon as we are
> aware that it is a cheat, no one will remain long listening to the song
> which before was counted so charming. . . . It must be nature or be re-
> garded as nature if we are to take an immediate interest in the beautiful
> as such, and still more is this the case if we can require that others
> should take an interest in it too. (145)

One might well want to argue that the little prank Kant describes
does not really harm anyone and that one should not be overly
scrupulous about anything that prompts our "immediate interest
in the beautiful," but Kant's point is that the "merry host" of the
example gains a kind of mastery over his guests by revealing the
means through which he has produced "an art obviously directed
designedly to our satisfaction."

One might formulate the difference between Burke and Kant
by saying that Burke wants to insist that legislation is natural
whereas Kant, while recognizing the conventionality of human
perceptions of nature, is outraged when the legislation behind
nature or art appears. Kant is thus being more than gratuitously
high-minded when he insists upon the disinterestedness of aesthetic judgments. A work of art cannot appeal, by his definition,
to the disinterested judgment as natural beauty does, because it
continually runs the risk of arousing the suspicion that we may be
imposed upon. And similarly, the sublime in nature is preferable
to the beautiful in nature because its very formlessness makes it
impossible to counterfeit; its purposiveness is thus always clearly
purposeless in relation to the human viewer.

Kant's position, curiously enough, echoes Locke's in the *Second*

Treatise of Government, both in its attachment to the notion of freedom and in some of the problems that beset it.[10] For Locke, the man makes the property; that is, while all men's claims to the world's land might be theoretically equivalent to one another, it is labor that transforms land into property. One can see that this argument parallels Kant's in making human participation crucial to a definition of nature; what is always at issue for both of them is not what something might be intrinsically and before all society but what humans make of it. Yet a difficulty arises for Locke and for Kant because of the embarrassing possibility that one human might treat another like a portion of nature, that is, might make property of him. Locke argues the case for freedom by discrediting any apparently natural claim that one person might make for legitimate sway over another, and, in attempting to forestall any arguments about the natural legitimacy of paternal power, he moves to the rather peculiar position of asserting that paternal power (which might be taken for a conjunction of the natural and the social that authorizes one person's control over another) is not like the power of ownership but is merely a case in which a father has his child's freedom on loan, as it were.[11] Kant argues the case for freedom by insisting that the aesthetic be so much a realm of freedom that the possibility of an aesthetic object's having an effect becomes increasingly attenuated. He recognizes that aesthetic judgments are a product of society when he remarks, as we earlier observed, that a man on a desert island would make no effort to adorn his hut or his person; he seeks, however, an aesthetics that will be a by-product of society but will involve none of the constraints imposed by one man on another in society. Whereas Burke derives resemblance among men ultimately from the similarity of their internalization of external objects, Kant adopts the infinitely more sophisticated position that the mind, rather than any external object, produces the sublime: "All that we can say is that the object is fit for the presentation of a sublimity which can be found in the mind, for no sensible form can contain the sublime properly so-called" (pp. 84-85).

One sees a progressive refinement—or purification—in the *Critique of Judgment* as Kant presents an ascending order of beautiful art, beautiful nature, and sublime nature; and it is an essential aspect of that refinement that Kant specifically disallows any place in the sublime to artifacts. While Burke is perfectly content to embrace various arts as sublime and to see poetry as the most sublime among them, Kant excludes all productions of human art from the sublime because of his insistence that the judgment upon the sublime must be equally imputed to and expected of everyone (p. 105). Whereas an artist might (mistakenly) be seen as having a privileged relation to the artifact that he had produced, the judgment that locates a feeling of the sublime in nature cannot have any greater or any less validity for one person than for another; the sublime can never be taken out of circulation and made private property.

In fact, Kant's insistence that our judgments always involve our "assuming" a standard that is the "same for everyone" establishes a particularly interesting kind of legislation of taste, inasmuch as it suggests Kant's ultimate privileging of a power that is seen as valid *only* because of an individual's *refusal* to inflict himself and his judgments on other human beings. Kant may have learned from Rousseau respect for the masses, but the legislation of judgment converts the mob into a completely noncoercive — that is, a merely abstractly powerful — force. Whereas Burke's account of aesthetics pays tribute to the force of the sublime mob in which natural force ravages all the accomplishments of civilization, Kant's finally sacrifices the very notion of human society for the sake of keeping the external noncoercive.

There is, therefore, a particularly powerful logic to the fact that the notion of God should fulfill the movement toward an understanding of freedom in the *Critique of Judgment*. Whereas Kant declares that we cannot present any proof of the existence of God, the notion of God issues from our notion of freedom. For God is the supreme version of individual autonomy, having the freedom to remain always undeceived (and uncoerced) and having his isolation constantly preserved intact. Burke might well have seen Frankenstein's monster as a version of the distasteful but impressive sublime mob that attempts to attack the legitimacy of any claims based on an individual's external connections, but one can easily imagine that Kant might well have seen the monster not only as sympathetic but also as a particularly godlike creature. The monster, after all, has enormous strength and what seems like omniscience and omnipresence, and his commitment to internally derived rights converges with Kant's account of freedom. The monster would perhaps have puzzled him, however, both with his violence against others and with his peculiar eagerness to find companionship. A Kantian God may be happy in his isolation, but the monster refuses to know his blessedness in being forcibly excluded from society. Although he obviously represents a strange variation on the effort to relate the human to the natural, he converts a problem that has revolved around the notion of human freedom into one that revolves around human bondage in his desire to be treated as property, to be owned by another man. He dogs Frankenstein as ducklings hounded Lorenz, begging for society and all the compromises it would impose upon his sublime freedom.

NOTES

1. Mary Wollstonecraft Shelley, *Frankenstein,* ed. James Rieger (Indianapolis: The Bobbs-Merrill Company, 1974), pp. 138-139. Subsequent references are to this edition.

2. For an interesting discussion of the domestic in *Frankenstein,* see Kate Ellis, "Monsters in the Garden: Mary Shelley and the Bourgeois Family" in *The Endurance of* Frankenstein, eds. George Levine and U. C. Knoepflmacher (Berkeley, Los Angeles, London: University of California Press, 1979), pp. 123-145.

3. Edmund Burke, *A Philosophical Enquiry into the Origin of Our Ideas of the Sublime and Beautiful,* ed. J. T. Boulton (Notre Dame: University of Notre Dame Press, 1968), p. 139. All subsequent references are to this edition.

4. For a more extensive discussion of the force of habit in Burke's distinction between the sublime and the beautiful, see my essay "The Sublime of Edmund Burke, or The Bathos of Experience," *Glyph* 8 (Winter 1981): 62-78.

5. See in particular Burke's remarks on the composition of the French National Assembly. Edmund Burke, *Reflections on the Revolution in France,* ed. Conor Cruise O'Brien (Harmondsworth, England: Penguin Books, 1968), pp. 129ff.

6. Ronald Paulson, *Popular and Polite Art in the Age of Hogarth and Fielding* (Notre Dame: University of Notre Dame Press, 1979), p. 61.

7. Immanuel Kant, *Observations on the Feeling of the Beautiful and Sublime,* trans. John T. Goldthwait (Berkeley and Los Angeles: University of California Press, 1965), pp. 99-100. Subsequent references are to this edition.

8. See Goldthwait's Translator's Introduction to *Observations on the Feeling of the Beautiful and Sublime,* p. 11.

9. Immanuel Kant, *Critique of Judgment,* trans. J. H. Bernard (New York: Hafner Publishing Co., 1966). Subsequent references are to this edition.

10. John Locke, *The Second Treatise of Government,* ed. Thomas P. Peardon (Indianapolis: The Bobbs-Merrill Co., 1952). Subsequent references are to this edition.

11. Locke, pp. 31-32.

VI

THE AESTHETICS OF MOURNING

Ronald Paulson

I am a member of a group of historians that meets every fall to discuss the uses of visual objects by the historian. Last fall we examined a painting by Joseph Wright of Derby, *The Blacksmith's Shop* (1771, Yale Center for British Art, fig. 1). Looking at this painting one of the historians suggested that the boy leaning toward us in the foreground was trying to light a cigarette. There was much concern with the time of day portrayed: When did a blacksmith shop close? Was it winter or summer? If, as the moon might suggest, it is after-hours, is an emergency therefore implied? If the emergency is a broken horseshoe, as the pictorial evidence seems to indicate, why is one being forged when a supply of ready-made horseshoes is visible on the wall at the rear? Is not the ingot on the blacksmith's anvil too large for a horseshoe?

What fascinated me, however, was one feature that all the historians were bothered by, and kept returning to: the intensity of the light was far in excess of the apparent source, the ingot. One historian said there had to be a furnace or some other source of light out of our range of sight in order to explain the brightness.

I appreciated this puzzlement because these historians, though they had not read my essay on Wright of Derby, confirmed my thesis in the best possible way: that the light generated by the ingot is a modern equivalent of the supernatural, a substitute for a Nativity or some other transcendent event.[1]

Most scholars still prefer to see Wright as his modern cataloger Benedict Nicolson does, as a "Painter of Light" whose paintings never leave the spectator "in any doubt as to what is meant."[2] The light for Nicolson designates a naive realism, a faith in empiricism and the technology of both industry and art: "To maintain that Wright transported his forges into imaginary settings," Nicolson writes, "is to misunderstand his whole approach to industry, which was a reverent acceptance of things as they were."[3]

The art historian Frederick Cummings provides a second example of a faith in ontological security. Unlike Nicolson, Cummings recognizes that "it is unlikely that any forge he visited would have been housed in a crumbling basilica reminiscent of Botticelli's shelter for the kneeling Virgin and Child in a Medicean 'Adoration of the Magi,'" but such differences only reveal the similar ontological concerns of the two scholars. The Nativity or Adoration architecture is secularized according to Cummings, who views it as creating "a setting of Roman grandeur for... modern steel-forgers," a subject outside the range of official art in the 1770s.[4] Blacksmiths, of course, were not laborers but traditional English craftsmen. If the Industrial Revolution is in any sense alluded to in the painting it is through a foreshadowing of industrialization by a memory of the ancient craft of the blacksmith.

All of these scholars, intent on seeing Wright as either "scientific" or proto-Marxist, overlook the excessive intensity of the light source or regard it merely as a way of elevating inappropriate subject matter.[5] Such naive ontological assumptions are surprising in Cummings, a critic who demonstrated Wright's interest in traditional structures of meaning in his portrait of Brooke Boothby (1780-81, Tate, fig. 2). In this case an appreciation of naturalistic detail and high finish does not satisfy Cummings, who observes a disquieting effect from his observation of the work, and traces its source. Boothby's dark dress is elegant, but incongruous in this wooded scene—as is his reclining on the ground. He lies deep within a forest, his back turned upon the distant sunlit meadow, the *locus amoenus,* to meditate in this quiet glade. These are details that Cummings has identified in the iconographic tradition of Melancholy. Recalling Elizabethan miniatures, Burton's *Anatomy of Melancholy,* and poetry of the mid-eighteenth century, Cummings identifies Boothby as a melancholic.[6]

There is more to the portrait, however, than the melancholy pose. Boothby also holds a volume titled *Rousseau,* which has been identified as the manuscript of the first dialogue of *Rousseau, Juge de Jean-Jacques,* entrusted to Boothby by Rousseau himself for publication in England. In the context of that manuscript with its Rousseauian doctrine of the superiority of nature over society, Boothby is also posed as Rousseau's hero St. Preux, solitary in the forest near Lake Geneva, in the most popular of all his works, *La Nouvelle Héloïse.*

But we have not finished yet with Boothby's poses. He has closed his Rousseau with a negligent fold, rendering it unreadable; he lies so near the picture plane that nature itself (except for a few flowers) is behind his back. What he would have suggested first to a contemporary Englishman (and undoubtedly to Boothby himself, an enthusiast of the subject) was a reclining figure on a funerary monument. As Cummings has recognized, melancholy and tomb sculpture coincide in this pose: reclining thus, "his right arm supporting his head, [was] the traditional motif of melancholy reflection especially as found in tomb portraits from Sansovino's Cardinal Sforza (Rome, s. Maria del Popolo) to Thomas Carter's Chaloner Chute of 1775."[7] (See fig. 3.)

There is, of course, the question of priority: Which came first, the topos of melancholy that is used on funerary monuments or the tomb pose of the deceased that is appropriate to the topos of melancholy? Visually in the 1780s it seems likely that the image of the reclining figure on a tomb was the more common experience.

My point is that though the portrait of Brooke Boothby, with every feature delineated in precise clear-focused detail, is so different from the Blacksmith's glowing ingot, in fact Boothby is a figure of equal ambiguity. The man Boothby in all his particularity is qualified by the poses of the melancholic solitary, of Rousseau's romantic St. Preux, and above all of the dead-yet-alive figure on a tomb.

Before asking what it may mean to portray Boothby in this way, let me turn to a literal representation of a tomb, one of

Wright's more schematic paintings, *Miravan opening the Tomb of his Ancestors* (1772, Derby, fig. 4). Miravan, according to the story, read the inscription of his ancestors' tomb, "a greater treasure than Croesus ever preserved," to mean that the inside was filled with gold. He broke open the tomb but found instead of wealth only his ancestors' bones — which, however, conveyed to him the wisdom that the "treasure" referred to in the inscription was "eternal repose." The moral is being revealed to Miravan — and Miravan *and* the moral to the spectator, including the observer who, having helped him break open the tomb, points out the skeleton to Miravan, who averts his eyes. Miravan's gesture of covering his eyes suggests, among other things, a progression from the outward form of the tomb to the interiorization of its significance in the spectator's mind. He is like the spectators we saw within and without *The Blacksmith's Forge* responding in various conflicting ways to the glowing ingot on the blacksmith's forge. Thus the tomb is both hollow receptacle of bones and dust and — something in excess of that — of moral wisdom.

In this painting two concerns characteristic of Wright's art are added to that juxtaposition of the scrupulous detail of presentation and the questionableness of a central object. First, the extension of the architectural form of the sarcophagus to the mausoleum in which it is housed, and, by implication to any human dwelling, implies the instability of all human structures, or at least of the relationship between inside and outside. A complex linking of observers to a central object, which is not what it first seems, thus induces a recognition of the questionable state of their response as well. Miravan may be the positivist historian, as the slick surface and sharp detail were intended for his eye — before he broke open the tomb. Now that it is broken Miravan and the other spectators beyond him respond to the full suggestiveness of the tomb. What separates this painting from the others is that Wright portrays the moment in which its emptiness-yet-fullness is established, recognized, and internalized by the spectator.

The dissolution of an immediately perceived solidity, both of objects and persons defined in their relation to objects, is a recurrent feature in the experience of Wright's scenes. Miravan's tomb is a useful point of departure because the tomb in Western tradition is a place of transition, where a dead body is placed. The common French tomb structure of the fourteenth to seventeenth centuries was two-layered, on the top an idealized figure of the man as he was in heaven (i.e., remembered, idealized), and below the *transi* in process of decomposition as he was in fact underneath the slab. Miravan's discovery is therefore only literarily—in terms of the story Wright quoted in his notebook entry on the painting—about the absent treasure, present bones, and edifying moral concerning "eternal repose"; more deeply it reveals the hope that something else will be found there, in the manner of the opening of Christ's tomb, not the bones and dust that we know, especially in the scientific age of Wright, to be there.

In the second place, that oil lamp, whose feeble light illuminates the scene, is itself an inversion of the dominant architectural form of the sarcophagus and mausoleum, and its limited light implies a comparison with the greater scene opening out from the shattered architecture. Miravan's arm, instinctively thrust away from the enclosing tomb, leads out of such man-made, lamplit interiors to a vague but extensive natural landscape illuminated by the natural light of a full moon.

Usually included in Wright's subject pictures is a contrast between the human and the natural, the man-made and the unchanging, as in the ingot, the lamp, the illuminated air pump, and the real sun or moon—or Brooke Boothby's elaborate pose and the natural world on which he (with his various artificial poses) has turned his back.[8] In fact, Wright's concern for the subjectivity of perception, his recognition of the inadequacy of reason to define experience, is frequently as observable as his intense interest in clarity of expression, in the technique of craft, and in the application of reason to the representation of nature. In Wright, as in many eighteenth-century English writers and artists, these two concerns are equally compelling.

I have begun by posing an aesthetic experience from the second half of the eighteenth century. My plan now is to go back to the aesthetic experience posed in the first half, and show how the aesthetic "principles" that can be educed from works of the earlier period are modified in Wright's paintings, and how the Wright paradigm reflects other art forms. As you may have gathered, my pivotal model is going to be the funerary monument.

But let me first remind you that "principles" is a word that refers to treatises rather than paintings: aesthetic treatises (on association, on the Beautiful, Sublime, and Picturesque), practical painting manuals, and guides or conduct books like those written by the Richardsons for connoisseurs taking the Grand Tour. A painting that embodies principles tends to be a second-rate one, at least in eighteenth-century England. The great paintings tend to be those that question principles. Even Reynolds's principles in his *Discourses* are after the fact in terms of his own practice and tell us relatively little about his best paintings (though I believe they may sidestep rather than question principles).

Indeed, the aesthetic principles to be found in Shaftesbury, Hutcheson, and Jonathan Richardson can be summed up as an equation of aesthetic and moral qualities in the work of art, external and internal states in the subject. They all argue that the harmony perceived as beauty of form is also perceived as virtue of the person. Reynolds does try, and often succeeds, to convey something of this synonymy in his painted portraits. In Shaftesbury's phrase "Harmony perceived as beauty," however, we must recognize *perceived* as the operative word, for with all his platonic optimism Shaftesbury was still thinking within the English empiricist tradition. For less sophisticated thinkers the model was Addison's *Spectator,* whose persona Mr. Spectator writes: "When I see a Man with a sour rivell'd Face, I cannot forbear pitying his Wife; and when I meet with an open ingenuous Countenance, think of the Happiness of his Friends, his Family, and Relations."[9]

Hogarth is the major painter of the first half of the century in England, and he also happened to write a treatise specifically on aesthetics, *The Analysis of Beauty* (1753). In the words of his text Hogarth can accept the Shaftesbury-Hutcheson assumptions that equate virtue and beauty, and so make aesthetics a branch of morality. In words he can urge a concordia discors of the Hutchesonian ration of unity and variety. But in images, as a glance at his painted or engraved works will show (and more interesting, a look at the illustrations for *The Analysis* shows), he cannot countenance such ontological security.

Hogarth grows out of the tradition of the Augustan moralists, Dryden, Swift, and Pope, all of whom worry about the relationship of beauty of form to beauty of virtue. One kind of beauty is defined by use, appropriateness, or fitness to function, and so a Pope satire that depicts ugliness is nevertheless itself elegant of form. Much more problematic is the relationship between the beauty of physical form in a man or woman and his or her moral actions. In *The Analysis of Beauty* this dichotomy reappeared in the (comic) discrepancies between Hogarth's text, concerned with formal beauty, which says in essence that beauty is a serpentine line wherever it is found, and the illustrative plates.

In the first of these plates (fig. 5) he shows (from left to right) the Farnese Hercules, the Antinous, the Venus de Medici, and the Apollo Belvedere, and in the background the Laocoön and in the foreground the Vatican Torso. These were the great works of the classical canon of taste around which the artist's (or poet's) imagination had circled from the Renaissance into the eighteenth century—which he copied in his academies, arranged into his own compositions, and from which he drew his ideas, expressions, iconography, and forms; which country gentlemen arranged in their houses and gardens to signify their prosperity and Roman ideals. These sculptures were collected, copied, and revered for their ancient historical associations and—above all—for their ideal beauty.

But this is a statuary's yard, a particular one (John Cheere's at Hyde Park Corner), where were stored lead castings of these canonical sculptures. Based on plaster casts taken from copies of doubtful originals, they were intended for use in landscape gardens throughout England. At the left, the serpentine beauty of the sculptured Antinous is ironically contrasted with the stiff pose of the foppish dancing master who stands next to him. This human figure was a portrait of one John Essex, a well-known dancing master (author of books on the subject), who assumes a more statuesque pose than the statue. The juxtaposition forces us to ask more particular questions of the Antinous than the connoisseurs and collectors were accustomed to doing. If we are as particular with the Antinous as with the dancing master, we have to acknowledge that Antinous was the Emperor Hadrian's minion, celebrated throughout the ancient world in versions of this statue erected by the emperor in memory of his drowned lover.[10] In the context of Hogarth's composition he is being approached (indecently propositioned?) by the effeminate dancing master.

In the same way, the Venus and Apollo, representing (in terms of the canonical tradition and the verbal text of the *Analysis* itself) Beauty, are here exchanging amorous looks (a symbolic pair of doves mate at Venus's feet, Laocoön is entangled with snakes in the background) while the older Hercules' back is turned in both his partial and full-length forms. What is revealed beneath the canonical assumptions is a romantic triangle and an undercurrent of human desire. In another gestalt Apollo seemingly knocks on the head an eighteenth-century stage Brutus who is (again seemingly, for it is only a rolled speech he holds) stabbing in the back Julius Caesar, who falls forward because a rope is hoisting his statue into a standing position.

Hogarth is asserting that the canonical sculptures were now essentially empty signs waiting to be filled by the experiential interpretations of the first passerby. These statues derived from a conventional code (aesthetic and iconographic) with no counterpart in the objective world. Hogarth reads them—or rather forces us to read them—as an unfolding sequence: First, in the conventional code of the connoisseur, as an ideal beauty; second, as an arbitrary iconography in which one statue is Venus, another Apollo, another Hercules. Then Hogarth empties them of their iconographical as well as their aesthetic significance by placing them as lead copies in a sculpture yard (thus turning them into vanitas symbols) waiting to be sold and crated and delivered— and so to be subjected to yet another context. Finally he places them as if in an existential situation, with at least one human who is both bystander and actor, so as to force us to read them within the unequivocally empirical sensory data of London in the eighteenth century, which fills the now empty signs—or perhaps we should say aesthetic forms—with a new meaning: a meaning, however, that does not entirely replace those others but ironically augments them. Though Hercules stands in for Vulcan and Apollo for Mars (or some other), the romantic triangle is part of the original iconography, an armature for a different set of gods as well as for the denizens of eighteenth-century London.

This is of course Hogarth's idea of how to revitalize English art—by infusing new, contemporary life into old forms, old myths. But the Venus and Apollo, the Brutus and Caesar lead the eye rightward to the climactic object: a tomb sculpture of the sort found in Westminster Abbey. This is a magistrate with a full-bottomed wig and heavy robes (which in Hogarth's *Analysis* designate dignity, artificial and often unearned), a pentecostal flame atop his head and a mourning putto holding a square signifying justice. However, in the existential context of the scene the square resembles a gallows, the putto's tears are for justice rather than the judge, and we may assume that the tomb like the wig and robes are trappings that cover meager fallible bones, whose judgments evidently produced only the ruins depicted around the base of his tomb—ruins equally consequential in the causal sequence that runs from Venus to Brutus to Caesar. In this sequence the climax of the Westminster Abbey funerary monument at one end (the sequence is framed by memorials to Antinous and to the dead magistrate) imposes a sense of the memorial and dead that equally applies to the Venus, Brutus, and Caesar; just as from the other direction, the live John Essex, dancing master, imbues them with the fitful half-life of contemporary London.

The plate expresses a doctrine Hogarth does not stipulate in his text: the Venus and the Apollo are, seen in one way, paradigms (or more specifically memories—memorials) of beauty; but seen in another way they are infused with human feelings, desires, and subterfuges. Something that appears to be an art object is naturalized, popularized, or filled with a different meaning; something seen as a public, political act (bashing the murderer of Caesar) is also revealed as a private act of passion. What is revealed as the living reality of the aesthetic object is not precisely moral wrong but human desire. In Hogarth's own terms (one point at which text and illustration connect in the *Analysis*), the revelation is the living, breathing, sensuous reality that is beneath—and preferable to—even the greatest but dead art object.

But Hogarth, being Hogarth, builds his iconoclastic act upon ancient doctrine (as he claimed in *A Harlot's Progress* to be only following Aeneas in seeking out his "ancient Mother"). In his *Monumens de Rome* (1700) the Abbé Raguenet described the classical sculptures as depicting "states which are neither Life, nor Death, nor Agony, such as the Niobe who is neither alive nor dead nor dying but turned to stone." *The Dying Gladiator* represents "the very moment from Life to Death, the instant of the last breath."[11] Raguenet suggested that the power of the great canonical sculptures lies in their showing better than any others the transitional states of expression, gesture, and being. This I am convinced was a view still shared by Hogarth, as earlier by Watteau (whose garden sculptures are often indistinguishably stone or flesh) and by other artists. The moment of transition is the one shown in Hogarth's examples: Apollo turning or reaching out, Venus (a *Venus pudica*) caught unaware and modestly covering herself, and Laocoön and his sons in process of being crushed to death by the serpent. (These transitions fit into the spectrum of aspects and attitudes of the human body that is the chief point of the illustrative plate: from caricature to diagram, anatomical figure, statue, and tomb effigy to a human overdressed dancing master to the man in the foreground looking at Dürer's rules for drawing the human figure. The latter wears a mob cap of the sort Hogarth wears himself in his self-portrait *Gulielmus Hogarth* of 1745 and so may represent the artist.) Hogarth's context makes us see these moments as morally transitional as well: Venus is choosing between preoccupied husband and gesturing lover, as Hogarth's contemporary heroes are shown choosing between right and wrong courses of action in the *Harlot's Progress* and *Rake's Progress*. Indeed the particular transitional moment of choice was the one recommended to modern history painters by Shaftesbury himself.[12] Hogarth represents the transitions between flesh and stone, life and death, human desire and a chilly idealism, as well as between good and evil.

As he ridiculed the static equation of formal and moral beauty, he also rejected the disinterestedness Shaftesbury attributed to the "moral sense" (in *Moralists* III) that pleasures in both aesthetic and ethical harmony, thereby suggesting that disinterestedness is an essential characteristic of the aesthetic attitude. The disinterestedness that can coldly separate aesthetic from other considerations or that includes this detachment in the aesthetic experience, which is distinct from either the moral or the purely existential experience, has become central in the doctrine of Edmund Burke.

In his *Philosophical Enquiry into the Origin of our Ideas of the Sublime and Beautiful* (1757), he defines beauty as "love" without desire, and sublimity as "terror" without danger. The Burkean spectator has to be aesthetically distanced from frightening objects or phenomena, which "are simply painful when their causes immediately affect us." They are better held at one or two removes — by a safe platform over an abyss or by the perspective that allows us to see over the shoulders of participants: such objects, he says, "are delightful when we have an idea of pain and danger, without being actually in such circumstances ourselves."[13]

If Hogarth is one stage of aesthetic theory, Burke is a second, as can be seen by comparing Burke's description of the sublime with Hogarth's interpretation of it in his *Tailpiece, or The Bathos* (1764, fig. 6). The form again is that of a funerary monument in Westminster Abbey, perhaps a cross between François Roubiliac's Hargrave monument with images of Death and Time and tottering masonry, and Rysbrack's reclining Sir Isaac Newton. The reclining Time is surrounded by emblems of mortality and Burkean sublimity — broken, burning, discontinuous, and decaying objects, including shattered Lines of Beauty. Hogarth could be illustrating Burke's image of sublimity "in images of a tower, an archangel, the sun rising through mists, or in an eclipse, the ruin of monarchs, and the revolutions of kingdoms." The spectator's mind is, as Burke says, "hurried out of itself, by a crowd of great and confused images" (p. 62). But what Burke regards as sublimity Hogarth clearly designates chaos, or (as he put it in *The Analysis*) "variety uncomposed, and without design, [which] is confusion and deformity."[14]

The difference we cannot avoid noticing between the image of the *Analysis of Beauty* plates and the *Tailpiece* is that one is still comic, the other is memorial, even funerary: Hogarth knows he is at the end of his life and is making a tailpiece for the folio of his engraved works, his earthly memorial. Those broken objects, and that image of Father Time breathing his last surrounded by decay, are Hogarth's program for his own funerary monument.

What Hogarth depicts as the end of all coherent values Burke obviously sees (at the moment at least — perhaps less so later when the French Revolution emerged to test his theory) as the highest sort of aesthetic object. He would like to maintain the relationship between aesthetics and morality, as he wishes to retain the reality of the beauty or sublimity he envisions in the object itself. To do this he has to postulate a uniformity of response to it and a continuum of the object and the responding subject. Although, as Frances Ferguson has said in her paper in this volume, Burke "stipulates that a human observer be the passive instrument of the external object," he leaves it not very clear how any but the most overwhelming "object" can fulfill the requirement. His argument requires that "the *mind* is so entirely *filled* with its object, that it cannot entertain any other nor by consequence reason on that object which employs it."[15]

But, as Hogarth's response to the "sublime" object in the *Tailpiece* suggests, one comes away from Burke's *Philosophical Enquiry* suspicious that there is only a conventional object and a conditioned subject ("the greater attention and habit," the more cultivated the taste, Burke argues, the more uniform the response to the sublime object [p. 22]). This subject and object are not very different from those supposed by David Hume:

> Euclid has fully explained all the qualities of the circle; but has not in any proposition said a word of its beauty. The reason is evident. The beauty is not a quality of the circle.... It is only the effect which that figure produces upon the mind.... In vain would you look for it in the circle, or seek it, either by your senses or by mathematical reasonings, in all the properties of that figure.... Till such a spectator appear, there is nothing but a figure of such particular dimensions and proportions: from his sentiments alone arise its elegance and beauty.[16]

Burke and Hume return us to Wright of Derby, who attempts to interpret their principles mythically. He reverses the situation of Burke's real avalanche distanced by imitation for the delight of the spectator. He paints a real (naturalistic, positivistic, illusionistic) perception or response distanced by the absolute ambiguity of the object that is its stimulus. Not a Nativity or an Adoration but an ingot in a blacksmith's shop; not a tomb full of wealth but containing a bare skeleton; not a solid likeness of Brooke Boothby that catches his stable character but a giant funerary figure registering his contradictions. And yet by this very negation each of these objects becomes much more. If Burke distances the physiological aspect of terror, Wright empties the phenomenological aspect and registers the responses to emptiness.

His paintings are about and embody the relation between a stimulus and a response, but the question is whether the thing at the center is only empty, a vanitas emblem or the result of a Humean skeptical-empirical reduction, or whether it is an ambiguous object embodying both nothingness and transcendence or in some sense even transubstantiation. If vanitas emblem, then Wright has purged science of its mystery and returned it to a conventional status. But even the tomb contains both emptiness and the moral that Miravan learns from it. There may be a rough parallel with Humean skepticism which clears away the pretensions of reason in order to present a positive area of agreement in belief based on the relative strength of feelings operating within a range of subjectivity narrowed by the categories of custom.

Wright's *Experiment with an Air Pump* (1767-68, London, Tate) shows a glass sphere enclosing a bird on the edge of extinction, attempting to prolong its life—and the sometimes anxious, sometimes unconcerned responses of the spectators to the experiment. The proof of the vacuum will be the asphyxiation of the bird in the airless glass sphere. But the wingspread bird, lit so dramatically and centrally, has to be in some sense a replacement for the Paraclete of a prescientific tradition. The bird is remythologized in the same way that Hogarth revived classical statues by placing them in contemporary situations in his *Analysis of Beauty* plate. But its exact function and status remain more doubtful than in Hogarth's statues.

The emphasis in Wright's painting seems not so much on transformational iconography as on another sort of transformation, from the surface of the glass sphere to the vacuum within, from a living bird to inanimate matter, that is, primarily from beauty to death.[17] The validation of the both-and quality of the object-in-transition is in the expressions of the spectators. Take the case of the early paintings that show a girl reading a letter by candlelight: It is the letter that is transfigured by the light, and its reflection in the girl's face indicates the power not of that phenomenologically trivial object—but of her reading of it. Something is in the letter, but I presume only "sweet nothings," that in fact express desire but are reflected as love on her transfigured face and anger on a second lover's (as he discovers desire for another man in her heart).

Looking back, we can see different ways to explain Wright's paintings: We can say that he starts with a Nativity Scene and a blacksmith's forge, with a melancholy tomb figure and a Brooke Boothby, and blurs the lines, questioning the nature of flesh and metal and stone, as one is turned into the other in the manner of the great canonical sculptures. But if in Hogarth's practice this change was depicted as a process of image-breaking and remaking (or re-filling), in Wright's practice it becomes a depiction of a person or object of uncertain status. Wright may be thought to have reduced the statuary's yard to a single art object and changed the predominantly moral-aesthetic contrast in Hogarth (and in another follower, Zoffany) to a more elemental contrast of man-made and natural objects. In his *Academy by Lamplight* (1768-69, Yale Center for British Art) he takes as a model Hogarth's satiric subscription ticket, *Boys Peeping at Nature* (1731). All the virtue or vice, the beauty or ugliness or sublimity, indeed the reality or art of the object itself, is in the perception of the living viewers within and without the painting (at least one of whom has fallen in love with the statue).

We could also explain Wright's paintings as a conscious reaction to the figure who poses and dresses and in some Reynoldsian sense *is* a god, goddess, or hero. Reynolds is consciously elevating these figures as a painter in the tradition and style of his canonical models Michelangelo, Raphael, and Titian. (He comes closest to Wright when he paints actors and actresses dressing for a role in a play.) The ontological security of Reynolds's *Sarah Siddons as the Tragic Muse* (1784, Huntington, fig. 7) is stunning compared with the insecurity of *Brooke Boothby*. Reynolds's figures and their poses, costumes, and settings are unified by the clear synonymy of forms and brushwork; while Wright's every detail emphasizes contingency and difference, and while this can simply be called realist painting or portraiture, I think we have seen enough of Wright's subject paintings by now to know that his subject is an ontological uneasiness, whether in the direction of transcendence, negation, or only difference.

In order to connect Wright's fables with larger issues of the time, however, I am going to argue for another explanation: that he finds his deeper reverberation of transcendence by building on a branch of the portrait tradition for which *Brooke Boothby* can stand as an example. I am not suggesting that all of Wright's many portraits function in this way, but only that *Brooke Boothby* overlaps with his history paintings in a way that allows us to ask whether Wright paints from different assumptions than those enunciated by Reynolds. While Reynolds ostensibly paints the living image, Wright finds a model in the tradition of funerary sculpture.

Both are attempts to use the artist's image in order to hold something that is passing or will be lost through aging or death, to maintain its presence while acknowledging its absence. But the funerary sculpture is more immediately an image that tries to recover something that is irrecoverable; it is apparent that an image can outlast what it represents—it has a survival power denied to humans, though it is trivial set against the objects and forces of nature.

In portrait painting the perceiver—the patron, the subject, or, even later, the survivors—can take pleasure in the imitation and in the beauty of the image. Funeral sculpture builds into its image, if in no other way than through the presence of the sar-cophagus and inscription, the stronger aesthetic pleasure of catharsis resulting from the ambiguous jointure of beauty and death, or the memory of a loved one and death, or fulness and absence. It may be that artists like Wright realized that it is pos-sible to elicit the feeling of beauty or sublimity in the spectator *because* of the loss or absence objectified in the empty object—and (in the terms of Freud's "Mourning and Melancholia") inter-nalized by the mourner.

The great majority of sculpture in England were funerary monuments. After the Reformation and the powerful tradition of iconoclasm that followed, there were no religious icons, relatively few statues of kings and heroes, and little or no opportunity for pure expression in sculpture. As portraiture offered the English painter the greatest opportunities, so funerary monuments offered English sculptors the assumptions with which to develop their aesthetic powers. A history of these monuments would yield the same aesthetic principles I have outlined above in painting. In the Hogarthian period (the 1730s), for example, it is not sur-prising to find one sort of commemorative monument built around the Good Samaritan or Christ healing the sick. These story-telling images of public charity (the equivalent of Hogarth's painted Samaritans and Christs as well as Harlots and Rakes) sur-vive into the 1770s in John Bacon's monument to Thomas Guy and in the 1780s in his monument to the prison reformer John Howard.

The most prominent funerary monument in the early eigh-teenth century, however, was the casually standing figure, still appearing very much alive. It was introduced to England by Guelfi's cross-legged James Craggs in Westminster Abbey (1727), but was best known in Scheemakers's Shakespeare (1740, fig. 8), which is also in the Abbey. As Nicholas Penny says, "a concern to portray the deceased in a pious or devotional posture is not particularly conspicuous in grand monuments erected in England during the first two-thirds of the eighteenth century."[18] But the source of this pose is what I want to indicate: the antique *Pothos* or "longing" statue (attributed to Scopas) that was thought to be a funerary monument, perhaps because longing was an appropriate funerary sentiment.[19] It presumably represented the longing or desire of the mourner, but in England this was translated into an image of the dead as caught in a moment of casual indifference—a private, personal matter that in some sense stimulates the *Pothos* in the mourner who remembers this aspect of the deceased. It is, I presume, a confusion of the figure who longs (mourns) for the deceased and the figure of the mourned, longed-for deceased.

That something of the ambiguity of this figure on a funerary monument was recognized I will suggest by reminding you first of Hogarth's Antinous, the model for an ancient monument to a lost beloved, and second of Gainsborough's tongue-in-cheek portrait (fig. 9) of David Garrick in the cross-legged pose of Scheemakers's Shakespeare but with his arm proprietarily around the frozen bust of Shakespeare against which he leans. Gainsborough's conflation of poses and images implies that Garrick regards himself as both "longing" for the lost Shakespeare and longed-for by his own spectators, as both proprietor of Shakespeare and (though still living) a monument in his own right.[20]

The ambiguity that is apparent in the simple standing figure—of life-death, celebration, commemoration, and nature-art—is allegorized in the grandest monuments in Westminster Abbey. These relate to Hogarth's history paintings as the cross-legged standing figure does to Augustan portraiture. Roubiliac's Nightingale monument of 1761 (fig. 10) sums of the Hogarth tradition in the idiom of the monument. It is constructed of three figures like those in Hogarth's painting *Satan, Sin, and Death* (London, Tate) of the late 1730s (itself a genteel echo of the conversation-picture situations of lover, daughter, and father in *The Beggar's Opera* of 1728). This is the formulation used by almost all the later illustrators of Milton, showing the woman trying to hold apart the rival men, the husband-lover Satan, the son-lover Death.[21] Roubiliac's version has the husband pathetically trying to intervene between his wife and Death brandishing his deadly dart. He reverses the preordained order of the female mediator in so many of Hogarth's pictures, focusing instead on the contrast of beauty and corruption, drawing by this time also on the chapter in Burke's *Philosophical Enquiry* in which Satan's confrontation with Death is an example of terror and obscurity. The spectator in this sculpture is the individual passerby in the aisle of Westminster Abbey who is on the same level as Death emerging from a metal door that seems to open directly out of the wall. This is the same gate Death fought over with Satan, but in the aisle of the Abbey it seems part of the sarcophagus above, and one is primarily aware of the empty darkness beyond the door which seems to indicate the whole edifice as one great hollow shell.[22]

The reclining figure on the sarcophagus, most impressively present in the Rysbrack-Kent memorial to Newton in Westminster Abbey, was a replacement of the old recumbent figure, and in a way a more dignified version of the seemingly alive figure who stands upright, cross-legged. The reclining figure is alone, retrospective, and (if you will) melancholy, but above all *transitional* between the states of life and death. If, as was sometimes the case (as Carlini's monument to Lady Milton or in Scheemakers's Page Monument), the reclining figure was accompanied by a recumbent one, it became a reference to the survivor regarding or mourning (or preparing to follow) the deceased mate. The point is that he is alive; the effigy refers to the living man, but is represented on his sarcophagus in which resides (at the moment) only the corpse of his wife. If he is still alive, his sarcophagus is itself empty, or at least half-empty. When he is in fact dead, the ambiguity is only increased, thrust unrelieved upon the live spectator-survivor, who cannot look on the tomb without awareness of the metamorphosis.

This is, of course, the echo we catch in Wright's *Brooke Boothby* (who was himself an active planner of funerary monuments for others)[23] and in Wright's other paintings of objects that are in a state of transition. In Wright's own time the popular funerary monument showed *Pothos* as a kneeling figure, praying or mourning the deceased, often mourning over an urn—sometimes an idealized widow mourning, sometimes an allegorical figure. Joseph Wilton's monument to Lady Anne Dawson (1769-1974), shows the urn with her husband and son approaching to be met by an angel assuring them by its gesture that the soul of the deceased has risen to heaven: the urn, like Christ's sepulchre, is empty because of the implied transfiguration,[24] but (as in the tomb of Miravan's ancestors) the fullness is imparted to the mourners.

Angelica Kauffmann's *Cleopatra decorating the Tomb of Mark Antony* (Burghley House, fig. 11) is a literal transference of the funerary convention into paint, of which the primary source is, I suppose, Poussin's *Et in Arcadia Ego*.[25] But Wright again shows us the implications of the structure: one form is the widow kneeling by the body of her dead husband within a tomblike tent (1789, Yale Center for British Art) and another is the girl in the fable of the origin of painting who traces the profile of her sleeping lover on the wall just before his departure for the wars (National Gallery, Washington). The woman mourning her dead husband is the conventional funerary symbol, whereas the girl outlining the profile of her sleeping but present lover is mourning in a more special sense: she is herself creating his monument. If the other paintings are fables of the function of the art object in relation to the response of spectators, this one is a fable of the artist himself. There are no spectators; there is not yet an absence, though the preparation for mourning, for filling the absence is at hand.

We might call this the fable of portrait painting. It can be done by a careful copying that recovers and preserves something experienced, loved, and lost (or feared to be passing). In these terms we can see Wright's *Blacksmith's Shop* not as Cummings's elevating of "modern steel-forgers" but rather as a preservation of the lost blacksmith—as within the scene the ingot is a preservation of an even more remote loss—mediated by the people gathered around. Again, we might see Reynolds as the Englishman who tries to use the classical canon not (in Hogarth's or Wright's way) by abstracting principles of form but by treating the sculptures and paintings as though they were themselves the departing lover and copying out their forms as tried and true sepulchres in which to inter the living figures of friends and patrons.

Reynolds's portraits rather than Wright's painting of the widow and the dead soldier lead to the related phenomenon of all those paintings of deathbed scenes so popular from Gavin Hamilton's *Death of Hector,* based on Poussin's *Death of Germanicus,* to West's *Death of General Wolfe* and Copley's *Death of Chatham* or *Death of Major Pierson*. West's mourners are all in harmony with one another, sharing a common grief, which (sharing Burke's assumptions) is objectified in Wolfe's body. But the center of the composition is also — as has often been noted — based on a Pietà, and so there is a sense of joy in the observers and transcendence in the dead body. Wolfe dies at the moment of the British victory of Quebec and the rise of the British Empire. (The painting was made ten years after Wolfe's death when all the political consequences were clear.) West is doing something quite different from Wright — celebrating I would say rather than analyzing — and yet the very composition of the Pietà, the very grief of the mourners now expresses an alienation from the man Wolfe who is no longer man but something like a funerary monument in relation to the bones within and the mourners without.

I am suggesting that the form adopted and explored for beauty in the 1760s and 1770s was the pathetic response (among other responses) to a center of emptiness and/or transcendence, or the one becoming the other, and that a model — or at least an analogue — was tomb sculpture, which was per se a filling of absence, a surrounding of emptiness, a representation of transition. The aesthetic is now attached to, or in congruence with, the pathetic, and by means of the inscription on the tomb (the good deeds of the deceased) with the moral. Wright's paintings are merely a more sophisticated, self-aware version of these monuments. They are about the aesthetic experience as developed by Shaftesbury and Hutcheson and remorselessly analyzed by Hume. The reactions projected by the apothegm "Beauty is in the eye of the beholder," materialized, look something like a Wright subject painting — and in turn reflect upon the straightforward, unselfconscious demonstrations of the tomb sculpture.

But I cannot end without mentioning the literary version of the aesthetics of mourning: I am thinking of the death of brother Bobby in Sterne's *Tristram Shandy*. The fact of Bobby's death, like so many other things in *Tristram Shandy*, has no independent existence of its own. Book V begins with an account of the word "whiskers" which has no stable meaning and so eventually gravitates to the dirtiest possible sense — and Book V ends with the well-known employment by Walter Shandy of auxiliary verbs to establish the reality of a white bear nobody has ever seen. The dead and never-glimpsed Bobby is nowhere to be found in the funeral oration of his father Walter Shandy. He is finally materialized only in Corporal Trim's dropping of his heavy, dark, claylike, tomblike hat—a hat that later, unsurprisingly in the world of this novel, is turned into another sexual symbol. As in Hogarth's *Analysis of Beauty,* Sterne finds under every aesthetic or monumental structure a trace of human desire—in this book which, we should also recall, is one enormous funerary memorial erected by Tristram to himself and his father, mother, uncle, and friend Yorick. Yorick's death, recall, was marked by a black page and the epitaph "Alas Poor Yorick," a symbol of both fullness and emptiness which is hard to match in the monuments of Roubiliac and Wilton. *Tristram Shandy* is only the most complex, ambiguous, and profound example—because, I suspect, it is written in the greater tradition of English literature—of the sort of structure I have been analyzing in English painting and sculpture.

NOTES

1. Paulson, "Zoffany and Wright of Derby: Contexts of Art in the Late Eighteenth Century," *Eighteenth-Century Studies* 3 (1969): 278-295; revised, *Emblem and Expression: Meaning in English Art of the Eighteenth Century* (Cambridge, Mass., 1975), pp. 184-203. Of course, the phenomenon of the excessive light could be explained in a slightly different (though complementary) way as the influence of a kind of painting Wright was imitating: the candlelit tradition (Honthorst, La Tour) in which a Christ Child is over-illuminated by a nearby candle simulating his own holy luminescence.

2. See *Joseph Wright of Derby, Painter of Light* (London, 1969), esp. pp. 50-51, 111-112, and 120-121.

3. Ibid., p. 121.

4. "Joseph Wright at the National Gallery," *Art Quarterly* 34 (1971): 476. See also F. D. Klingender, *Art and the Industrial Revolution* (London, 1947; revised ed., 1968), pp. 60-61 (where he makes the point that Cummings elaborates).

5. Behind them is Wright himself, the primary empiricist, who left a written program for his painting: "Two men forming a bar of iron into a horseshoe, from whence the light must proceed. An idle fellow may stand by the anvil in a time-killing posture, his hands in his bosom or yawning with his hands stretched upwards, & a little twisting of his body. Horse shoes hanging up ye walls, and other necessary things

faintly seen, being remote from the light. Out of this room shall be seen another, in wch a farrier may be shoeing a horse by the light of a candle. The horse must be sadled, and a traveller standing by. The servant may appear with his horse in hand, on wch may be a portmanteau. This will be an indication of an accident having happened, and show some reason for shoeing the horse by candlelight. The moon may appear, and illumine some part of the horses, if necessary" (Account Book, quoted by Nicolson, p. 51). "It is gratifying to know that we see in the pictures what he saw," says Nicolson; and Cummings: "Such explanations of Wright's views and the tradition of ideas upon which he relied are essential for understanding his painting" (ibid.). The passage reveals Wright to be an artist in the candlelit tradition of Honthorst and La Tour, and it shows that at some point he wanted to tell a story—or felt he should tell a story. But I prefer to focus on the artist's telling phrase "if necessary": "The moon may appear, and illumine some part of the horses, if necessary." Among the numerous discrepancies between Wright's apparent program and his finished painting we may note that the horse is not illuminated by a moon, but rather by a guttering candle, whose precarious flickering is emphasized by a pointing figure, and we may question whether Wright chooses to make clear that the scene concerns the shoeing of a horse (certainly not evident in the painting).

6. "Boothby, Rousseau, and the Romantic Malady," *Burlington Magazine* 110 (1968): 659-666.

7. Cummings, "Boothby," p. 660.

8. See Paulson, *Emblem and Expression,* p. 190.

9. *Spectator,* no. 86, in *The Spectator,* ed. Donald F. Bond (Oxford, 1965), 1: 365-366. For Shaftesbury, see *The Moralists, A Philosophical Rhapsody* (1709). To bring the matter down to graphic art, see (for example) Richard Haydocke's version of Lomazzo's *Trattato dell-Arte* (1598), p. 81: "As in all naturall things, heither *goodness* can stande without *beauty,* nor *beauty* without *goodnesse*: so in things artificially framed and composed, nothing can promise *profite* or *commoditie* without *comlinesse,* which consisteth wholy in due proportion: So that profite and commodity, ariseth as well from Arte, as Nature." Or see Giovanni Battista della Porta, *Della Fisonomia dell'Huomo* (Vicenza, 1615), Bk. IV, folios 171, 174: "It is an old axiom, and one ratified by all those who make a profession of Physiognomy, that the pleasing arrangement of the parts of the body demonstrates as well a pleasing disposition of the mind.... On the contrary, the ugly of face, are hideous of mind, and ugliness is a defect of nature, and an effect of disproportion, an object abhored by the visual faculty, and finally like a deliberate image of the Infernal" (tr. Giulia Giuffre).

10. On the Belvedere *Antinous,* its identification as "Antinous," and its fame, see Francis Haskell and Nicholas Penny, *Taste and the Antique: The Lure of Classical Sculpture 1500-1900* (New Haven and London, 1981), pp. 141-142.

11. Haskell and Penny, who quote these remarks of Raguenet, pass

them off as "absurd" (Raguenet, *Monumens de Rome* [Rome, 1700], pp. 321-326; Haskell and Penny, p. 30). In their otherwise invaluable catalogue of the classical canon, Haskell and Penny make no attempt to register what a contemporary may have thought these sculptures meant, besides associations of ancient history and ideal beauty.

12. *A Notion of the Historical Draught or Tablature of the Judgment of Hercules* (1713).

13. *A Philosophical Enquiry into the Origin of our Ideas of the Sublime and Beautiful*, ed. J. T. Boulton (London, 1967), p. 51.

14. *The Analysis of Beauty*, ed. Joseph Burke (Oxford, 1955), p. 35.

15. See p. 132; Burke, *Philosophical Enquiry*, p. 57.

16. Hume, *An Enquiry concerning the Principles of Morals* (1777 ed.), App. I. 242, ed. P. H. Nidditch (Oxford, 1975), pp. 291-292.

17. Wright's fascination with transmutations appears as an almost compulsive feature of his work. His iron forges and smithies, for example, show none of that detail of metalworking machinery, of stock forms, shapes, and products so carefully chronicled in the plates of Diderot's *Encyclopedie*. We perceive, in contrast to Diderot's documentation, an appearance that undoes our conceptual expectations, replacing our faith in the solidity of objects with an experience of transmutation. In his late series of burning cottages and Vesuvian eruptions, which certainly demonstrate his mastery of light, Wright makes use of his mastery to undermine our faith in a stable ontological center in our relationship to apparently unchanging objects.

18. Penny, *Church Monuments in Romantic England* (New Haven and London, 1977), p. 66. For Guelfi's monument to Craggs, see Penny, pl. 43 (p. 64).

19. The statue is in the Conservatori Museum, Rome. See Gisela Richter, *A Handbook of Greek Art* (London, 1959), pl. 199; cited, Joseph Burke, *English Art 1714-1800* (Oxford, 1976), pp. 106-107. See Emily Vermeule, *Aspects of Death in Early Greek Art and Poetry* (Berkeley, Los Angeles, London, 1979), pp. 145-147, 154-155: "*Pothos* is generally a feeling of longing in the nighttime for someone who is not there, a lover gone overseas, or the absent dead" (p. 154).

20. See Paulson, *Emblem and Expression*, pp. 208-209.

21. See Paulson, *Book and Painting: Shakespeare, Milton, and the Bible* (Knoxville, Tenn., 1982), pp. 104-114.

22. I should mention the rise of the mausoleum. Hawksmore's at Castle Howard, completed in 1742, was the first in Western Europe since antiquity, and another of his Roman allusions. Several followed in the 1750s and 1760s, and dozens in the 1770s and 1780s (Penny, *Church Monuments*, pp. 44 and 210 n. 13). This structure gave added importance to the individual tomb or family tombs, by enclosing them in a similarly tomblike structure, dimly lit, often from an opening in the ceiling, recalling the architectural structures that were also available by the 1750s in Piranesi's prints.

23. Penny, *Church Monuments*, pp. 21, 116; pls. 10, 87.

24. Dartrey Mausoleum, County Monaghan, in Penny, *Church Monuments,* pl. 33, pp. 47-48.

25. See Erwin Panofsky, "Et in Arcadia Ego: Poussin and the Elegiac Tradition," in *Meaning in the Visual Arts* (New York, 1955), pp. 295-320. Versions of Poussin's painting are in Chatsworth and the Louvre; Cipriani's painting of the subject, with the full tomb shown, is reproduced by Panofsky; Reynolds' version, *Mrs. Bouverie and Mrs. Crewe* (1769) is in Crewe Hall. In Richard Wilson's version, *"Ego fui in Arcadia"* (1755), as Panofsky says, "the shepherds and the funerary monument — here a slightly mutilated *stele* — are reduced to a *staffage* accentuating the muted serenity of the Roman Campagna at sundown" (p. 319).

Fig. 1. Joseph Wright, *Blacksmith's Shop* (1771). New Haven,
Yale Center for British Art.

Fig. 2. Joseph Wright, *Sir Brooke Boothby* (1780-81). London, Tate Gallery.

Fig. 3. Louis-François Roubiliac, Monument to John, Duke of Argyl (1745-1749). London, Westminster Abbey.

Fig. 4. Joseph Wright, *Miravan opening the Tomb of his Ancestors*
(1772). Derby Museum and Art Gallery.

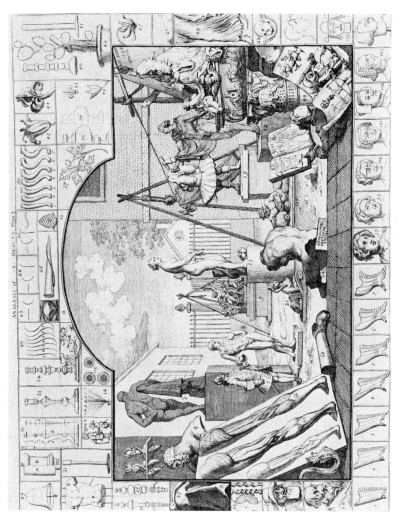

Fig. 5. William Hogarth, *Analysis of Beauty* (1753), pl. 1.

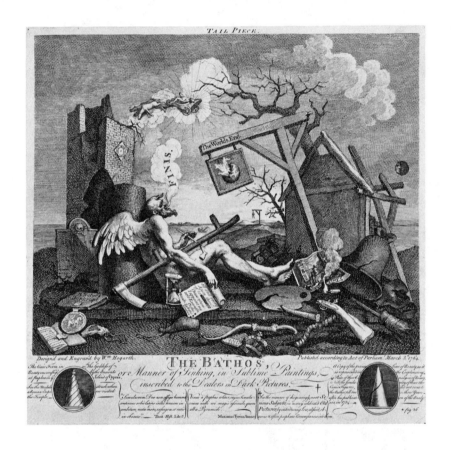

Fig. 6. William Hogarth, *Tailpiece,* or *The Bathos* (1764).

Fig. 7. Sir Joshua Reynolds, *Sarah Siddons as the Tragic Muse* (1784). San Marino, California, Henry E. Huntington Library and Art Gallery.

Fig. 8. Peter Scheemakers, *Shakespeare* (1740). London,
Westminster Abbey.

Fig. 9. Thomas Gainsborough, *Garrick with a Bust of Shakespeare* (1760). Painting destroyed. Mezzotint by Valentine Green.

Fig. 10. Louis-François Roubiliac, *Monument to Lady Elizabeth Nightingale* (1761). London, Westminster Abbey.

Fig. 11. Angelica Kauffmann, *Cleopatra decorating the Tomb of Mark Antony.* Burghley House, Collection of the Marquess of Exeter.

VII

FROM TOPOS TO TROPE, FROM SENSIBILITY TO ROMANTICISM: COLLINS'S "ODE TO FEAR"

Harold Bloom

Doubtless there are many perspectives that could reveal to us the essential continuities between four apparently disjunctive entities: the topics of classical rhetoric, the ideas of Associationist psychology, the tropes of High Romantic poetry, the mechanisms of defense named by Sigmund Freud and eventually codified by his daughter Anna. But I have only my own perspective to offer, and I seek here to develop certain critical notions that have obsessed me in a series of works, culminating in an essay called "Poetic Crossing," to be found as a coda to my book on Stevens. Much that I have to say will be rather technical, but at least it will not be dry. I propose to take William Collins's "Ode to Fear" and to read it rhetorically and psychologically, so as to contrast within it the representations of two related but distinct poetic modes, Sensibility (as Northrop Frye suggested we call it) and Romanticism.

The "Ode to Fear," a remarkable poem by any standards, is perhaps too Spenserian in its diction, and too Miltonic in its procedures, to sustain its own implicit prayer for originality, its own yearnings for strength. Collins was a very learned young poet of real genius, and he seems to have intuited how few years of sanity and control would be available to him. His "Ode to Fear" is a daemonic exercise, a desperate gamble with his poetic limits that rightly reminds us how attractive he was to Coleridge and to Hart Crane, poets who shared his temperament and his ambitions. The modern critical theorist who best illuminates daemonic or Sublime poetry is Angus Fletcher, both in his remarkable early book, *Allegory* (1964), and in his more recent essays on threshold rhetoric and personification. But before I expound Fletcher's liminal visions, I need to say something about the puzzling gap between the poets, in their advanced conceptions of rhetoric and psychology, and the critics of later eighteenth- and early nineteenth-century Britain.

We are currently in a literary situation where much critical theory and *praxis* is more on the frontier than most of our best poetry tends to be, a situation infrequent though hardly unique in the history of culture. The criticism and formal psychology of the Age of Sensibility and of Romantic times lagged considerably behind the experiments of Collins and Shelley. When I began to write criticism, in the mid-1950s, it seemed to me that Wallace Stevens was well out in front of available criticism, though not of the speculations of Freud. We are catching up to Stevens, and perhaps we begin to see precisely what Freud was *not* doing, anyway. Collins implicitly had a Miltonic theory of imagination, as presumably the commentaries on Aristotle that he wished to write would have shown. But what marks both British psychology and literary theory from the mid-1740s down to (and beyond) the time of Coleridge is its conservatism. Hazlitt is a formidable exception, and his theories helped to free Keats from some of the inadequacies of British intellectual tradition, but the main story is elsewhere, with Wordsworth and Coleridge, where the puzzles of the relation between thought and art are still just beyond the analytical range of our critical scholarship.

Dr. Johnson, who wrote of Collins with personal warmth but lack of critical discernment (rather like Allen Tate on Hart Crane) was of course the strong critic contemporary with Collins's experiments in the ode. With his Neoclassic bias, Johnson was critically just not what Collins needed, though humanly the compassionate and sensible Johnson did Collins much good. Poetically, I would say, Collins needed a vital critic to tell him that the trope for time, particularly *literary* time, could be only irony or else metalepsis (also called transumption) and Collins was deliberately one of the least ironic of all gifted poets. He needed a critic rather like Angus Fletcher, who is discussing Coleridge in the passages I am about to quote, but who might as well be describing Collins:

> Coleridge, whose heart is so full, if sometimes only of its own emptiness, its desire to be filled, seems fully aware that the betweenness of time-as-moment, pure thresholdness, barren liminality, at least in what Einstein would call a "space-like" way, must be a nothingness. Between the temple and labyrinth there must be a crossing which, viewed from the perspective of time, does not stand, stay, hold or persist. Yet the poet craves persistence and duration. . . .
>
> A new or renewed Renaissance mode of personification would seem to be the main yield of the poetry of threshold. . . .
>
> Formally, we can say that personification is the figurative emergent of the liminal scene. . . . Personifications come alive the moment there is psychological breakthrough, with an accompanying liberation of utterance, which in its radical form is a first deep breath.

A Sublime or Longinian critic this acute would have strengthened Collins where he needed it most, in his own sense of poetic election. The "Ode to Fear" could have been called "Ode to Poetic Election," and its opening invocation makes us wonder just what the personification Fear can mean:

> Thou, to whom the world unknown
> With all its shadowy shapes is shown;
> Who see'st appalled the unreal scene,
> While Fancy lifts the veil between:
>   Ah Fear! Ah frantic Fear!
>   I see, I see thee near.

Why name one's own daemon or genius as Fear? Indeed as "frantic Fear"? Is this a free choice among available personifications, a kind of Aristotelian "fear" to be dispelled by an aesthetic catharsis, or is it an overdetermined fear, belonging more to Freud's cosmos than Aristotle's? Perhaps these questions reduce to: is there not a sexual, perhaps a sadomasochistic element, in what Collins calls Fear? The "mad Nymph," Fear, is nothing less than Collins's Muse, rather in the sense that Lacan called Freud's earliest patients, those gifted and charming hysterical young women of Jewish Vienna, Freud's Muses.

The most illuminating reading of the "Ode to Fear" that I know is by Paul Sherwin in his superb book, *Precious Bane: Collins and the Miltonic Legacy* (Austin, 1977). Sherwin rightly emphasizes Collins's teasing technique; we never do see anything of the presumably attractive mad Nymph beyond her "hurried step" and "haggard eye." I agree with Sherwin that there is an affinity here between Collins and Burke. Collins too favors sympathy over imitation, the effect of things on the mind over a clear idea of the things themselves. Milton's "judicious obscurity," as Burke admiringly called it, is followed by Collins, who also rejects mere mimesis. Sherwin approvingly quotes Mrs. Barbauld, that Mrs. Alfred Uruguay of her age, as remarking that Collins's Fear is at once the inspirer of passion and its victim. And so, in Sherwin's reading, is Collins:

> If, on the one hand, his sympathy is drawn out by Fear's all-too-human vulnerability, it is perplexed by her apparent divinity; and whereas the former aspect of the personification establishes the possibility of intimacy, it is the latter aspect, enticing the speaker with the dangerous allure of numinous experience and heightening his sense of self, that provokes him to seek out this precarious communion.

I don't wish to be accused of assimilating William Collins to Ernest Dowson, but I am going to urge a reading rather less ontological and more sexual even than Sherwin's. How after all, experientially speaking, does one go about renewing the link between rhetorical personification and daemonic possession? There is religion of course, presumably more in its esoteric than in its normative aspects. There is intoxication, by drink and by drug, and there is, yet more poetically, the always beckoning abyss of sexuality as taken to its outer limits, where pleasure and pain cease to be antithetical entities. I am not going to give us a William Collins as heroic precursor of the Grand Marquis, or a critical vision of the "Ode to Fear" as a grace note preceding *The Hundred and Twenty Days of Sodom and Gomorrah*. But the pleasures of the "Ode to Fear" are uneasily allied to its torments, and there is an element of sexual bondage in those torments. That even this element should be, ultimately, a trope for influence-anxieties is hardly a revelation, since I know no ampler field for the study of belatedness than is constituted by the sadomasochistic elements in our psyches.

Is it too much to say that Collins, throughout his Ode, attempts to work himself up into a frenzy of fearful apprehension, in the hope that such frenzy will grant him the powers of the tragic poet, of Aeschylus, Sophocles, but above all of Shakespeare? Yes, that is to say too much, because we then underestimate what Freud would have called Collins's overvaluation of the object, when his Fear is that object. Fear indeed is Collins's wounded Narcissism, and so becomes the entire basis for the aggressivity of his poetic drive. But that requires us to name more clearly the Nymph or daemon, since Aristotle's tragic fear hardly seems an apt name for the Sublime hysteria that Collins confronts and desires.

Shall we not call her the Muse of repression, and so of the Counter-Sublime? Perhaps, in Freudian terms, we could call her the Counter-Transference, the analyst's totemic and repressed apprehension that he is in psychic danger of being, as it were, murdered and devoured by his devoted patient. Fear, as Fletcher and Sherwin tell us, is Collins's *own* daemon, his indwelling Urania. Our twentieth-century Collins was Hart Crane, and I turn to Crane for his versions of Collins's Nymph. In a late, unfinished lyric, "The Phantom Bark," Crane rather strangely alludes to Collins, and evidently not to any actual poem Collins wrote:

> So dream thy sails, O phantom bark
> That I thy drownèd man may speak again
> Perhaps as once Will Collins spoke the lark,
> And leave me half adream upon the main.

The reference is purely visionary, as though Collins came back from the dead, say, in Shelley's "Skylark." In some truer sense Collins speaks to his Nymph Fear again when Crane addresses his nymph Helen in *For the Marriage of Faustus and Helen.* Crane too cries out: "Let us unbind our throats of fear and pity," while he goes on to give us his version of "*Vengeance,* in the lurid Air, / Lifts her red Arm, expos'd and bare" as "the ominous lifted arm / That lowers down the arc of Helen's brow / To saturate with blessing and dismay." Crane's later versions of this antithetical Muse include the Paterian Venus of *Voyages* VI, who "rose / Conceding dialogue with eyes / That smile unsearchable repose—," and the woman of "The Broken Tower," a Collinsian poem where the Muse's "sweet mortality stirs latent power" in her poet. A late fragment by Collins actually prophesies Crane's death lyric: "Whatever dark aerial power, / Commission'd, haunts the gloomy tower." Like Collins, Crane invokes the Evening Star as the gentlest form of his Daemon, though Crane's invocation necessarily is more desperate: "O cruelly to inoculate the brinking dawn / With antennae toward worlds that glow and sink; — "

What Crane helps us see is that Collins's Fear is a Muse not so much called on to help the poet remember, as one invoked to help the poet forget. A Muse who forgets, or who needs to forget, is en route to Moneta in *The Fall of Hyperion,* but Collins is rather more Coleridge's precursor than he is Keats's. Except for Scripture and Milton, and perhaps Shakespeare, what passage in poetry haunted Coleridge more productively than this:

> Through glades and glooms the mingled measure stole,
> Or o'er some haunted stream with fond delay,
>> Round an holy clam diffusing,
>> Love of peace and lonely musing,
> In hollow murmurs died away.

From "The Passions" to "Kubla Khan" is a movement from one threshold to another, and liminal poets have a particularly intense way of recognizing their family romance and its nuances. Fletcher, the theoretician of thresholds, reminds us that etymologically the *daemon* is the spirit of division, a reminder that I remember using as a starting point in working out the revisionary ratio of *daemonization* or the Counter-Sublime. The Sublime trope for such dividing tends to be breaking, a making by breaking, or catastrophe creation. I return to the "Ode to Fear" to trace just such a breaking.

How specific ought we to be in finding an identity for Collins's "world unknown" and "unreal scene"? The late Thomas Weiskel brilliantly argued for something like Freud's Primal Scene Fantasy, but here as elsewhere I would prefer some version of what I have theorized as the Scene of Instruction. Not that the two fantasies are wholly exclusive, since what passes between the Poetic Father and the Muse has its sexual overtones in the evening ear of the belated ephebe. Yet Collins's scene can be called more Yeatsian than Freudian, more at home in the world of *Per Amica Silentia Lunae* than in that of *Totem and Taboo.* This may be simply because Collins's "sources" are mostly Spenserian (Masque of Cupid, Temple of Venus), but I suspect a more crucial reason also; Fear is indeed Collins's own Daemon, but he has not yet possessed her or been possessed by her. The scene she partly inhabits by seeing is populated by the fathers, by Spenser, Shakespeare and Milton, but not by Collins himself. As the Ode begins, Fear sees the visionary world, but all that Collins sees is Fear. We are in the ancient topos of Contraries and Contradictories but not yet in the trope of Romantic Irony. And there I touch at last upon my first theoretical speculation in this essay; Sublime Personification seems to me an uneasy transitional phase or crossing between Associationist topos and Romantic trope. Collins's Fear is a commonplace burgeoning but not yet burgeoned into an irony, or as Freud called it, a reaction-formation. Fear *sees* and is frantic; Collins sees *her,* and becomes rather less persuasively frantic:

> Ah Fear! Ah frantic Fear!
> I see, I see thee near.
> I know thy hurried step, thy haggard eye!
> Like thee I start, like thee disordered fly.

That repetition of "I see, I see" is already quite Coleridgean, so that we almost expect Collins to burst forth with "And still I gaze — and with how blank an eye!" What restrains Collins is an awareness still just short of irony, certainly short of Spenserian irony, regardless of all the Spenserian diction. The contraries of seeing and not-seeing the visionary scene yield to the topoi of definition and division in the remainder of the strophe, as Collins enumerates the monsters appearing in Fear's train. Division is properly daemonic here, with one giant form, a Spenserian Danger, thousands of phantoms: "Who prompt to deeds accursed the mind," as well as an indefinite number of fiends who: "O'er natures wounds and wrecks preside." All these lead up to a highly sadistic Vengeance, who requires considerable scrutiny. But even Danger has his peculiarities:

> Danger, whose limbs of giant mould
> What mortal eye can fixed behold?
> Who stalks his round, an hideous form,
> Howling amidst the midnight storm,
> Or throws him on the ridgy steep
> Of some loose hanging rock to sleep;

The sources here — in Spenser and Pope — are not developed with any particular zest or inventiveness on Collins's part. But we should note the obsessive emphasis again upon the eye of the holder, the horrified fixation that is one of the stigmata of repression. Spenser's Daunger, that hideous Giant, was associated with hatred, murder, and treason, which may have been daily intimations for Spenser to dread, whether in Ireland or at court, but cannot have had much reality for Collins in the years when he still was sane. His Danger "stalks his round" amid more commonplace sublimities, storm and impending rock fall. These represent surely the psyche's potential for violence, whether aggressivity is to be turned against others or against the self:

> And with him thousand phantoms joined,
> Who prompt to deeds accursed the mind;
> And those, the fiends who, near allied,
> O'er nature's wounds and wrecks preside;

Those wounds and wrecks of nature include internalized disorders, which is what prompts the vision of a ferociously personified feminine superego, as it were, an image of sadomasochistic Vengeance:

> Whilst Vengeance in the lurid air
> Lifts her red arm, exposed and bare,
> On whom that ravening brood of fate,
> Who lap the blood of sorrow, wait;

Again the sources (Milton, Dryden, Pope) are of little consequence except for Collins's own noted reference to the hounds of vengeance in Sophocles' *Electra*. The curious doubling, almost redundant, of Vengeance's lifted arm as both "exposed and bare" enforces how lurid Collins's scopic drive dares to become. There is a troubling ambiguity in the image, as Weiskel noted. Vengeance is a kind of phallic woman, appropriate to a masochistic fantasy, and in some curious way Collins blends her into an Artemis figure, waited upon by destined hounds. There is thus a hint of an Actaeon identity for poor Collins himself, a hint taken up in the couplet closing the strophe:

> Who, Fear, this ghastly train can see,
> And look not madly wild like thee?

Like his daemonic Muse, Collins really does expect to be hunted down and torn apart by the Furies, for his tone lacks any playful element. That he more than half desires his fate is clear enough also. What is beautifully not clear is just who is seeing what in this rather confused scene of sadomasochistic instruction. Fear sees it all, yet Collins is by no means as yet fully one with his own Fear. She sees and yet does not wish to see; Collins sees only in and by visionary fits, yet he does want to see, whatever the cost. Lacan's grim jest about the scopic drive comes to mind: that which we are fixated upon, obsessively stare upon, is precisely what cannot be seen. Only the creativity of Fear can impel Collins beyond this daemonic threshold.

Of course, like Weiskel or to some extent also Sherwin, or Paul Fry in his fine reading of this Ode, I am giving a kind of Freudian reading (broadly speaking) and Collins's own overt psychology was Associationist. But the line between Associationism and Freud is a blurred one, for a number of reasons. One is merely genetic, despite all Freudian denials. Freud's theory of language essentially came from John Stuart Mill (whom Freud had translated) and so was essentially a late version of Associationism. But far more crucially, both the Associationist categories and the Freudian mechanisms or fantasies of defense rely implicitly on rhetorical models, these being the topoi or commonplaces for Associationism and the prime topos or figures for Freud. Romanticism is of course the connecting link here between topos and trope, association and defense, or to phrase this more saliently, Collins's "Ode to Fear," though a monument of and to Sensibility, is itself a version of that connecting link, a poem verging on High Romanticism and kept back from it mostly by two barriers. Call one of these decorum or diction, and the other Collins's own anxieties, human and creative, and you may be calling a single entity by two misleadingly different names.

I am aware that I am telling what is hardly a new story, scholarly or critical, but this twice-told tale always does need to be told again. The story's troublesome phantom is what we go on calling personification, an old term I have no desire to protest provided we keep remembering that primarily it means not humanization but masking, or as Fletcher has taught us, masking at the threshold, at the crossing between labyrinth and temple, or as I want to say, between limitation and a representation that is a restitution. Such masking, in Associationist terms, is a movement through categorical places. In Romantic or Freudian terms, it is a movement between tropological or defensive configurations, marked always by ambivalence and duplicity.

The masterpiece of emotive ambivalence, in Freud or in the poets, is called variously the Oedipal conflict, taboo, and transference, and this is where Collins chooses to center his Epode:

> In earliest Greece to thee with partial choice
>   The grief-full Muse addressed her infant tongue;
> The maids and matrons on her awful voice,
>   Silent and pale, in wild amazement hung.
>
> Yet he, the bard who first invoked thy name,
>   Disdained in Marathon its power to feel:
> For not alone he nursed the poet's flame,
>   But reached from Virtue's hand the patriot's steel.
>
> But who is he whom later garlands grace,
>   Who left awhile o'er Hybla's dews to rove,
> With trembling eyes thy dreary steps to trace,
>   Where thou and Furies shared the baleful grove?
>
> Wrapped in thy cloudy veil the incestuous queen
>   Sighed the sad call her son and husband heard,
> When once alone it broke the silent scene,
>   And he, the wretch of Thebes, no more appeared.

Sophocles of course is hardly Collins's poetic father, but the Oedipal scene is very much Collins's own, and the echo of *Comus* in the condition of the maids and matrons has considerable force. Freud has taught us to look for meaningful mistakes, and the learned Collins errs remarkably here. The "sad call" in *Oedipus Coloneus* is not sighed once by Jocasta, but frequently by the god, who is summoning Oedipus to join him. I take it that Collins himself is being summoned, not by Apollo but by the Oedipal Muse, for whom another name, we now can see, is Fear:

> O Fear, I know thee by my throbbing heart,
>   Thy withering power inspired each mournful line,
> Though gentle Pity claim her mingled part,
>   Yet all the thunders of the scene are thine!

Pity here is as little Aristotelian as Fear has been. Collins now recognizes Fear as being not only daemon and Muse but as mother, a recognition scene that is the Sublime crisis point of the Ode. In Associationist terms, the Epode has moved from the categories of Contiguity to those of Comparison, from matters of cause and effect to those lying, beyond causation, in the heights and depths of the daemonic Sublime. Collins's heart recognizes what his occluded sight could not, and so he learns, as Stevens phrased it, that the mother's face is the purpose of the poem. But a mother who is more fear than pity, whose power is withering, and who inspires a thunderous Scene of Instruction, is a most extraordinary version of the mother, and suggests an Orphic as well as an Oedipal fate for poor Collins.

But this is of course Collins's own direct suggestion, and the puzzle of the "Ode to Fear" grows ever greater. The Pindaric, from its origins through Collins on to Shelley courts disaster, as suits the most overtly agonistic of all lyric forms. Paul Fry charmingly suggests that all the "monsters" Collins invokes: "appear to be nothing other than Pindaric odes." I would modify Fry by observing that Collins is a strong enough poet to know that anything he wishes to get into his Pindaric ode must be treated as if it already was a Pindaric ode. A motherly Muse so fearful, indeed so hysterical as to require the analog of Jocasta, belongs to the same principle of strength and its costs. Collins is frightening himself to some purpose, and I swerve for a brief interval from Collins into Freud not to seek a reductive version of that purpose but rather to show that every strong anxiety is in some sense an *achieved* anxiety, so that Collins mimes a profound constant in the civil wars of the psyche.

Freud, in his later (post-1926) revision of his theory of anxiety, wrote a kind of commentary upon the Sublime ode, not least upon the "Ode to Fear." In Freud's earlier theory, neurotic anxiety and realistic anxiety were rigidly distinguished from one another, since neurotic anxiety was dammed-up libido, caused by unsuccessful repression, while realistic anxiety was caused by real danger. But after 1926, Freud gave up the notion that libido could be transformed into anxiety. Anxiety, Freud came to insist, is prior to repression, and indeed was the motive for repression. The causal distinction between neurotic anxiety and real fear was thus abandoned for good. The doctrine of the priority of anxiety depends on a mapping of the psyche in which the ego itself is viewed as being in large part unconscious, so that we must say we are lived by the id. Oppressed from the other side by the super-ego, or the ego's own abandoned earlier affections, the poor ego is exposed to the death drive, the final form of sadomasochistic ambivalence aggressively turned in against the self. Real fear and neurotic anxiety alike become interchangeable with the fear of castration, which is to say, the fear of death. But the hapless ego's surrender of its aggressivity, whether against the self or others, does not appease the superego, which progressively grows more murderous toward the ego.

Associationist psychology had no such vision of man, but Collins's "Ode to Fear" does, probably against Collins's own desires and intentions. Weiskel shrewdly observed that Collins had discovered "a fantasy code appropriate to the special crisis of discourse in his day." Freud admitted that the poets had been there before him, and it is uncanny that Collins was more *there* than poets far stronger. We think of Blake in this dark area, but Blake was enough of a heroic vitalist to disengage from his own Spectre of Urthona. Collins, like Cowper, is all but one with that Spectre, with the temporal anxiety that cannot be distinguished from the poetic ambition of the Sensibility poets.

If we glance back at the Strophe of the "Ode to Fear" we can see that its hidden subject is the tormented question: "Am I a poet?" Collins indeed is the Muse's true son, but can the Muse be Fear and nothing more? In the Epode the question is altered, since there the true poet, Aeschylus, is revealed as being fearless. The question therefore becomes: "Can I love, or get beyond poetic self-love?," and the answer seems to be highly equivocal, since Oedipal love is narcissistic beyond measure. In the Antistrophe, much the strongest of the poem's three divisions, Collins makes a fierce endeavor to introject poetic immortality, but the Miltonic shadow intervenes, with startling results. The question becomes not what it should be, more life or a wasting death, but the truth and decorum of the romance mode. Collins is, I think, creatively confused throughout the Antistrophe but the confusion, as in so much of Tennyson, becomes an aesthetic gain:

> Thou who such weary lengths hast passed,
> Where wilt thou rest, mad nymph, at last?
> Say, wilt thou shroud in haunted cell,
> Where gloomy Rape and Murder dwell?
> Or in some hollowed seat,
> 'Gainst which the big waves beat,
> Hear drowning seamen's cries in tempests brought!

The sentiment here, though not the mode, suggests Thomas Lovell Beddoes and George Darley, a good three generations later. The "mad nymph" desperately requires rest, but the Miltonic verb "shroud" for "shelter" suggests that no rest is possible for this personification of the poetic. A rested Fear would cease to fear, and so the poem would have to close prematurely. But the transmogrification of personification into phantasmagoria moves Fear from visual to auditory hallucination, which increases psychic disorder, both in the Muse and in her poet. What seem to me the poem's most effective lines mark Collins's crisis of identification, as he seeks to internalize Miltonic power while continuing his avoidance of naming that source of paternal strength:

> Dark power, with shuddering meek submitted thought
> Be mine to read the visions old,
> Which thy awakening bards have told:
> And, lest thou meet my blasted view,
> Hold each strange tale devoutly true;

The Archangel Michael, instructing Adam just before the expulsion from Eden, says it is time to wake up Eve, who has been calmed with gentle dreams: "and all her spirits compos'd / To meek submission." Collins here takes up that feminine and passive stance imposed on Eve by angelic power, and so I think that his union with his Muse Fear now has become a very radical interpenetration. In this progressive internalization, the topos of Resemblance engenders characteristic metaphor, in which nature and consciousness bewilderingly perspectivize one another. Weiskel, acutely aware of this progress from Sensibility to Romanticism, caught it up in an eloquent formulation:

The "reader's" mind is deeply divided between the powerful and dark appeal the fantasies are making and his conscious renunciation of the desires they excite. An attitude of meek submission holds off his recognition of these desires, but it also prevents his Longinian appropriation of the precursor's power as his own. The power remains dark, instinct with danger; the liberating power of a symbolic identification with the bards is just what is missing.

Sherwin emphasizes "the radical bivalence of the daemon" here, saying of Collins that:

... He has so thoroughly absorbed the rage of his dark angel that the daemon, no longer threatening the poet with engulfment, is viewed as a guide leading beyond itself to the special prerogatives of the prophetic seer.

Both these critics of Collins's Sublime help us to see that Collins is on the verge of strength, yet hesitant to cross over into it, though Sherwin's tone is more positive than Weiskel's. I would add that Collins's baffled version of the Longinian or reader's Sublime is very difficult indeed to interpret. Unlike the idealized Eve's, Collins's meek submission is a "shuddering" one, and that modifier "shuddering" is his ironic response to Milton as an "awakening" bard, that is, a bard who imposed upon the reader a very intense affective burden. So empathic is this response, however ironic, that Collins's eyes are threatened with being blasted, darkened by shock, unless he assents to the Miltonic fable, however strange. If the precise tale here be the expulsion from Eden, then one sees why Collins's subsequent passage returns to the Milton of *L'Allegro* and *Il Penseroso,* and of *Comus,* and perhaps to the Shakespeare of *A Midsummer Night's Dream*:

> Ne'er be I found, by thee o'erawed,
> In that thrice-hallowed eve abroad,
> When ghosts, as cottage-maids believe,
> Their pebbled beds permitted leave,
> And goblins haunt, from fire or fen
> Or mine or flood, the walks of men!

That an urbane tone has entered cannot be questioned, but what has departed is the voice of William Collins. We hear the octosyllabic Milton, and not his venturesome and daring ephebe. Had Collins dared further, he would have found the Miltonic rhetoric of transumption or metalepsis for a triumphant closure, but instead he ends quite elegantly but weakly, in an interplay of the topoi of Antecedents and Consequences:

> O thou whose spirit most possessed
> The sacred seat of Shakespeare's breast!
> By all that from thy prophet broke,
> In thy divine emotions spoke,
> Hither again thy fury deal,
> Teach me but once like him to feel:
> His cypress wreath my meed decree,
> And I, O Fear, will dwell with thee!

Collins was capable of strong closure, as the "Ode on the Poetical Character" demonstrates. What defeated him here? Para-

doxically, I would assert that the relative failure is in the generation of sufficient anxiety. What fails in Collins is his own capacity
for an infinite Fear. Not that courage becomes the issue, but
trauma. Apathy dreadly beckons, and Collins prays for the power
to feel. Yet I do not think he means affect. His knowing failure is
in cognition, and I want to look closely at Dr. Johnson's moving
dispraise of his learned and gifted young friend in order to see if
we can recover a clue to Collins's self-sabotage:

> . . . He had employed his mind chiefly upon works of fiction, and sub-
> jects of fancy; and, by indulging some peculiar habits of thought, was
> eminently delighted with those flights of imagination which pass the
> bounds of nature. . . .
> This was however the character rather of his inclination than his
> genius; the grandeur of wildness, and the novelty of extravagance, were
> always desired by him, but were not always attained. . . . His poems are
> the productions of a mind not deficient in fire . . . but somewhat ob-
> structed in its progress by deviation in quest of mistaken beauties.

To pass natural bounds, to wander beyond limits, *extra
vagans,* that surely was Collins's poetic will, his intended revenge
against time's: "It was." Johnson is shrewd, as always, in saying
that Collins not only desired too much, but beyond the range of
his genius. The fault was not ambition, but rather that Collins
had to ask his inventive powers to give him what neither contemporary criticism nor contemporary psychology afforded. Milton
stands on the verge of the European Enlightenment, but when it
begins to reach him it breaks over him, confirming only his recal-
citrant furies. Collins puzzles us because he is spiritually close
enough to Milton to acquire more of the Miltonic power than
actually came to him. Geoffrey Hartman's sad summary is just,
noble, and restrained, and joins Johnson as the classical verdict
upon Collins:

> Collins rarely breaks through to the new poetry. . . .
> Collins does teach us, however, that the generic subject of the sublime
> ode (as distinct from that of individual poems) is the poetical character:
> its fate in an Age of Reason. The odes are generally addressed to invited
> powers and, like the gothic novel, raise the ghosts they shudder at.
> Their histrionic, sometimes hysterical, character stems from the fact
> that they are indeed theatrical machines, evoking a power of vision that
> they fear to use. Collins, like a sorcerer's apprentice, is close to being
> overpowered by the spirit he summons.

My friend's simile of the sorcerer's apprentice is particularly effective if associated with the version of Dukas in Disney's *Fantasia*. The vision of William Collins as Mickey Mouse overcome by a host of mops is more than any poet's reputation could sustain. Poor Collins indeed! I would prefer another vision of Collins's limitations, one that emphasizes the odd splendor, or splendid oddness, of his liminal achievements. Daemonic poetry is a strange mode, whether in Collins, Coleridge, Shelley, Beddoes, or Hart Crane. When Collins gets it exactly right, then he has the uncanniness of an original, as this cento intends to illustrate:

> And she, from out the veiling Cloud,
> Breath'd her magic Notes aloud:
> And Thou, Thou rich-hair'd Youth of Morn,
> And all thy subject Life was born!

> To the blown *Baltic* then, they say
> The wild Waves found another way,
> Where *Orcas* howls, his wolfish Mountains rounding;
>   Till all the banded West at once 'gan rise,
> A wide wild Storm ev'n Nature's self confounding,
>   With'ring her Giant Sons with strange uncouth Surprise.

> Now Air is hush'd, save where the weak-ey'd Bat,
> With short shrill Shriek flits by on leathern Wing,
>   Or where the Beetle winds
>   His small but sullen Horn,
> As oft he rises 'midst the twilight Path,
> Against the Pilgrim born in heedless Hum:

> What though far off, from some dark dell espied
>   His glimm'ring mazes cheer th'excursive sight,
> Yet turn, ye wand'rers, turn your steps aside,
>   Nor trust the guidance of that faithless light;
> For watchful, lurking 'mid th'unrustling reed,
>   At those mirk hours the wily monster lies,
> And listens oft to hear the passing steed,
>   And frequent round him rolls his sullen eyes,
> If chance his savage wrath may some weak wretch surprise.

These are among the breakthroughs from Sensibility into Romanticism, though never into the Wordsworthian mode. What Collins could not learn was what Wordsworth had to invent, a transumptive or time-reversing kind of troping as original as Milton's own, yet plainly *not* Miltonic. Collins's stance was neither ironic nor transumptive, and so temporality remained for

Collins a choking anxiety. If Collins was no mere sorcerer's apprentice, it must be admitted he was also no sorcerer, as the baffled closure of the "Ode to Fear" renders too obvious. I circle back to the question prevalent in all criticism of Collins: What made him poor? Why was his psychic poverty, his imaginative need, so scandalously great? To have crossed into the Romantic Sublime only a year or two after the death of Pope was hardly the act of a weak poet, yet Collins will never lose the aura that Johnson gave him and that Hartman has confirmed.

I go back to Collins's true spiritual companion among the critics, Fletcher, though Fletcher alas has published only a few remarks about Collins. In his early masterpiece, *Allegory*, Fletcher has a fine observation on the function of the Sublime:

Graver poems like the sublime odes of Collins and Gray, and later of Shelley, have the direct and serious function of destroying the slavery of pleasure.

I interpret Fletcher as meaning that Collins, Gray, and Shelley, in their uncanny Pindarics, are bent on persuading the reader to forsake easier in exchange for more difficult pleasures. Paul Fry, acutely but perhaps too severely, says of the School of Collins and Gray: "An ode that remembers the pastness of others and not the otherness of the past can have nothing to say of fallen experience as a distinct phase." I think that Collins met Fry's challenge by refusing to admit that fallen experience *was* a distinct phase. As Coleridge's precursor, Collins pioneered in representing what Thomas McFarland calls the "modalities of fragmentation" or "forms of ruin" in Romantic poetry. As McFarland is showing us, these *are* modalities, these *are* achieved forms, with aesthetic arguments and structured intensities all their own.

Repetition, as Paul Fry has noted in this context, is very much the issue when we bring Collins to an aesthetic judgment:

Repetition is what unlearns the genealogical knowledge of the ode, which creates a world and a god with every stroke of the pen, only in the same movement to absent these creations from the poet's field of vision.

Fry knowingly follows Paul de Man's theory of lyric here, but I would suggest Kierkegaard's "repetition" rather than de Man's as being closer to Collins's Sublime project. Kierkegaard's "repetition" literally means in Danish "a taking again," and is described by Mark Taylor as "the willed taking-again of a transcendental possibility." Collins wills to take again the transcendental possibility of poetry as he knows it in Spenser, Shakespeare and Milton. Or rather, he wills to will such a taking-again, so as to affirm again the possibility of poetic strength. But a will two degrees from the possibility is a troubled will, too troubled to attempt what McFarland, following Plato, calls "the Place Beyond the Heavens," the "true being, transcendence, and the symbolic indication of wholeness" that make up the synecdoches of visionary poetry. Collins's synecdoches are wounded aggressivities, turned in against themselves, sadomasochistic vicissitudes of the thwarted poetic drive against time's "It was." Collins cannot say: "I am," in his poems. Instead of the synecdoches of wholeness, Wordsworthian or Keatsian, he can offer only the Associationist categories of Definition and Division.

Yet the "Ode to Fear" remains a unique poem, as do three or four other major performances by Collins, and its deep mutual contamination of drive and defense is far closer to the psychic cartography of Freud than to Locke. Collins survives not so much as a voice but as the image of a voice, perhaps even as the topos of image-of-voice itself. What Collins knows in that daemonic place is the "continuous present" that Northrop Frye said was representative of the mode of Sensibility and of its exercise of repetition. Gray and Cowper and Smart perhaps were more at home in that "continuous present" than Collins was, and what we know of his life shows us how little Collins ever felt at home anywhere. Only the place of the daemon could have been home for Collins, and to that occult place I turn for my conclusion.

Collins, as all his critics rightly say, is a poet always engaged at invocation, in calling, until he seems quite giddy with the strain. Recall that our word "god" goes back to a root meaning "called" or "invoked," and that the word "giddy," possessed by god, has the same root. Yeats, in his beautiful daemonic reverie, *Per Amica Silentia Lunae,* gives us the formula for Collins's sense of place, for the exact topos of Sensibility:

The Daimon, by using his mediatorial shades, brings man again and again to the place of choice, heightening temptation that the choice may be as final as possible, imposing his own lucidity upon events, leading his victim to whatever among works not impossible is the most difficult....

Collins's odes enact that drama over and again. That there should have been a religious element in his final mania is not surprising, for he is nothing but a religious poet, as Shelley and Hart Crane are Orphic religionists also. But to be an Orphic prophet in the mode of Sensibility was plainly not possible, and again it was not surprising that Collins and his odes alike were slain upon the stems of Generation, to adapt a Blakean conceptual image. Yeats, so much stronger a poet than Collins ever could be, must have the final words here. The tragedy of Sensibility is that it could suffer but not write this liminal passage of High Romantic self-revelation, which again I quote from *Per Amica Silentia Lunae*:

> ... when I have closed a book too stirred to go on reading, and in those brief intense visions of sleep, I have something about me that, though it makes me love, is more like innocence. I am in the place where the Daimon is, but I do not think he is with me until I begin to make a new personality, selecting among those images, seeking always to satisfy a hunger grown out of conceit with daily diet; and yet, as I write the words 'I select,' I am full of uncertainty, not knowing when I am the finger, when the clay.

ODE *to* FEAR.

Thou, to whom the World unknown
With all its shadowy Shapes is shown;
Who see'st appall'd th' unreal Scene,
While Fancy lifts the Veil between:
    Ah *Fear!* Ah frantic *Fear!*   5
    I see, I see Thee near.
I know thy hurried Step, thy haggard Eye!
Like Thee I start, like Thee disorder'd fly,
For lo what *Monsters* in thy Train appear!
Danger, whose Limbs of Giant Mold   10
What mortal Eye can fix'd behold?
Who stalks his Round, an hideous Form,
Howling amidst the Midnight Storm,
Or throws him on the ridgy Steep
Of some loose hanging Rock to sleep: 15
And with him thousand Phantoms join'd,
Who prompt to Deeds accurs'd the Mind:
And those, the Fiends, who near allied,
O'er Nature's Wounds, and Wrecks preside;
Whilst *Vengeance,* in the lurid Air,   20
Lifts her red Arm, expos'd and bare;
On whom that rav'ning* Brood of Fate,
Who lap the Blood of Sorrow, wait;

---

*Alluding to the Κυνας αφυκτους of *Sophocles.* See the ELECTRA.

2 shadowy] shadow *Pearch* (*misprint?*)

Who, *Fear,* this ghastly Train can see,
And look not madly wild, like Thee?   25

EPODE.

In earliest *Grece* to Thee with partial Choice,
   The Grief-full Muse addrest her infant Tongue;
The Maids and Matrons, on her awful Voice,
   Silent and pale in wild Amazement hung.

Yet He the Bard* who first invok'd thy Name,   30
   Disdain'd in *Marathon* its Pow'r to feel;
For not alone he nurs'd the Poet's flame,
   But reach'd from Virtue's Hand the Patriot's Steel.

But who is He whom later Garlands grace,
   Who left a-while o'er *Hybla's* Dews to rove,   35
With trembling Eyes thy dreary Steps to trace,
   Where Thou and *Furies* shar'd the baleful Grove?

Wrapt in thy cloudy Veil th' *Incestuous Queen* †
   Sigh'd the sad Call ‖ her Son and Husband hear'd,
When once alone it broke the silent Scene,   40
   And He the Wretch of *Thebes* no more appear'd.

O *Fear,* I know Thee by my throbbing Heart,
   Thy with'ring Pow'r inspir'd each mournful Line,
Tho' gentle *Pity* claim her mingled Part,
   Yet all the Thunders of the Scene are thine!   45

ANTISTROPHE.

Thou who such weary Lengths hast past,
Where wilt thou rest, mad Nymph, at last?

Æschylus.   † *Jocasta.*

‖ ―――― ουδ ετ' ορωρει βοη
Ην μεν Σιωπη; φθεγμα δ'εξαιφνης τινος
Θωυξεν αυτον, ωστε παντας ορθιας
Στησαι φοβω δεισαντας εξαιφνης Τριχας,
See the Œdip, Colon, of *Sophocles.*

Say, wilt thou shroud in haunted Cell,
Where gloomy *Rape* and *Murder* dwell?
Or in some hollow'd Seat,   50
'Gainst which the big Waves beat,
Hear drowning Sea-men's Cries in Tempests brought!
Dark Pow'r, with shudd'ring meek submitted Thought
Be mine, to read the Visions old,
Which thy awak'ning Bards have told: 55
And lest thou meet my blasted View,
Hold each strange Tale devoutly true;
Ne'er be I found, by Thee o'eraw'd,
In that thrice-hallow'd Eve abroad,
When Ghosts, as Cottage-Maids believe,   60
Their pebbled Beds permitted leave,
And *Gobblins* haunt from Fire, or Fen,
Or Mine, or Flood, the Walks of Men!
    O Thou whose Spirit most possest
The sacred Seat of *Shakespear*'s Breast!   65
By all that from thy Prophet broke,
In thy Divine Emotions spoke:
Hither again thy Fury deal,
Teach me but once like Him to feel:
His *Cypress Wreath* my Meed decree,   70
And I, O *Fear,* will dwell with *Thee!*

VIII
"MORE THAN MOTION WITHOUT MEANING": EIGHTEENTH-CENTURY BRITAIN AND THE BALLET D'ACTION

Selma Jeanne Cohen

One of the most frequent and most mistaken allegations made against the intellectual status of dance is that practically nothing serious has been written about it. When for "serious" we substitute the still more demanding "theoretical" or "aesthetic," the accusation becomes more sweeping still—only Susanne Langer, we are told, has ever discussed dance in terms of philosophy. Of course this verdict depends on how "serious," "theoretical," and "aesthetic" are defined. But if we accept Langer's own concept of a philosophical question as it relates to art, if we accept the idea that such a question will relate to the meaning of key concepts that pertain to that art, then we will find—if we really look—that a rather large number of writers have asked questions about the qualities of dance as art, about its necessary and sufficient conditions, about the sources of its creativity, and about the nature of the dance experience, both for the performer and for the audience. True, more has been written about literature and painting, and with good reason, for of all the arts dance is the most resistant to intellectual scrutiny because it does not stand still. In "A

Dialogue Concerning Art" (1744), James Harris remarked that "dance has its being or essence in a transition: call it a motion or an energy."[1] It's hard to catch. Still, some brave souls — even philosophers — have tried to analyze this volatile thing. The first I know of was Plato.

Most important for our purposes is the fact that the eighteenth century produced an especially impressive assortment of writings on the dance. Not all of them, I must admit, treat it with respect. Sir Joshua Reynolds, in his third discourse on art (1770), likened dancing masters to hairdressers and tailors, characters who distort and disfigure the human form. Of the more kindly discussions, however, a number can be called at least serious; at best, philosophical. That they have been largely ignored by scholars, with the notable exception of the late Artur Michel, may be because most dance researchers look exclusively at books with "dance" in the title, which allows them to discover only two Frenchmen, Louis de Cahusac and Jean Georges Noverre, and a single Englishman, John Weaver. Where are the rest hiding? In books about the arts in general and even in some volumes that bear only "poetry and painting" on their covers. It is necessary, unfortunately, to open these books to find that they contain sections on dance. The task has evidently appeared too onerous for most otherwise eager inquirers to undertake.

Why this burgeoning attention to dance in the eighteenth century? I believe several factors contributed to it. First, while it was not considered a major art, dance was accepted into the hierarchy of the arts and was consequently eligible for inclusion in any discussion of aesthetic matters. Certainly it was amenable to the basic questions that the century asked about a work of art: Did it represent *la belle nature*? Did it exhibit harmony and order in its composition? Was its imitation just and lively? Did it teach and delight?

Interest was stimulated as dance rose in popularity on the stage. All those "entertainments of dancing" that concluded so many performances of plays on the London stage were apparently box office attractions, for their titles and the names of their performers are writ large in the advertisements, and their number increased with the years. Among others, the author of *A Satyr Against Dancing* (1702) was not happy about the situation:

> The fair thus wave what Betterton will say,
> And only talk how finely danc'd L'Abee;
> Those cuts in the'air, how sudden nice and clean;
> These Entertainments ruin ev'ry Scene.[2]

Further, the art of dance itself was undergoing an exciting transformation. In the seventeenth century little distinction had been made between the dance of the court ball and the dance of the theater. Decorum was the rule for both; spontaneous response, display of emotion, natural exuberance were all considered contrary to accepted etiquette. Order and control had to be visible. Of course, any obvious exhibition of individual skill would be frowned upon. However, beginning with the founding of the royal academy of dance in Paris in 1661, the gulf between ballroom and stage gradually widened. The new concentration on training professional dancers encouraged the development of better teaching methods, as technical expertise emerged as a desirable quality. In the eighteenth century, Marie Camargo shortened her skirt and became the first woman to perform an entrechat quatre; Anna Heinel perfected the pirouette; Gaetano and Auguste Vestris were famous for their virtuosity. In 1729, Soame Jenyns remarked in his *The Art of Dancing*:

> 'Tis not a nimble Bound or Caper high
> That can pretend to please a curious Eye;
> Good judges no such Tumblers Tricks regard,
> Or think them beautiful because they're hard;
> Yet in *Stage-dancing,* if performed with Skill
> Such active Feats our Eyes with Wonder fill.[3]

Competition bred virtuosity, and virtuosity led some to question if this was the ballet or the circus. Cahusac admitted the brilliance of the ballerinas of the Paris Opera while he lamented that his age lacked the art of dance.

In the opinion of some, dance would become an art only when choreographers disdained the lure of pyrotechnics and concentrated their efforts on the imitation of actions, manners, and passions. Actually, it was the same separation between social and theatrical dance that had stimulated the development of virtuosity that also made possible the evolution of the ballet d'action. As long as the social prescriptions of restraint and decorum had to be observed, portrayals of strong emotion were considered as improper in the theater as in the ballroom. The actor or singer could utter passionate phrases, but if he stood stiffly erect, his arms still and face expressionless, he would appear in control and therefore acceptable. The dancer, however, was hopelessly vulnerable. As Martha Graham was to say two centuries later: "Movement [i.e., natural movement] never lies." Eighteenth-century society demanded lies. But when ballet became more distinct from social dancing, the rules could be modified. What could not be countenanced in the intimacy of the ballroom could be tolerated when observed from the distance that separated the stage from the auditorium of the theater; on that stage, the skills of the performers marked them as beings apart from the inhabitants of the everyday world and consequently exempt from at least some of its conditions.

Despite their common origin in the separation of stage and society, however, virtuosity and dramatic expressiveness were often at odds, emphasis on either one tending to lessen the claims of the other. The grounds for theoretical controversy were laid in France with the works of Michel de Pure (*Idées des Spectacles,* 1658) and Claude Menestrier (*Des Ballets Anciens et Modernes,* 1682). But the arguments were waged on both sides of the channel.

In his *Essay Towards a History of Dancing* (1712), Weaver claimed only to be arguing for a return to the principles of the Roman pantomime. His way was not easy, for in London then audiences showed little interest in dance drama. Favorite numbers on the stage included various "national" dances — "the Dutch Skipper," the "Highland Lilt," "A French Peasant and his Wife." In the early years of the century prestige was contributed by such visiting French artists as Marie Thérèse Subligny and Jean Balon who showed the English audience how polished dancing could be. Most conceded that the guest stars displayed their virtuosity with taste, but some remarked that their imitators employed such skills with less refinement. In *The Spectator,* Richard Steele questioned the approbation of those "impertinents as fly, hop, caper, tumble, twirl, turn round, and jump over their Heads, and in a word, play a thousand Pranks which many Animals can do better than a man."[4]

A most serious threat to Weaver's interests was John Rich, whose antics and mechanical effects made him rich indeed. Harlequin was hatched from an egg, turned into a flower; volcanos fumed, and men were transformed into wheelbarrows, Alexander Pope saw in the Empire of Dullness as described in the *Dunciad*:

> a sable Sorcerer rise,
> Swift to whose hand a winged volume flies:
> All sudden, Gorgons hiss, and Dragons glare,
> And ten-hornéd fiends and Giants rush to war.
> Hell rises, Heav'n descends, and dance on Earth:
> Gods, imps, and monsters, music, rage, and mirth,
> A fire, a jig, a battle and a ball,
> Till one wide conflagration swallows all.[5]

Weaver fought his battles in both ballets and books. Like most of his contemporary theorists he looked for dual values in art, looking to it for both pleasure and instruction. The excellency of dance he assigned to its imitative powers: "to explain Things conceiv'd in the Mind, by the Gestures and Motions of the Body, and plainly and intelligibly representing Actions, Manners, and Passions; so that the Spectator might perfectly understand the Performer by these his Motions, tho' he say not a Word." Communication was assured because "Nature assign'd each Motion of the Mind its proper Gesticulation and Countenance, as well as Tone; whereby it is significantly and decently express'd."[6] But the beauties of dance were something else, though they too depended on the laws of nature; movements are beautiful when they are "built upon the Fundamentals of Anatomy; agreeable to the Laws of Mechanism; consonant to the Rules of harmonical Proportion, and adorn'd with the Beauty of a natural and cultivated Gracefulness."[7] Dancing for Weaver, then, is "an elegant and regular Movement harmonically composed of beautiful Attitudes and contrasted graceful Postures of the Body."[8] But true elegance involves also the appropriateness of the motion to the manners and passions to be expressed. If imitation is ignored, dance is only an amusing trifle. Weaver condemned those performers who were more concerned "how to please than [with] what is natural, fit, or proper."[9]

Fortunately Weaver has left us some evidence of how he put his ideas into practice. The most significant and detailed of these is his libretto for *The Loves of Mars and Venus* (1717), which he described as "A Dramatick Entertainment of Dancing, Attempted in Imitation of the Pantomimes of the Ancient Greeks and Romans." Colley Cibber produced it at Drury Lane, claiming his mission "to give even Dancing therefore some Improvement, and to make it something more than Motion without Meaning. . . ."[10] True to his precepts Weaver allowed his dancers to "speak not a word." Where the ballets of the preceding century had relied on spoken verses and songs as well as on telling costumes, symbols, and masks to identify their characters and situations, Weaver was determined to depend only on naturally expressive gesture to tell his story. The libretto describes some specific instances: "Power. The Arm, with impetuous Agitation, directed forwards to the Person, with an awful Look, implies Authority"; "Grief is express'd by hanging down the Head, wringing the Hands; and striking the Breast."

Venus was danced by Weaver's favorite ballerina, Hester Santlow, who later became well known as an actress. Her histrionic talents were probably already noticeable and may well have accounted for the choreographer's choosing her for his heroine. Another ballerina who might have been influenced by Weaver, since she was in London at the same time, was Marie Sallé. Lacking the technical brilliance of her chief rival, Camargo, Sallé was known for her dramatic expressiveness. In 1734 she both choreographed and performed *Pygmalion,* a "ballet-pantomime," in which she dared to appear with her hair down, without a single ornament on her head, and wearing only a simple muslin dress draped about her in the manner of a Greek statue. *Pygmalion,* which drew London audiences for more than two months, told its whole story through movements and gestures of the body. But by this time Weaver was ready to quit the theater scene of the city, and Sallé soon returned to Paris.

In the end, the influence of Camargo proved the stronger. It was the divertissements designed for brilliant technicians, rather than the ballet d'action that dominated London during most of the remainder of the century. But as virtuosity gathered popular acclaim, it provoked philosophical censure.

The author of *The Polite Arts* (1749), drawing much of his material from *Les Beaux Arts* of Charles Batteux (1746), viewed the arts as modes of imitation of la belle nature. He distinguished three means of expressing ideas and sentiments: words, tone of voice, and gesture. The last two, he claims, have the advantage of

being more natural and more universally understood; words convince by way of thought, but tones and gestures move the heart
directly. Like the materials of the other arts, the gestures of
dance are naturally significant, and their significance must be
preserved, though the artist enhances them with measure, modulation, and harmony. In addition, the author insists that the
expression be clear, just, lively, easy to understand, and novel
enough in its form to alert the spectator who might otherwise be
unimpressed.

The most famous of the eighteenth-century advocates of
expressive dance was French. But Jean Georges Noverre super-
vised productions of his own choreography for the London stage
in 1755 and again from 1781 to 1794; further, his *Lettres sur la
danse et les ballets* appeared in an English translation in 1783, so
we may feel entitled to consider him here. Brought to London by
David Garrick, Noverre met with disaster on his first visit to
England; the timing was bad, for anti-French feeling was strong
and the audiences rioted. Noverre's second sojourn, however, met
with great success, and London saw many of his ballets in these
later years. Unfortunately, the newspaper accounts tell us little of
what his works looked like, and Noverre's librettos, unlike Weaver's, give us only the narrative and reveal nothing at all about the
nature of the dancing.

We know from the first pages of the *Lettres* exactly where
Noverre stands: "Poetry, painting and dancing, Sir, are, or
should be, no other than a faithful likeness of beautiful nature."
He continues with a stern criticism of contemporary practice:
"This art has remained in its infancy only because its effects have
been limited, like those of fireworks designed simply to gratify the
eyes; although this art shares with the best plays the advantage of
inspiring, moving and captivating the spectator by the charm of
its interest and illusion. No one has suspected its power of speaking to the heart."[11] The fault he lays not to the art but to the artist who ignores its imitative powers. Throughout his writings Noverre likens ballet to drama, urging the choreographer to divide
his work carefully into scenes, to observe the rules of probability,
to make his characters individual. He admits, though, some
relaxation of the laws of the unities.

Applied to dance, his dramatic ideas led him to favor the use of
asymmetrical stage groupings as more expressive than the usual,

nicely balanced rows of fixed bodies; perhaps he also found them more picturesque in Wiebenson's use of the term. Noverre also had a good deal to say against formula-type composition, a matter that Kerman would have noted with delight. What we cannot tell, either from his own words or from those of others, is precisely how he carried out his ideas in practice. No notated scores remain — probably they were never made.

Noverre's statements may lead us to wonder. He refers to "dancing united to pantomime," to "the graces which dancing affords to gestures," to "dancing embellished with feeling." He urges the performer to "divide his attention between the mechanism of steps and movements proper to express the passions." He seems to admit conventional technique for the legs but asks that the arms and the face be expressive. The dichotomy appears frequently in the *Lettres*. If their words are to be believed, Noverre seems less innovative than his predecessor Weaver, who wrote of Venus and Vulcan in a manner that seems to synthesize "dance" movement and expression: "They perform a dance together; in which Vulcan expresses his Admiration; Jealousie; Anger; and Despite; And Venus shows Neglect; Coquetry; Contempt; and Disdain." But Weaver did not push his claims in the manner of the aggressive Noverre. In 1733 the English theorist gave up choreography in London for teaching in his native Shrewsbury, and was soon practically forgotten. Noverre staged his ballets and published his books in Paris, London, Stuttgart, and Vienna over a period of more than forty years. Had their personalities been reversed, how might ballet have developed?

Some eighteenth-century theorists were not so insistent on dance as an imitative art. In fact, considerable attention was paid to concepts of beauty and grace in dancing without reference to their appropriateness to an object that was represented. In 1752 Joseph Spence claimed in his *Crito: Or A Dialogue on Beauty* that expression was common to all the arts, but grace to few, and he favored the importance of the rarer quality. Distinguishing two sorts of grace, the majestic and the familiar, he did admit that they could be observed most clearly in those dances that express character and passion.

In *The Analysis of Beauty* (1753), William Hogarth too is concerned with graceful movement, which he contrasts to that which is utilitarian. The lines of the latter are straight, but graceful movement is serpentine, a quality which makes the minuet the finest of all dances. Its varied movements exhibit these attractive wavy lines, while the floor path followed by the dancers is also composed of serpentine patterns. Hogarth quotes Shakespeare's *A Winter's Tale*:

> What you do,
> Still betters what is done,
> When you do dance, I wish you
> A wave of th' sea, that you might ever do
> Nothing but that; move still, still so,
> And own no other function.

With "no other function." This is nonrepresentative dance, dance as sheer visual design. Hogarth notes, however, another kind of theatrical dancing from which the serpentine line is excluded, but which, when "made consistent with some character, and executed with agility, it nevertheless is very entertaining." For purposes of characterization, then, the line of beauty is deliberately violated: "The attitudes of the harlequin are ingeniously composed of certain little, quick movements of the head, hands and feet, some of which shoot out as it were from the body in straight lines, or are twirled about in little circles."[12]

Henry Home, Lord Kames, proposed another explanation for the appeal of the serpentine. In his *Elements of Criticism* (1762) he claimed that the undulating line is more pleasing because it is more free and natural. Motion, Kames remarked, is agreeable by itself but also by its utility as a means to a beneficial end. Thus we can admire machines and horses. "But the grace of motion is visible chiefly in man, not only for the reasons mentioned, but because every gesture is significant."[13] Motion shows character and sentiment, therefore grace arises from elegance of motion accompanied by expressiveness. "Dancing," he concludes, "affords great opportunity for displaying grace."[14]

The eighteenth century's concern with the nature of grace, that enchanting attribute of human motion, appears in many of the era's discussions of dance. Grace is that "je ne sais quoi" that seems utterly natural and that cannot fail to charm. Some thought that this most desirable quality might be taught, but only up to a point; essentially grace is a natural gift. Further, grace is exhibited only in movement and in movement of a very special kind. In his *Essays on the Nature and Principles of Taste* (1790), Archibald Alison notes that grace always engenders respect and admiration for the person because it is expressive of self-command. Grace becomes especially admirable when it meets an obstacle and remains unfazed by it; to exhibit superiority to a threat makes an especially pleasing impression:

The common motions of walking, running, &c., have in themselves nothing of difficulty, and are therefore, in general, incapable of producing any emotion. But dancing is an art of real difficulty, and we observe it always with the consciousness of this difficulty.... When, accordingly, we see all this well performed, when we see the dancer move without hurry or disorder; perform all the steps of the dance with ease, accommodate his motions with justice to the measure, and extricate himself from all apparent intricacies of the figure with order and facility, we feel a very perceptible sentiment of surprise and admiration, and we are conscious of the grace of the gestures, in which so much skill and composure, and presence of mind are displayed.[15]

Alison claims a still higher degree of grace in movements that express serenity and self-possession in cases of danger—he cites horsemanship and tightrope walking. But here he admitted a potential problem, warning that such feats must not degenerate into tricks of mere agility. He is also aware of instances in which qualities other than grace might be even more desirable, for he sees beauty in motion that is appropriate to the age, sex, and character of the mover. He also distinguished between expressions of permanent character, or disposition of mind, and attitudes or gestures that express temporary or occasional passions or affections. This, theoretically, opened the way for dramatic dance, but Alison did not follow the path. He considered the imitative function of dance to be secondary.

In his essay on the imitative arts, Adam Smith agreed. "Dance," he asserted, "is not necessarily imitative and it can produce very agreeable effects without imitating at all." Those dances that do without imitation "consist almost entirely of a succession of such steps, gestures, and motions, regulated by the time and measure of Music, as either display extraordinary grace or require extraordinary agility." The imitative powers of dance, he remarked, though not necessary are still considerable; however, he finds them limited in scope. For Smith, dance is most satisfactory for the representation of adventures of love or war, but not very good at depicting matters of understanding or judgment. Yet in portraying the sentiments, emotions, and passions of the heart—here he found dance superior to music, though inferior to poetry. He analyzed the pleasure or witnessing skillful representations: "That pleasure is founded altogether upon our wonder at seeing an object of one kind represent so well an object of a very different kind, and upon our admiration of the art which surmounts so happily that disparity which Nature had established between them."

Still, Smith seems capable of enjoying—even preferring—that dance which is simply itself. Dance movement is so fascinatingly different from what we see around us all the time. In social situations a person's intention of "showing off" is reprehensible; it is the avowed intention of the performer. "The display [of grace and agility] is in reality the proper purpose of the action; there can never be any disagreeable vanity or affectation in following out the proper purpose of any action. . . . Every Dance is in reality a succession of airs and graces which, if I may say so, profess themselves to be such. The steps, gestures, and motions which, as it were, avow the intention of exhibiting a succession of such airs and graces, are the steps, gestures, and motions which are peculiar to Dancing, and when these are performed to the time and measure of Music, they constitute what is properly called a Dance."[16]

Grace and agility. The intention of exhibiting airs and graces. Yet Alison had warned that these could degenerate into tricks. The dancer was—somehow—different from the horseman and the tightrope walker. But how? For the early theorists of the century the answer lay in imitation, since the dancer uses his skills in order to create a character. For the later writers formal values begin to take precedence. Smith finds skills offensive when they are "unsuitable to the nature of the Dance." Since he is not here referring to imitative dance, we may suspect that what Smith has in mind when he cites the nature of the dance is style. Here the eighteenth century starts to sound very modern.

In 1757 Jean Jacques Rousseau urged the theater to banish all dance that represented nothing but itself. "I start [a dance] with the movement. . . . But then out of this the action begins to assume its own proportions. . . . It can take a momentum of its own," said Merce Cunningham in 1968.[17] Apart from occasional deviations in favor of spectacular effects, Western theatrical dance has wavered between these two poles for much of its history. Weaver tried and Noverre was convinced that he had succeeded in making the ballet d'action the accepted form, but their admonitions had to be repeated at the end of the nineteenth century and again in the middle of the twentieth. Why this recurring need for the same kind of reform?

One reason may be repeated overstepping, repeated carrying of an idea to such an extreme that dance begins to impinge on another genre altogether. Carry virtuosity too far and we get the circus. Carry expression too far and we wonder at the absence of words. Each rebel has claimed to be recalling dance to its true nature: to its true status as an imitative art, or to its true status as an art needing to serve no end outside of itself.

Within any performing art there is an intrinsic tension. The dancer, like August Baron's fictional Sophie of 1825, has struggled for years to acquire suppleness in the hips, facility in the ankle; she has daily executed her battements for hours in front of the mirror. Now she is to perform in a ballet d'action, and all those years at the barre count for nothing.

"Children of Terpsichore," cried Noverre, "renounce *cabrioles, entrechats* and over-complicated steps; abandon grimaces to study sentiments, artless graces and expression."[18] Poor Sophie! Or poor Noverre?

On certain rare occasions, though, the miracle has happened when the technical skills developed by the dancers and the form of expression desired by the choreographer complement one another—perfectly. Not long after the close of the eighteenth century, it happened. All the work the women had been doing to vitalize their insteps, their knees, their backs, finally gave them the strength to dance on the tips of their toes. Not for long at first, but enough to give the impression of an ethereal creature, one that—according to Théophile Gautier—looked as if she could run over grass without bending a blade of it. Simultaneously came the vogue of tales of the sylph, the ondine, the peri— the unattainable, ideal woman whom the man pursues through misty glades and mysterious forests, their atmosphere enhanced by the newly introduced gas lighting. The technique, achieved to serve the aims of virtuosity, lay waiting for the poets of romanticism to use for the embodiment of their dreams. The romantic ballet, one of the greatest periods in all theatrical dance history, was born.

When Marie Taglioni danced *La Sylphide* in London in 1832, the eighteenth century was, indeed, over.

NOTES

1. James Harris, *The Works of James Harris* (London: Wingrave, 1801), I: 23.

2. *A Satyr Against Dancing* (London: A. Baldwin, 1702).

3. Soame Jenyns, *Works* (London: T. Cadell, 1790), I: 20-21.

4. *The Spectator*, no. 466 (25 August 1712).

5. The *Dunciad*, ed. James Sutherland, Vol. V, *The Twickenham Edition of the Poems of Alexander Pope*, gen. ed. John Butt (London and New Haven: Methuen and Yale University Press, 1963), pp. 331-332 (Bk. III, 11.233-240).

6. John Weaver, *An Essay Towards the History of Dancing* (London: J. Tonson, 1712), pp. 160-161.

7. John Weaver, *Anatomical and Mechanical Lectures Upon Dancing* (London: J. Brotherton, 1721), p. 2.

8. Weaver, *Lectures Upon Dancing*, p. 137.

9. Weaver, *Essay*, p. 159.

10. Colley Cibber, *An Apology for the Life of Mr. Colley Cibber*, ed. Robert W. Lowe (London: J. C. Nimmo, 1889), II: 180.

11. Jean Georges Noverre, *Letters on Dancing and Ballets*, trans. Cyril W. Beaumont (London: C. W. Beaumont, 1951), p. 11.

12. William Hogarth, *The Analysis of Beauty* (London: J. Reeves, 1753), p. 158.

13. Henry Home, Lord Kames, *Elements of Criticism* (Edinburgh: A. Kincaid and J. Bell, 1762), I: 236.

14. Home, *Elements*, I: 364.

15. Archibald Alison, *Essays on the Nature and Principles of Taste* (Edinburgh: J. J. G. and G. Robinson, Bell, and Bradfute, 1790), p. 437.

16. Adam Smith, *Essays on Philosophical Subjects* (London: T. Cadell, Jr. and W. Davies, 1795), pp. 239-242.

17. Merce Cunningham et al., "Time to Walk in Space," *Dance Perspectives*, 34 (1968): 47.

18. Noverre, *Letters*, p. 29.

IX

THEORIES OF LATE EIGHTEENTH-CENTURY MUSIC

Joseph Kerman

Late eighteenth-century music is called classical *not* because it has anything to do with the issues of classicism and neoclassicism that so occupied literary and artistic theory at the time. We call this music classical (as the eighteenth century did not) not because of what it looked back to, but because of the way we look back to it. For a variety of reasons it has assumed for musicians an authority as great as, however different from, that of the literary and artistic monuments of ancient Greece and Rome for later poets, architects, painters, men of letters, and historians of the fine arts. This authority was achieved very rapidly in the early decades of the nineteenth century. In the later decades it was personified by the powerful figure of Brahms and embodied in his oeuvre. It is still felt today in any musician's education and in the conduct of his or her professional life.

As a consequence, any music critic or scholar who makes any claim to generality, even if he is not a specialist in the eighteenth century, as I am not, thinks he has something to say about Haydn and Mozart. It is a little like the situation in literary studies, where so many people seem to be ready and eager to talk about Shakespeare. Further, the criticism of this music can be taken as a fair spectrum of modern attitudes toward music in general. There has been intensive and distinguished work in other fields too, of course, but in none other, I believe, have different and sometimes divergent theories jostled so powerfully. My intent here is to examine critically the work of several important authors, in order to trace the main outlines of a developing modern view of classical music.

I

Let us begin with Charles Rosen's *The Classical Style: Haydn, Mozart, Beethoven* (1971), a book which offered, without much doubt, the freshest prospect on this music that had been seen since the dissertations of Kurt Westphal and Rudolf von Tobel in the 1930s, or—if we may take a viewing-point across the Channel—since the collecting and publication of Sir Donald Tovey's program notes and essays, starting around the same time.[1] Charles Rosen is principally a pianist, of course. As a critic he has adopted much from many quarters, and a broad kinship between his work and that of Tovey has often been observed. Later we shall discern another influence—perhaps less conscious, perhaps more profound.

In any event, whether or not Rosen's eclecticism demonstrates sound common sense, and even if it betrays a regrettable lack of rigor, as some of his critics evidently feel, it probably accounts for the consensus of approval that has been accorded to *The Classical Style*. There is something in the book for everyone. Especially in view of the book's broad sweep, then, we will do well to identify clearly at the start the intellectual tradition to which the author owes his central allegiance.

This is the tradition that musicians call "analysis." American academic music criticism today, as distinguished from journalistic criticism, is dominated by analysis; and as I have argued elsewhere, all the various methodological currents and eddies of musical analysis flow from a single theory, indeed from a single guiding ideology.[2] The theory is the analogue in music of a closely related pair of aesthetic theories that are discussed by M. H. Abrams elsewhere in this volume. The "contemplative" theory of art, developed primarily in reference to painting, and the "heterocosmic" theory, developed in reference to poetry, especially narrative poetry, can be traced back to the eighteenth century, though, as we know, it was in the nineteenth century that they surged and in the twentieth that they threaten to engulf us. (They do, at least, in music.) According to the contemplative and heterocosmic models, a work of art may be analyzed "as having distinctive elements, made coherent by a variety of internal relations, and unified by subordination to an internal end"; this pithy characterization by Professor Abrams applies just as well to the vision of the musical analysts. The problem of artistic form and content is solved (when it is posed at all) by equation, by decreeing that expression, meaning, beauty, and so forth, must reside in the music's internal relations and nowhere else.

Some analysts explain the autonomous perfection of the musical masterpiece according to the familiar metaphor of an organism, others do not. But analysis as a critical theory can absorb organicist theories of art much more easily than other theories we have learned to identify through Abrams's work—more easily than expressive theories, for example, or than the mimetic, imitative, didactic theories that still dominated the thought of the late eighteenth century. Music analytic writings say nothing about the work of art as an expression of the composer's imaginative vision, his ideology, or indeed any other such personal category. They say nothing about how music might uplift, educate, or please the nonprofessional listener. I shall return to these lacunae later. Analysis is a strictly professional type of criticism and it is essentially a formalist type of criticism. Analysts deal with internal musical relations in technical language, and their values are expressed in such terms as coherence, integration, and unity—not infrequently, organic unity.

And so with Rosen, although "organic" is a word he tends to stay strictly away from. Like most serious analysts and other music critics, he takes up a position at some distance from the full-fledged organicist theories that are still current. *The Classical Style* begins with a number of polemic chapters disposing of some ideas that the author thought needed to be countered. The chapter—entitled, significantly, "Theories of Form"—offers a convenient point of entry to his own position.

Formenlehre is the German term for the doctrine of form taught in the old conservatories and modern music-appreciation mills, with its patterns of A and B sections and phrases, its abstract norms and categories. Among the components prescribed for classical sonata form are the first and second "subjects," the modulatory bridge section, the development section consisting of motivic working-out, and so on. Rosen begins with a spirited destruction of this naive account, and holds it up to ridicule on more than one occasion later in his work. Though as he himself admits, this is "a game too easy and too often played": indeed, it was Tovey, seventy-five years ago, who polemicized decisively against what he called the "jelly-mold" view of sonata form, form conceived as something prior and rigid into which musical material is mindlessly poured. Nonetheless, the appreciation of classical music that Tovey instilled depends on form fundamentally. Music exists in time—time is its primary level, what Susanne Langer calls its primary illusion; musical sounds moving through time create the contrasts, balances, and symmetries we call form; we cannot do without it, we must only try to understand it as flexibly as did the masters. Near the end of his preliminaries Rosen remarks, somewhat wistfully, that "an understanding of the sense of continuity and the proportions of classical style would enable us largely to dispense with a further discussion of 'sonata form.'"[3] It was not to be. Two chapters later he presented a concise, essentially conventional summary of the various sonata forms. Nine years later he published another book, actually called *Sonata Forms* (1980), in which such taxonomic urges are carried to unusual and surprising lengths.

Also somewhat equivocal are Rosen's attacks on what he describes as the most sophisticated theories of form developed in the twentieth century, those of the *Urlinie* and *Ursatz* on the one hand, and of *Substanzgemeinschaft* on the other. Of these two eminently Germanic, unabashedly organicist theories,[4] Schenker's *Ursatz* was, I think, less to Rosen's purpose, except insofar as he felt inclined to take account of high fashion in the academy, and is indeed, less to the purpose of anyone concerned with classical music. I therefore forego the nearly impossible task of trying to characterize it briefly. For all the "considerable validity" of Schenkerian analysis, Rosen remarks, "the rate of progression from one point of the basic line [*Urlinie*] to another and the proportions of the form . . . are completely irrelevant to the theory."[5] And for him any account of classical music that slights movement, proportions, and temporal symmetries—in short, form—goes clearly and outrageously against the basic postulates of the style.

More significant are theories of *Substanzgemeinschaft,* or, as we would do better to call them, thematicist theories. Thematicist critics see the unity of musical compositions in the community of thematic or motivic material among their various parts or levels. While in criticism this idea can be traced at least as far back as E. T. A. Hoffmann's famous reviews of Beethoven in the ealy 1800s, thematicism did not really come into its own until this century, especially under the impetus of Gestalt psychology. Tracing deep-level thematic relationships, which may not be easily or immediately perceived, has become the characteristic pursuit of modern thematicists. The figure best known in this country, Rudolph Reti (at one time a follower of Schoenberg, Reti emigrated to America and wrote several books in English), is also the most extreme, the most vulnerable, and in consequence possibly the most frequently attacked of any modern writer on music. But Schoenberg himself, in some rather shadowy comments he made about the derivation of musical compositions from a single *Grundgestalt,* or "basic shape," provided a less systematic but highly suggestive theory along the same lines. The analogue between thematicist theories of criticism and the development of twelve-tone composition is obvious enough and has often been remarked.

Rosen approaches theories of *Substanzgemeinschaft* or thematicism obliquely, by first undermining the antithematicist position in the person of its most outspoken adherent, who was Tovey. As I have suggested elsewhere,[6] ideology appears to have got in the way of Tovey's ear in this matter; he was so determined to rest art upon a bed of Victorian verities that he refused to admit the evidence of his senses in respect to any thematic relationships that were not made absolutely clear by the composer. Once one accepts the obvious possibility that composers may not have wanted to make their intentions all that clear, one is free to accept more imaginative thematicist insights. But Rosen is no gentler on Reti than he is on Tovey. When the extreme thematicists treat music as a purely relational field that is static and nondirectional (or, as is sometimes said, "ontic"), they do not recognize that relational structure in music is created by sound in time. Even more than Schenker, Reti minimizes (even denies) the importance of form in classical music. Compared to these men, Rosen can even begin to look like a *Formengelehrter.*

At a closer look he will be discovered on middle ground. Like many critics of this century, he has worked out for himself a critical practice that tries to reconcile the claims of both "inner form" and "outer form," in the dialectic formulation of the German theorist Ernst Kurth. These claims have been recognized ever since sonata form was categorized, a little uneasily, by A. B. Marx in the 1840s;[7] for however deeply some critics have wished to view classical compositions as autonomous individual works of art, none except the most ideologically committed have been able to ignore those compositions' recourse to patterns, formulas, and even molds on a variety of different compositional levels. When Tovey equated "freedom" with "normality" in music, and when Schoenberg contrasted "musical prose" with "poetry" (as *patterned* discourse), each was dealing in his own way with this same basic dialectic.[8]

Rosen is less inclined to address it in theoretical terms; his strength is as a practical critic, not as a theorist. But in his criticism, a key concept is the relation between material and structure, between the detailed musical gesture and large-scale formal proportions. All the elements of style—line in Schenker's sense, motif in Reti's, tonality, harmony, rhythm, phrasing, texture, figuration, dynamics—work together to produce that most perfect and autonomous of musical objects, the masterpiece of classical music. Or as Edward T. Cone put it in a well-known article, in reference to what he called "the Golden Age of functional tonality,"

The tension between detail and whole was here brought into equilibrium; musical suspense was under complete control; the shapes demanded by the respective needs of melody, harmony, and rhythm were integrated into a rich, multidimensional whole.... [E]verywhere we look, whether at general proportions, at phrase structure, at harmonic rhythm, or at rhythmic motifs, we find patterns interesting not only for their own sake but also, and especially, for the way in which they control, and are controlled by, the other elements.[9]

The elucidation of this central insight occupies focal chapters in each of Rosen's books, "The Coherence of the Musical Language" in *The Classical Style* and "Motif and Function" in *Sonata Forms*. This drawing together of so many elements in an eclectic and comprehensive sweep is no doubt the most impressive aspect of Rosen's work.

How much, for Rosen, coherence depends on deep-level thematic connections appears from his treatment in the latter chapter of Beethoven's "Lebewohl" motif in the Sonata in E-flat, op. 81a, as compared to Tovey's. However, thematic connections do not enter at all into his discussion of the first movement of Mozart's C-major Concerto, K.503, the coherence of which is demonstrated in terms of mass, rhythm, and modality. Here his discussion is much closer to Tovey's well-known essay than to the elaborate thematicist attack on it by Hans Keller, a follower of Reti.[10]

We have the sense, says Rosen in a striking sentence, that in classical music "the movement, the development, and the dramatic course of a work all can be found latent in the material, that the material can be made to release its charged force so that the music . . . is literally impelled from within."[11] This seems a classic statement of the organicist's creed of an entelechy generating a work of art from within. Yet once again, where Rosen wants to apply this idea is in the sphere of form, sonata form. The sonata exposition's inevitable modulation in the bridge passage is not to be thought of as a prescriptive "rule" or formula but as the outcome of charged forces latent in the particular opening theme. The nature of the so-called "second group," after the modulation—its thematic substance, its graded series of cadences—emerges from all that has preceded it. The development section dilates upon thematic, tonal, and textural conflicts established in the exposition. As for the recapitulation section, its true function is that of "symmetrical resolution"—a catch-phrase of Rosen's that seems to me a little clearer when turned around as "resolving symmetry." Symmetry is a requirement of all eighteenth-century art; what the sonata required was a symmetry that would also reinterpret material so as to resolve prior tensions—a resolving symmetry rather than the purely decorative symmetry of earlier musical genres such as the da capo aria.

In summary, the following seem to me to be the main points about Rosen's view of late eighteenth-century music. While his stance as a critic is eclectic, his central concern—like that of other analysts—is with the internal coherence of works of art con-

ceived of as autonomous entities. While he grumbles a good deal
about sterile formalism as applied to classical music, his own criticism holds stubbornly to the concept of form. But his is a concept
of form growing out of and articulated by musical material, by
musical material in all its aspects, all seen (and shown) as working
together, without dogmatic emphasis on any single one.

II

When *The Classical Style* appeared in 1971 it was received with
mixed feelings, if not outright distrust, by many musicologists in
the academic establishment. It was a foregone conclusion that
historians of eighteenth-century music would find at least one of
the book's basic postulates unacceptable.[12] For musicologists style
is a normative concept; for Rosen it is an ideal one, embodied
perfectly only in the works of Haydn, Mozart, and Beethoven—
whose names form, indeed, the subtitle of his book. Other composers are almost completely ignored in *The Classical Style*. More
attention is paid to history in *Sonata Forms*. But even assuming
that the differences with the historians have been papered over—
which would be assuming too much[13]—there still remain other
problems with Rosen's theory of classical music. His classical synthesis is a powerful but not an easy concept, which shades easily
from the demonstrable to the mystical. How does one distinguish
purely formal or merely tautological resemblances among artistic
phenomena from manifestations of vital coherence? Exactly what
is meant by "impulsion," "latency," "emergence," even symmetry? What does Cone mean by "control"? What tests are offered by the validation of these qualities?

I shall attempt to deal with some of these questions later, in
reference to an actual piece of music. Before doing so, however, I
should like to show how they are avoided in more orthodox
accounts of classical music. Let me take as an example the article
"Sonata Form" written for the recent *New Grove Dictionary of
Music and Musicians* (1980) by James Webster, a leading younger
specialist in the music of Haydn and his contemporaries. That a
major statement specifically about sonata form may fairly be
taken as indicative of a total conception of classical music will be
clear from what has already been said. It is also clear that while

Webster has read Rosen with care and appreciation, he is prepared to follow him only so far.

Webster begins, as one does in dictionary articles, by casting the net wide:

Like any form in tonal music, a sonata-form movement creates its designs in time. The form is a synthesis of the tonal structure, the rhythmic organization and the development of the musical material. . . . The meaning of each event depends both on its function in the structure and its dramatic context. Sonata form is thus not a mould into which the composer has poured the contents; each movement grows bar by bar and phrase by phrase. (XVII: 497)

This is unexceptionable, and it is only after reading the article to the end that we notice not much more is said about the synthesis. Whether or not this was due to the compression inevitable in such articles, it seems that for Webster the matter of synthesis cannot be crucial. He delivers a routine slap at the jelly-mold theory of sonata form, but just how each movement grows bar by bar and phrase by phrase is something he does not enlarge upon.

Also noticeable is a disparity in treatment between the three elements of the classical synthesis—"the tonal structure, the rhythmic organization, and the development of the musical material." Tonal structure receives adequate coverage, considering the limited amount of space Webster allows himself for a discussion of "Principles of Sonata Form" (most of his article deals with its history). The main business of the sonata-form exposition is to establish "a large-scale dissonance (Rosen) that must be resolved"; the development should be viewed as "a (gigantic) transition from the end of the exposition to the beginning of the recapitulation," and this beginning counts as "the central aesthetic event in the entire movement [produced by] a return to the main theme . . . timed to arrive simultaneously with the return to the tonic [key]." Rhythmic organization is also given its due, if not in the actual prose—rhythm is an extremely difficult thing to write about—at least in the annotations provided along with Webster's main musical example, which is the whole first movement of Mozart's *Eine kleine Nachtmusik*, K. 525, in a skeletal reduction. In classical music, "sections vary in phrase rhythm, level of activity, harmonic structure and cadential strength; this

Example 1: Mozart, *Eine Kleine Nachtmusik,* first movement (reduction).
From James Webster's article "Sonata Form" in *The New Grove Dictionary of Music and Musicians* (London: Macmillan, 1980).
Reproduced by permission.

sense of varied pace is essential to the style," writes Webster, and
that is exactly what is revealed graphically by his rhythmic analysis of the Mozart. See example 1, pp. 226-227. We shall return to
this example later.

It is "the development of the musical material"—that is, the
melodic, thematic, and motivic material—which comes off less
well. The Mozart example is furnished with thematic as well as
rhythmic and harmonic annotations—the usual themes 1 and 2,
a's and b's and c's and c''s, etc.—but some of them are unper-
suasive and none of them illuminates the relation of the material
to the structure. Nor in the rest of the article is there much to be
learned about why tunes or motifs come when they do, or how
they function, or what role they play in the synthesis. The bias
noted here is characteristic. Historical musicologists of past generations nearly always regarded anything that smacks of thematicism with suspicion. And American musicologists of today, confronted by the two great Germanic "rigid linear dogmatisms," as
Rosen calls them, those of the *Urlinie* and of *Substanzgemeinschaft,* have proved more hospitable to the former, more resistant
to the latter. As I have tried to show, Rosen stands considerably
to the right of dogmatic organicist critics such as Schenker or
Reti. He is still too far to the left for most musicologists.

And if (as it appears)[14] Webster regards Rosen as a somewhat
radical thematicist, he is not alone. In a recent study issuing from
another sector of the music-academic establishment, the theorist
David Epstein specifically associates Rosen with Reti and Reti's
followers Keller and Alan Walker. To be sure, he absolves Rosen
from the one-sided emphasis on melodic shapes that characterizes
the Reti school, and by drawing attention to the discussion of
Haydn's intertwining of shapes and key structures in *The Classical Style,* he acknowledges the book's broader thrust.[15] As well he
might, for Epstein's own study, *Beyond Orpheus: Studies in Musical Structure* (1979), is probably the most forthright assertion
that has yet appeared of a modern all-embracing organicist position in musical criticism.

This study is not one we should pause over, for though it
includes illuminating material about Haydn, Mozart, and Beethoven, it does not deal centrally with classical music, still less
with classical style or form. Epstein walks the long gallery of mod-

ern music from Haydn to Brahms, with the door left invitingly
open, in more ways than one, to Schoenberg. The focus is not
critical or historical but theoretical — that is, in the last analysis,
philosophical, so that insights about music are secondary to ideas
about order. In view of what has been said above about Rosen's
eclecticism, however, it is interesting to see Epstein set out pro-
grammatically to synthesize Rosen's two "linear dogmatisms," to
infuse life into both of them, jointly, under the aegis of an arch-
ing theory of rhythm. It is also interesting to see him place as
antithesis to Schenker's linear reductionism not Reti's simplistic
"thematic process" but rather Schoenberg's much subtler concept
of the *Grundgestalt*. A *Grundgestalt* or "basic shape" is not
exactly equivalent to a melodic configuration; it is that and also
something more abstract. Thus when Rosen, in discussing
Haydn's Quartet in B-flat, op. 55 no. 3, shows how a "dead" semi-
tone interval between the first two four-bar phrases infects other
themes and controls formal junctures, he is dealing not with a
motif but a "shape," a Gestalt. Likewise his point about the opening orchestral sonority of Mozart's Sinfonia Concertante, K.364
(320d), and how this prefigures the music to come, recalls the
point made by Epstein and others about the two opening chords
of the *Eroica* Symphony. These are observations worthy of Schoenberg; they are beyond the range of the systems of Reti or
Schenker.

Of various influences on Rosen's criticism, the one that has
struck people most often is that of Tovey, whom Rosen seems
clearly to admire in everything but his antithematicism.[16] Once
past an initial skirmish on that score, which I have already mentioned, *The Classical Style* includes references to Tovey in far
greater number than to any other author. Tovey too never tired
of proclaiming the equation of artistic form and content; but
Tovey tied himself into paradoxical knots by refusing to admit
any but the simplest kinds of thematicism. Consequently he was
never quite able to translate his organicist ideology into his actual
criticism, as Schoenberg did in his fugitive but brilliant analytical
aperçus — to say nothing of what he revealed (though not to
Tovey) through his own music. It is probably no accident that
next after *The Classical Style* Rosen wrote a book for the "Modern Masters" series on Schoenberg.

III

To move from Epstein's *Beyond Orpheus* to the new book by
Leonard G. Ratner, *Classic Music* (1980), is to move from theory
to history; it is also almost like moving into history. Ratner is a
musicologist who has spent a lifetime studying eighteenth-century
writers on music theory and composition. He has studied them so
devotedly—so uncritically, I am afraid—that he has ended up by
absorbing not only their limited insights but also their limitations. This is true even in a narrow chronological sense. Not
much gets quoted in Ratner's *Classic Music* that was written later
than around 1820.

The book's subtitle is *Expression, Form, and Style;* whole sections are devoted to "Expression," "Rhetoric," "Form," and "Stylistic Perspectives." This bold seizing of the category "expression"
is unnerving. Nothing of the sort happens in any of the other
recent literature; bring up the subject and Epstein throws up his
hands, Webster pretends not to hear, and Rosen waxes John-
sonian (" 'Expression' is a word that tends to corrupt thought").
But since the subject was the first brought up by systematic writers on music in the eighteenth century, Ratner makes it his first
order of business too. What interests most twentieth-century listeners who come to classical music is also, I think, expression—at
least, expression in some sense. Granted that this word is used by
different people to mean different things, some of them perhaps
regrettably imprecise. But given the general retreat from anything but technique as the subject for current American music
criticism, one turns with eager anticipation, even yearning, to
any account that offers to deal seriously with expression in almost
any of its meanings.

The trouble is that on the subject of musical expression, Ratner's late eighteenth-century authorities stumble and skim, pon-
tificate and prevaricate. Although the century was a time of un-
paralleled speculation about psychology and feeling, as we know,
not much of this rubbed off onto the writers of treatises on music
and manuals of practical composition. There were no minds of
the stature of a Rameau, a Kirnberger, or an Emanuel Bach
among the music theorists at the end of the century. They were
mostly modest individuals, who had enough trouble keeping up
with the latest trends of music in Vienna and Paris without

attempting serious contributions to musical aesthetics (a subject, let us remember, that still eludes thinkers of the present century, who have a good deal more to go on). The most conscientious and thoughtful among them was a violinist of Rudolstadt, a little town in Thuringia, named Heinrich Christian Koch. In 1793 Koch mentions Mozart (*"der sel. Mozard"*) in a single sentence; he had heard of Mozart's six quartets dedicated to Haydn but it is not clear that he had heard them. He discusses in detail only one Haydn symphony, from twenty years earlier—that is, from a quite early stage in the composer's career.[17]

What these men remembered was the baroque *Affektenlehre,* the doctrine of affects derived ultimately from Descartes, and still current in watered-down forms, which associated certain musical tropes with certain standardized sentiments. You could always convey the required sentiment by employing the correct trope; you could, indeed, do it just as well as Johann Sebastian Bach or George Frideric Handel, for it was no part of the doctrine to distinguish between one user of these universal nostrums and the next. Likewise analysis of later eighteenth-century music in terms of what Ratner calls "topics" gives us no way to distinguish between Haydn and Pleyel, Mozart and Süssmeyer—or between Haydn and Mozart. This is a more serious shortcoming because of a significant change over the course of the century. As is well known, musical expression became less emblematic and more personal. Even traditionalists who still thought in terms of the affects could no longer limit a musical composition or a movement to a single affect, as in the earlier period. Music was now made up of contrasting sections, sections with contrasting affects. This meant that musical expression became a function of musical form: another significant change, or another aspect of the first one.[18]

Ratner's procedure is to identify as many as possible of the topics or *topoi* which were used again and again at the time and therefore universally recognized. They are mostly melodic or rhythmic configurations—a thoroughly miscellaneous collection of tags, signals, and formulas to which he gives names such as minuet, contredanse, brilliant style, learned style, military music, Turkish music, Storm and Stress, and fantasia. And it is unnerving indeed to see the first-movement exposition of a late Mozart quintet, the E-flat major, K. 614, partitioned into successive segments labeled hunt, brilliant style, sensibility, learned style, brilliant style again, singing style, gigue, learned, brilliant, fanfare, and finally sensibility.[19] But what is most seriously wrong is that no topic label acknowledges the later reinterpretation of the first so-called "brilliant" passage: in the recapitulation section, Mozart turns this into something rich, unbrilliant, and deliciously chromatic. Expression in Mozart's music, if not in Bach's, is controlled by such reinterpretations. We can see this more clearly, perhaps, than could theorists of the time, to whom this music was new and exciting but also different and difficult.

Under the broad heading of "Rhetoric" Ratner discusses the construction, juxtaposition, and enjambment of musical phrases, techniques closely dependent on the placement and weighting of cadences. These are the areas that the instruction books dealt with most successfully and in the greatest detail. Hence Ratner's historically based account of sonata form, amply bolstered by contemporary citations, resembles Webster's in its bias toward the rhythmic and harmonic elements of the "classic synthesis" at the expense of the thematic. (Though perhaps this is putting the matter the wrong way around; Webster too has read Koch, and he has also read Ratner.) There is no use searching in this author for the ritual attack on the jelly-mold theory of sonata form; he is too close to the composition manuals, which were designed not for the Haydns and Mozarts of this world but for readers who needed, expected, and welcomed rules and patterns to follow. As he says, music of the time undoubtedly "had to be composed quickly, for immediate use, [and] composers relied on familiar and universally accepted formulas for its organization and handling of detail." Ratner likes to tell of the *ars combinatoria* that is promulgated by some of his writers, whereby standard phrases and even individual bars can be juggled around in many different permutations and combinations to produce plausible little classical compositions.[20] It is all very matter of fact. Perceptive critical comments and coarse ones rattle disconcertingly together.

A curious book, and never more curious than in its final chapter, "Beethoven and the Classic Style," which is given over to a continuously perceptive discussion of one piece, the first movement of the String Quartet in F, op. 59 no. 1, the first "Razumovsky" Quartet. This dates from 1805, early in Beethoven's so-called second period, shortly after the *Eroica* Symphony. Here, clearly, it was the author's laudable intention to break out of the heavily systematic manner adopted to explicate late eighteenth-century music in order to suggest horizons beyond. He breaks out with a vengeance: for now eighteenth-century terms such as topic and rhetoric are abandoned for the vocabulary of present-day analysis. After the "opening chord of the movement sets the mood" (I am now quoting almost entirely Ratner's own words),[21] the first four measures, which "appear as an expansion or elaboration of this [chord]," are perceived as "a pattern for the whole movement." This is because the opening scale figure "can be trimmed to various lengths" and quickened or slowed in such a way as to "penetrate and saturate the melodic action, contributing to the broad flow and unity of the movement." When Ratner sees "the 'vertical' and 'horizontal' exchang[ing] roles . . . to fuse even more strongly the continuous flow," he seems to look past the immediate technical point he is making to an almost ecstatic organicist vision; and when he derives the development section's fugue subject from the second theme of the exposition, as follows,

he comes before us in a new guise, as a thematicist to be reckoned with. There is no labeling of topics in this chapter. Nor, for once, is there a single citation from a contemporary authority. The unsuspecting reader might suppose that the insights presented here into Beethovenian unity are the product of a twentieth-century ear, not an eighteenth- or nearly nineteenth-century one.

However, Ratner's historical credentials are entirely in order. He might easily have cited E. T. A. Hoffmann's appreciation of Beethoven's music, which was referred to in passing above. The following familiar sentences appeared in a musical magazine as early as 1810, and then circulated widely in the *Fantasiestücke in Callots Manier* of 1814. In Beethoven's Fifth Symphony, Hoffman wrote,

The internal structure of the sections [Sätzen], their development, their orchestration, the way in which they follow one another — everything contributes to a single end; above all, it is the intimate relationship among the themes that engenders that unity which alone has the power to hold the listener firmly in a single mood....[22]

but lest we think that under the impact of Beethoven's V-for-victory motif Hoffmann is expressing no more than a superficial thematicism, he adds that although "this relationship is sometimes clear to the listener when he hears it in the [thematic] connection between two sections," nevertheless "a deeper relationship, which does not reveal itself in this way, speaks at times only from spirit to spirit..." Hoffmann is a good contemporary witness, all the better because he is not a theorist but a practicing artist — an important composer and a very important novelist and essayist. Unlike the theorists, moreover, who notoriously write for the most prosaic of human beings, namely students, Hoffmann writes for the most audacious, the most imaginative, the most poetic:

How does the matter stand if it is *your* feeble observation alone that the deep inner continuity of Beethoven's every composition eludes? If it is *your* fault alone that you do not understand the master's language as the initiated understand it, that the portals of the innermost sanctuary remain closed to you?

In spite of Hoffmann's taunts, sensitive critics from his time to the time of Ratner have seldom missed the "deep inner continuity" in compositions by Beethoven. Beethoven's music was made to order for the burgeoning organicist theory of music, and so was the music of the boldest composers who followed him in the nineteenth century. Even Brahms, widely considered to be one of the less bold, was shown by Schoenberg to have developed his own type of thematic procedure, what Schoenberg called "developing variation"; and Professor Webster, in an important two-part essay on sonata form in Schubert and Brahms, points to imaginative thematic relationships in Brahms of a kind unmentioned in his *Grove* article.[23] Here Webster goes beyond Schoenberg to touch on the dialectic between "inner form" and "outer form" in the work of this composer — that is, on the way Brahms's developing variation technique was made to meet the demands (as he saw them) of traditional sonata form. This topic is further developed with much sensitivity by a younger scholar, Walter Frisch, in a recent study.[24]

Rosen's major effort in regard to classical music can be viewed in similar dialectic terms, as I have already suggested. And what has always been provocative about Rosen's *The Classical Style* is that he has carried a familiar Romantic dialectic back to the eighteenth century—back to Mozart's first great piano concerto, the E-flat Concerto, K. 271, of 1775, which Alfred Einstein characterized as Mozart's *Eroica*; back especially to Haydn's op. 33 quartets of 1781 and his symphonies of the late 1770s. Speaking of the "deeper structural import between shape, as local idea, and its correspondence through tonal plan," David Epstein remarks that these relationships "are most striking, perhaps, in the music of Haydn, though the idea was adopted and extended by his successors throughout the next hundred years."[25] This would not have been said, I think, before the appearance of *The Classical Style*.

IV

I should now like to focus this discussion by means of a specific musical composition, and also to extend the base of the argument somewhat. To introduce the extension, here is another familiar quotation, this one from a letter from Mozart to his father, in 1782. Mozart is writing about his earliest Viennese piano concertos.

These concertos are a happy medium between what is too easy and too difficult; they are very brilliant, pleasing to the ear, and natural, without being vapid. There are passages here and there from which connoisseurs alone can derive satisfaction; but these passages are written in such a way that the less learned cannot fail to be pleased, though without knowing why.[26]

Ratner, who reminds us of this letter, thinks that when Mozart refers to difficult passages for connoisseurs he means passages in the topic he calls "learned style." This may be right, but it seems to me admissible also to read the passage in a broader context. If modern connoisseurs claim to derive satisfaction from the interpenetration of material and structure in Haydn's music, this is not likely to have escaped Mozart's attention. He may have been referring to compositional subtlety, rather than contrapuntal ostentation. Can we perhaps locate the two poles between which Mozart found his "happy medium" not only in his most ambitious and personal works, such as his piano concertos, but also in more modest, less learned, seemingly routine classical compositions? Can we locate them in a work like *Eine kleine Nachtmusik*?

Webster's selection of this particular work as his paradigm of sonata form gives pause. The piece belongs to the category of the serenade, a popular genre, *Gebrauchsmusik* for the open air, the minimalist art of the late eighteenth century. It was a genre abandoned by Mozart long before he came to write *Eine kleine Nachtmusik* in 1787, the year of *Don Giovanni*; and why he wrote it remains a mystery, for no record survives of its commissioning or its performance. "Vapid" it is not, but it breathes a refined simplicity of form, content, and procedure as the essence of its genre.

Eine kleine Nachtmusik would not, then, have been the obvious choice for an author who wanted to show the subtle synthesis of melody, harmony, and rhythm in classical music. In fact, I do not believe it would have been chosen by any true hater of jelly-molds. Tovey, at all events, did not choose such an example for his "Sonata Forms" article in the old *Encyclopaedia Britannica,* an article that must haunt any later writer on the subject. What Tovey chose was the first movement of the *Eroica* Symphony (all 689 measures of it, requiring three full folio pages in a condensed score). This is a movement that gloriously illustrates the horizons of classical form. The *Nachtmusik* would seem, at least at first glance, to exemplify its lowest common denominator.

What is more, the *Eroica* includes Tovey's favorite case of a pregnant thematic detail that is expanded into the total structure. Both Rosen and Epstein also write about it.[27] The famous dissonance in the *Eroica* main theme (bar 7) acts initially as a disturbance, a source of those charged latent energies that drive the music on and on through its extraordinary journeys. At the beginning of the recapitulation (bar 402) the dissonance is reinterpreted enharmonically so as to move the music in lyric, static, poignant directions. In a coda or final section of unprecedented extent it is finally accorded heroic resolution. There is nothing of this kind going on, surely, in *Eine kleine Nachtmusik.*

Or perhaps there is something. Not that much can be made of

the neutral, formulaic opening theme shown in Webster's line 1 (see example 1; in this example each new staff corresponds to what Webster calls a new "sentence" in the music). Label it "fanfare." Line 2 is the merest busywork, and the modulatory phrase of line 4 such as to cause a delicate critic discomfort, discomfort heightened by the suspicion that Mozart may be grinning at him. As for the charming melody in line 5, it would take a deeply committed thematicist to propose its derivation from the latent charge of anything ahead of it. Ever so gracefully, it might have been poured into a mold.

Halfway through this sentence, however, Mozart's interest became engaged. The first-violin part at bar 32, starting as an extended ticktock accompaniment—thirteen eighth-note A's—takes over the main melodic role as the A moves up the scale to echo the modulatory phrase and to prepare the cadence. There is a magical integration of the functions of theme and accompaniment here.[28] Then in line 6 this line is played backwards (more or less) to disclose another melody:

The scale-figure backward—that is, going down, not up—also occurs in the cadence figure (line 7, end) and stands out there because of the cadence figure's extreme brevity.

In this sonata exposition, then, there is a sense in which the end of the second group (lines 6 and 7) can be said to "emerge" out of its beginning (line 5, end).

To demarcate and initiate the second large section, the fanfare theme appears again, but with a harmonic change (spelled out in example 1 by Webster's bracketed chords at the end of line 8). Instead of the original neutral motion from tonic to dominant harmony, from I to V^7, the fanfare now goes from I (in D major) to V^7 of ii, from the tonic toward the supertonic. The important difference is the note D-sharp. This is slightly less neutral. For to an exposition of astounding harmonic simplicity, this same V-of-ii chord built on D-sharp had brought the one even slightly disturbing element. The chord had come twice, in two not unrelated passages, both of them repeated.

The harmonic content (slim as it is) of the exposition can therefore be said now to have infected the fanfare theme and thus to
have "impelled" the first harmonic gesture of the development
section.

The nature of this impulsion well illustrates the wit and also
the sense of balance that are so important to the classical style.
Whereas in the exposition the V-of-ii chord always resolved normally to ii, in the development section it resolves deceptively to
the lowered VII degree, C major. Once this slightly surprising
harmony has been proposed, it is maintained as the central plateau of the whole little section. And the route off of this plateau is
by way of a long bass E-flat, the punning equivalent (or enhar-
monic reinterpretation) of D-sharp.

So if we may venture a little further into metaphorical language, the "latent force" injected by D-sharp in the exposition
can be felt not only in the first gesture of the development section,
but over its entire course.

As for the melodic material in this section, it did not take a
composer of Mozart's genius to decide on using the little up-and-
down scale figures of lines 5 and 6. They are, after all, the most—
perhaps the only—interesting material at hand. As the scales are
treated rather intensively, at least by the standards of this piece,
it was a good idea to liquidate them rather definitely at the end of
the section. Mozart does this by carrying the upward scale up far-
ther, by slowing it down, and by introducing chromatic steps (B♭
B C C♯ D) which seem to trivialize the upward thrust at the same
time as the slow-down tends to make it more imposing. It is another very witty place. And the thematic procedure here—the
liquidation—can certainly be said to be coordinated with the
form. It can also be said to articulate the form. Perhaps it can be
said, without undue solemnity, to "engender" the form.

Rosen's term "reinterpretation," however, does seem too sol-
emn for what happens to the exposition material in the recapitulation. This 55 = bar passage is altered by a mere flick of the wrist
in the modulatory section (line 4) at bars 99-100 and by an extension to the tiny cadence figure (line 11). The only sense of resolution conveyed by this facile symmetry is the outcome of one of
Mozart's characteristic setups, as transparent as it is delightful. In
the exposition he holds the cadence figure down to two bars,
which is really too brief to discharge the relative intensity of the

music just preceding it (line 7). (This intensity itself depends on parallelism with a less intense earlier passage, as Webster indicates.) We are so used to the *Nachtmusik* that we may not notice — but Koch would probably have recommended four bars for the cadence figure, not two:

So in the recapitulation the composer of *Don Giovanni* resolves this rhythmic imbalance by the sort of expandable vaudeville exit repetitions that come so naturally to Leporello, and Figaro and Bartolo before him (line 11). Instead on the insinuating *"voi sapete..."* phrases of the Catalogue Aria, Mozart makes final reference to his much-used up-and-down scale figures — a "resolving" reference in that the upward chromatic line from the end of the development section now runs harmlessly down, and a comic one in that a diatonic scale now seems to grow out of a chromatic one. Since six bars have been used up by this, overshooting the required four, the further rhythmic imbalance requires further discharge in an overlapping six-bar coda. Though why the discharge takes the particular noisy and vacuous form it does here is not altogether easy to say, unless Mozart is grinning at us again. Label it "raucous."

V

How much of this was apprehended and appreciated by the man in the street who happened upon the (undocumented) first performance of Mozart's serenade, one night in 1787, we cannot say. Nor what effect it all has on his progeny who are still listening to Mozart in our own time. Perhaps what Mozart's "less learned" listener enjoyed in *Eine kleine Nachtmusik* was indeed "expression" in the sense of an agreeably varied series of "topics" that he could identify with comfortably: fanfare, busywork, charm, ticktock, vaudeville-exit, and the rest. Symmetry in art always pleased him, especially in recapitulations, where things are not obscured by improvised ornamentation as in the da capo arias he had grown weary of because of their fussy elaboration and faintly indecorous display. That he cared about the recapitulation resolving or reinterpreting anything is vastly to be doubted. He would have appreciated the raucous passage at the end of the first movement, and also the parallel place at the end of the last movement; at any rate, these we can at least feel fairly sure he would have apprehended. Mozart must have written them purposely to drown out the likely street noise.

As for the features of this music for the connoisseur, I suppose I am making two contrary points about them. They can be missed by the connoisseur, the specialist, or the musicologist who concentrates on Kurth's "outer form," on formula and pattern, at the expense of "inner form." However, in a classical work of this kind they amount to no more than occasional touches. They can hardly be said to permeate the entire fabric of the music.

Rosen likes to give the impression that the classical style depends critically on the perfect integration of melody, harmony, rhythm, and texture, something the minor composers of the time could scarcely achieve. Tovey wrote a major essay purporting to show the essential "freedom" of the one Beethoven sonata which looks suspiciously as though it were poured into a mold.[29] Yet I do not think we can seriously doubt that in writing his serenade Mozart relied, in Ratner's words, "on familiar and universally accepted formulas for its organization and handling of details." He would have lost his audience otherwise. I might mention parenthetically that even in the organization of the *Nachtmusik's* development section around D-sharp and E-flat Mozart was relying on a formula that he used in several other compositions, among them the E-flat String Quintet. When thirty years later Beethoven began to depart radically from accepted norms he did indeed lose his audience; Beethoven being Beethoven, the late sonatas and quartets were accorded a measure of mystical respect, but they were not understood for nearly fifty years after his death.[30] His earlier works that retained their enormous popularity did not depart too far from norms, despite Hoffmann's enthusiastic proclamations. And it is probably true that what made the Fifth Symphony a favorite with contemporary *Nichtkenner* was its series of powerful topics: fate knocking at the door, Storm and

Stress, the hunt, consolation, mystery music, military music, fan-fare—particularly, in those Napoleonic times, military music and fanfare.

By insisting in their matter-of-fact way on the importance of topic and formula, musicologists provide a corrective to esoteric modern theories of classical music. Whatever late eighteenth-century art was, it was not (and is not) esoteric. Immersion in the treatises and manuals of the time has at least allowed Ratner to keep the common touch, for while those books were written by and for professionals, in the eighteenth century no professional musician or writer on music ignored the essential audience for music as is the case in our time. Analysts like Schenker, Reti, and Epstein write as though the nonprofessional world did not exist, and it is this, when all is said and done, not the particular details of their theories, that makes them so profoundly unhistorical. Here too Rosen occupies middle ground, for his criticism is addressed to an educated lay public—to an elite public, if you will, but at least not to music professors. He is, in the best sense of the word, a popularizer of advanced modern critical insights. He writes for the same public he plays to.

There is still something to learn from Tovey in this matter, I believe. Tovey's final appeal was always to what he called the "naive listener," the interested, earnest nonmusician whom he could cajole again and again into appreciating the subtleties of tonality, invertible counterpoint at the twelfth, and so on. Rovey's very limitations as a critic were probably due, in part, to his refusal to venture into certain areas where he feared the nonpro-fessional would not be able to follow the professional. This naive listener, this amiable abstraction, this eminently Victorian inven-tion—clearly he is a grandchild in concept of the cultivated man of common sense to whom eighteenth-century writers addressed their work. Can we postulate a great-great-grandchild for our own time?

We need him to keep our criticism honest, and we will continue to appeal to him most urgently in respect to the music of the late eighteenth century, to the music we call classical. This is no longer for us, as it still actually was for Tovey, a touchstone for musical composition. It remains a touchstone for ideas about how music is to be apprehended and appreciated.

NOTES

1. On the German tradition, see Jens Peter Larsen, "Sonatenform-Probleme," *Festschrift Friedrich Blume zum 70. Geburtstag,* ed. Anna Amalie Abert and Wilhelm Pfannkuch (Kassel: Barenreiter, 1963), pp. 221-230. On Tovey, see Joseph Kerman, "Tovey's Beethoven," *Beethoven Studies* II (London: Oxford University Press, 1977), pp. 172-191.

2. Joseph Kerman, "How We Got into Analysis, and How to Get Out," *Critical Inquiry* 7 (1980): 311-331.

3. Charles Rosen, *The Classical Style: Haydn, Mozart, Beethoven* [rev. ed.] (New York: Norton, 1972), p. 53.

4. See Ruth A. Solie, "The Living Work: Organicism and Musical Analysis," *19th-Century Music* 4 (1980): 147-156.

5. *Classical Style,* p. 36.

6. In "Tovey's Beethoven" (see n. 1).

7. See Ian Bent, "Analytical Thinking in the First Half of the Nineteenth Century," in *Modern Musical Scholarship,* ed. Edward Olleson (Stocksfield: Oriel Press, 1980), pp. 151-166. Many writers, including Rosen, have misjudged Marx's role in the ossification of sonata-form theory.

8. Tovey, "Normality and Freedom in Music," in *The Main Stream of Music and Other Essays* (New York: Oxford University Press, 1959), pp. 183-201; Schoenberg, *Style and Idea* (London: Faber and Faber, 1976), p. 415.

9. "Music: A View from Delft" (1961), repr. in *Perspectives on Contemporary Music Theory,* ed. Benjamin Boretz and Edward T. Cone (New York: Norton, 1972), pp. 65-66.

10. Hans Keller, "K, 503: The Unity of Contrasting Themes and Movements" (1956), repr. in *Mozart: Piano Concerto in C Major, K. 503,* ed. Joseph Kerman, Norton Critical Score (New York: Norton, 1970), pp. 176-200.

11. *Classical Style,* p. 120.

12. See especially the review by Edward Olleson in *Musical Times* 112 (1971): 1166-1167. For criticism on somewhat different historical grounds, and from a less strictly academic position, see Alan Tyson in *New York Review of Books* 18 (June 15, 1972): 10-12.

In America *The Classical Style* was given the silent treatment by the "official" scholarly journals; no reviews appeared in *Journal of the American Musicological Society, Musical Quarterly, Music Library Association Notes,* or *Journal of Music Theory.*

13. See the review of *Sonata Forms* by Jan LaRue in *Journal of the American Musicological Society* 34 (1981): 557-566.

14. "As it appears": as it appears to me on the basis of careful analysis and my best understanding of Webster's article. It should be said, however, that Webster does not broach this issue in his review of *Sonata Forms* in *Musical Times* 122 (1981): 301-304.

15. David Epstein, *Beyond Orpheus: Studies in Musical Structure*

(Cambridge, Mass.: MIT Press, 1979), p. 53, n. 7. Rosen is linked with Reti, etc., on pp. 10 and 37.

16. A lengthy review of *The Classical Style* was entitled "Better Than Tovey?" (*Hudson Review* 25 [1972-73]: 633-646); to William H. Youngren, "Tovey's catalyzing influence" was "apparent on virtually every page of Rosen's book." See also the review of *Sonata Forms* by Joseph Kerman, *New York Review of Books* 27 (October 23, 1980): 50.

17. Heinrich Christian Koch, *Versuch einer Anweisung zur Composition* (Leipzig: A. F. Böhme, 1782-1793), III: 326-327, 179-190. There is a growing literature on Koch, who was first studied intensively by Ratner; recent items include *New Grove* articles on Koch (Ratner) and analysis (Bent), and Nancy Kovaleff Baker, "Heinrich Koch's Description of the Symphony," *Studi musicali* 9 (1980): 303-316. Baker discusses Koch's Haydn analysis in detail, and remarks that when Koch analyzes a more modern symphony, by Rosetti, he misattributes it to Pleyel (!).

18. "It is largely in the music of Haydn and Mozart after 1775 that structure replaced ornamentation as the principal vehicle of expression" (*Classical Style,* p. 395).

For the difficulties experienced by late eighteenth-century theorists and aestheticians with the element of contrast in contemporaneous music, see Bellamy Hosler, *Changing Aesthetic Views of Instrumental Music in 18th-Century Germany,* Studies in Musicology, no. 42 (Ann Arbor: UMI Research Press, 1981), esp. chap. 5, "Contrast, Change, and the Worth of Instrumental Music: Sulzer—Junker—Forkel."

19. Leonard G. Ratner, *Classic Form: Expression, Form, and Style* (New York: Schirmer Books, 1980), pp. 237-246.

20. For a fresher view of this matter, see Bent, "Analytical Thinking" (see n. 7).

21. *Classic Form,* pp. 423-431.

22. Oliver Strunk, *Source Readings in Music History* (New York: Norton, 1950), p. 778 (translation slightly modified).

23. "Schubert's Sonata Form and Brahms's First Maturity," *19th-Century Music* 1 (1978): 18-35; 2 (1979): 52-71.

24. *Brahms and the Principle of Developing Variation,* in California Studies in 19th-Century Music, no. 2 (Berkeley, Los Angeles, London: University of California Press, 1983).

25. *Beyond Orpheus,* p. 41.

26. *The Letters of Mozart & His Family,* ed. and trans. Emily Anderson (London: Macmillan, 1938), III: 1242.

27. *Classical Style,* p. 80; *Sonata Forms,* pp. 277-280; *Beyond Orpheus,* pp. 124-125, etc. Tovey's music example is reprinted in *Musical Articles from the Encyclopaedia Britannica* (London: Oxford University Press, 1944), pp. 221-228; see also his *Essays in Musical Analysis* I (London: Oxford University Press, 1935): 30-31, etc.

Incidentally, Schenker's nontreatment of this central matter in his book-length study of the *Eroica* has become a *locus classicus* for showing the limitations of his system; see "Tovey's Beethoven," p. 187 (see n. 1), and Milton Babbitt's remarks in the Foreword to *Beyond Orpheus*, p. x.

28. This is a style feature in classical music that has been repeatedly illuminated by Rosen (*Classical Style*, pp. 115-118, *Sonata Forms*, pp. 174-180). Rosen sees this feature as a key criterion of the style, and he sees it used consistently by Haydn and Mozart only after 1775-1780. Hence he dates the beginning of the classical style from that period (cf. n. 17) rather than from around ten years earlier — a point of issue between him and other scholars (see the reviews by Tyson and LaRue, nn. 12 and 13).

A little-noticed passage in one of Tovey's earliest essays draws attention to this same style feature. The finale theme in Haydn's great Sonata in E-flat "begins with a purely rhythmic figure on one note. If this rhythm is treated as an accompaniment (and Haydn so treats it from the outset), that accompaniment is *ipso facto* alive and thematic...It is interesting to note that Beethoven, in his 'second period,' developed a strong predilection for such rhythmic figures in his themes, and used them constantly as a most powerful means of giving life to inner parts without the necessity for the [introduction of independent] counterpoint" (*Essays in Musical Analysis: Chamber Music* [London: Oxford University Press, 1944], p. 104). (The words in square brackets are my attempt to fill an evident lacuna in the text.)

29. Op. 22: "Some Aspects of Beethoven's Art Forms," *Main Stream*, pp. 271-297.

30. See Amanda Glauert, "The Double Perspective in Beethoven's Op. 131," *19th-Century Music* 4 (1980): 113-120.

Designer: UC Press Staff
Compositor: Janet Sheila Brown
Printer: Thomson-Shore, Inc.
Binder: John H. Dekker & Sons
Text: Baskerville 11/13
Display: Baskerville